CHAPTER 1: INTRODUCTION TO NATURAL LANGUAGE PROCESSING

In this initial exploration of Natural Language Processing (NLP), we will delve into the core principles and significance of this multifaceted field. Natural Language Processing, a branch of artificial intelligence (AI) and computer science, focuses on the interaction between computers and human language. It aims to enable machines to understand, interpret, and generate human language in a way that is both meaningful and useful.

At its heart, NLP seeks to bridge the gap between human communication and computational systems. Human language is inherently complex, filled with nuances, ambiguities, and a rich variety of expressions that vary across different contexts and cultures. NLP attempts to unravel these complexities by providing machines with the capability to process and analyze large volumes of textual and spoken data, facilitating a range of applications from automated translation to sentiment analysis.

Understanding NLP begins with recognizing its historical evolution and foundational concepts. The origins of NLP can be traced back to the 1950s, with early research focusing on rule-based systems for machine translation. These systems relied heavily on hand-coded rules and dictionaries. However, the limitations of these early approaches became evident as the field evolved, necessitating more sophisticated methodologies. The advent of statistical methods and machine learning techniques in the 1990s marked a significant turning point, allowing NLP systems to learn from vast amounts of data rather than relying solely on predefined rules.

The importance of NLP in contemporary society cannot be overstated. It permeates numerous aspects of daily life, often in ways that go unnoticed. For instance, NLP is integral to the functionality of virtual assistants like Siri and Alexa, which rely on speech recognition and natural language understanding to interact with users. These systems use NLP algorithms to process spoken commands, interpret the intent behind them, and generate appropriate responses. Similarly, NLP underpins the recommendation engines used by streaming services and online retailers, which analyze user preferences and behavior to suggest relevant content or products.

Another significant application of NLP is in sentiment analysis, which involves assessing and categorizing the emotions conveyed in textual data. This technique is widely used in business and marketing to gauge public opinion about products, services, or brands. By analyzing customer reviews, social media posts, and other forms of user-generated content, companies can gain insights into consumer sentiment and adjust their strategies accordingly. For example, a positive sentiment detected in reviews might prompt a company to emphasize certain features of their product in marketing campaigns, while negative sentiment could signal areas for improvement.

Text classification is another crucial application of NLP, where text data is categorized into predefined categories based on its content. This task is essential for organizing and retrieving information, such as sorting emails into folders or filtering spam. Advances in machine learning and deep learning have significantly enhanced the accuracy and efficiency of text classification systems, enabling more sophisticated and context-aware categorizations.

Machine translation is perhaps one of the most visible and impactful applications of NLP. Services like Google Translate have revolutionized communication by breaking down language barriers and enabling people from different linguistic backgrounds to interact seamlessly. Machine translation systems use complex algorithms to translate text from one language to another, accounting for grammar, syntax, and cultural nuances. The continuous improvement of these systems relies on large-scale datasets and advanced models that learn from vast amounts of multilingual text.

Despite its many advancements, NLP is not without challenges. One major obstacle is the issue of ambiguity inherent in human language. Words and phrases can have multiple meanings depending on their context, which can complicate the process of understanding and generating language. For instance, the word "bank" could refer to a financial institution or the side of a river, and determining the correct interpretation requires contextual knowledge that can be difficult for machines to grasp.

Another challenge is the need for high-quality training data. NLP models typically require large and diverse datasets to learn effectively, and the quality of these datasets directly impacts the performance of the models. Issues such as bias and representativeness in training data can lead to skewed or unfair outcomes, highlighting the need for careful curation and evaluation of data sources.

Furthermore, NLP systems must address the intricacies of human language, including idiomatic expressions, slang, and evolving linguistic trends. These elements contribute to the richness of language but also pose difficulties for computational models that rely on fixed rules or predefined vocabularies.

To address these challenges, researchers and practitioners in the field of NLP are continually developing and refining techniques. Recent advances in deep learning, particularly in the development of neural network architectures such as transformers, have significantly improved the capabilities of NLP systems. These models leverage vast amounts of data and computational power to achieve remarkable results in tasks such as language generation, question answering, and summarization.

As we continue to explore the field of Natural Language Processing, it is essential to recognize both its potential and its limitations. The ability to process and understand human language opens up a multitude of possibilities for enhancing communication, automating tasks, and deriving insights from textual data. However, the complexity of language and the challenges inherent in NLP require ongoing research and innovation to achieve more accurate and meaningful results.

In summary, the study of Natural Language Processing offers a window into the intersection of language and technology. By examining its foundational concepts, applications, and challenges, we lay the groundwork for a deeper understanding of how NLP can transform various aspects of our lives. As we progress through this exploration, we will build on this foundational knowledge to uncover more intricate aspects of NLP and its impact on the future of artificial intelligence and data science.

Natural Language Processing (NLP) involves a broad spectrum of techniques and methodologies designed to enable machines to process and understand human language. One of the foundational components of NLP is tokenization, which involves breaking down text into smaller, manageable pieces, known as tokens. These tokens can be as small as characters or as large as words or phrases, depending on the application. Tokenization is crucial because it simplifies the complexity of language into discrete elements that can be analyzed and processed by computational algorithms.

Once tokenized, text is typically subject to further processing, such as normalization and stemming. Normalization involves converting text to a standard format, which might include lowercasing all letters, removing punctuation, and correcting misspellings. This step is essential for reducing the variability in text data, which can otherwise complicate analysis. Stemming, on the other hand, reduces words to their root forms. For instance, the words "running," "runner," and "ran" might all be reduced to the root "run." This process helps in consolidating similar words, making it easier to analyze text data at a more abstract level.

Another important aspect of NLP is part-of-speech tagging, which involves labeling each word in a sentence with its grammatical role, such as noun, verb, adjective, etc. This tagging provides valuable context for understanding the relationships between words in a sentence. For example, in the sentence "The cat sat on the mat," part-of-speech tagging helps the system understand that "cat" and "mat" are nouns, while "sat" is a verb, and "on" is a preposition. This contextual information is crucial for more advanced NLP tasks such as syntactic parsing, where the structure of a sentence is analyzed to understand its grammatical relationships.

Syntactic parsing is closely related to the concept of syntax, which refers to the rules governing the structure of sentences in a language. By analyzing syntax, NLP systems can determine the grammatical relationships between words and phrases. This understanding is essential for tasks such as machine translation, where preserving the grammatical integrity of the source language while converting it to the target language is crucial. Parsing techniques range from traditional rule-based systems to more modern approaches that leverage machine learning to infer syntactic structures from large corpora of text.

Semantics, the study of meaning in language, is another critical area in NLP. While syntax focuses on the structure of language, semantics deals with the meaning conveyed by words and sentences. Techniques for semantic analysis include word embeddings, which represent words as vectors in a high-dimensional space. These embeddings capture the semantic relationships between words based on their usage in context. For example, word embeddings can reveal that "king" and "queen" are semantically related, and "man" and "woman" are similar in their gender-based context.

Named entity recognition (NER) is a specific application of semantic analysis that involves identifying and classifying entities within text. Entities such as names of people, organizations, locations, and dates are extracted and categorized, allowing systems to better understand and organize information. For instance, in the sentence "Apple Inc. is headquartered in Cupertino," NER would identify "Apple Inc." as an organization and "Cupertino" as a location.

In addition to these foundational techniques, NLP encompasses a variety of applications that leverage these methods to solve practical problems. One notable application is sentiment analysis, which involves determining the emotional tone of a piece of text. This can be particularly useful in understanding public opinion, customer feedback, and social media interactions. Sentiment analysis models typically classify text into categories such as positive, negative, or neutral, based on the sentiment expressed. Advanced models may also detect nuances in sentiment, such as sarcasm or mixed emotions.

Machine translation is another prominent application of NLP, enabling the automatic translation of text from one language to another. Modern machine translation systems, such as Google Translate, use sophisticated algorithms and large-scale bilingual corpora to provide accurate translations. These systems have evolved from rule-based approaches to more advanced neural network models, which are capable of handling complex linguistic phenomena and providing translations that are contextually appropriate.

Chatbots and virtual assistants are applications of NLP that have become increasingly prevalent. These systems use a combination of natural language understanding (NLU) and natural language generation (NLG) to interact with users in a conversational manner. NLU involves parsing user input to understand intent and extract relevant information, while NLG focuses on generating coherent and contextually appropriate responses. The effectiveness of chatbots and virtual assistants relies heavily on the underlying NLP techniques that enable them to process and generate human-like responses.

In conclusion, the field of Natural Language Processing encompasses a wide array of techniques and applications that facilitate the interaction between humans and computers through language. From the fundamental processes of tokenization and part-of-speech tagging to advanced applications such as machine translation and sentiment analysis, NLP plays a crucial role in modern technology. Understanding these foundational concepts provides a solid basis for exploring more complex topics and innovations within the field.

The exploration of semantics in NLP encompasses the challenge of interpreting the meaning behind words and sentences. This dimension of NLP goes beyond syntax and focuses on understanding the intent and nuances embedded in human language. Semantics deals with how words combine to form meaningful phrases and sentences and how context influences the interpretation of those meanings. For instance, the word "bank" can refer to a financial institution or the side of a river, depending on its usage. Disambiguating such terms requires an understanding of context, which is a core challenge in NLP.

One effective approach to semantic analysis is named entity recognition (NER). NER involves identifying and classifying key elements in a text, such as names of people, organizations, locations, and dates. This process helps to structure unstructured text, making it easier to extract relevant information and establish connections between different pieces of data. For example, in the sentence "Apple Inc. is headquartered in Cupertino," NER would identify "Apple Inc." as an organization and "Cupertino" as a location, providing valuable contextual information for further processing.

Contextual understanding in NLP is significantly enhanced by the use of word embeddings. Word embeddings are vector representations of words that capture semantic relationships between them. Traditional methods, such as one-hot encoding, represent words as binary vectors, which fail to capture the inherent similarities between words. Word embeddings, such as those produced by Word2Vec or GloVe (Global Vectors for Word Representation), map words into continuous vector spaces where semantically similar words are positioned closer together. This allows NLP systems to understand and leverage the relationships between words in a more nuanced manner.

Advanced techniques in NLP involve the use of deep learning models, particularly those based on neural networks. Recurrent Neural Networks (RNNs) and their variants, such as Long Short-Term Memory (LSTM) networks and Gated Recurrent Units (GRUs), are designed to handle sequential data, making them well-suited for tasks involving language, where the order of words is crucial. These models can capture temporal dependencies and contextual information across sequences, which is vital for tasks like machine translation and text generation.

The introduction of transformer models, such as BERT (Bidirectional Encoder Representations from Transformers) and GPT (Generative Pre-trained Transformer), has marked a significant advancement in NLP. Transformers leverage self-attention mechanisms to weigh the importance of different words in a sentence relative to each other, allowing for a more sophisticated understanding of context. For instance, BERT s bidirectional approach enables it to consider the entire context of a word from both directions, improving its performance on tasks like question answering and sentiment analysis.

Another critical aspect of NLP is its application in generating human-like text. This task involves the creation of coherent and contextually relevant text based on input prompts. Models like GPT-3 have demonstrated impressive capabilities in generating text that can mimic human writing styles, making them useful for applications ranging from content creation to conversational agents. These models are trained on diverse datasets to capture a wide range of language patterns and can generate responses that are contextually appropriate and grammatically accurate.

Despite these advancements, challenges remain in NLP. One significant issue is the handling of ambiguity and context. Human language is inherently ambiguous and context-dependent, which can lead to difficulties in accurately interpreting and generating text. For example, sarcasm and idiomatic expressions can pose challenges for NLP systems, as they often require a deeper understanding of context and subtleties that are not easily captured by algorithms.

Bias in NLP models is another critical concern. Models trained on large datasets can inadvertently learn and perpetuate biases present in the data. This issue has implications for fairness and ethics in NLP applications, as biased models can reinforce stereotypes and lead to unintended consequences. Addressing bias requires ongoing research and the development of strategies to ensure that NLP systems are equitable and just.

The field of NLP continues to evolve rapidly, driven by

advancements in machine learning, computational power, and the availability of large datasets. Researchers and practitioners are constantly developing new techniques and refining existing methods to improve the accuracy, efficiency, and applicability of NLP systems. As we advance further into the realm of NLP, the goal remains to enhance the ability of machines to understand and generate human language in a way that is both meaningful and beneficial across a wide range of applications.

By gaining a foundational understanding of these concepts and techniques, you will be well-prepared to explore more complex aspects of NLP and engage with the ongoing advancements in this dynamic field.

CHAPTER 2: THE EVOLUTION OF LANGUAGE MODELS

The evolution of language models represents a fascinating journey through the development of technologies designed to understand and generate human language. Initially, language models were grounded in simple statistical methods, which provided a foundation for subsequent advancements. Early models relied heavily on basic probabilistic techniques to handle linguistic data. These early systems, often rule-based, were built upon hand-crafted rules and lexicons to process and interpret text. They were limited by their reliance on explicit, pre-defined structures and their inability to adapt to the variability and complexity of natural language.

In the early days of computational linguistics, the predominant approach was based on n-gram models. These models predicted the probability of a word or sequence of words based on the preceding n-1 words. For example, a bigram model (where n2) might predict the likelihood of a word based on the preceding single word, while a trigram model (where n3) would use the two preceding words. Although effective for certain applications, these models suffered from limitations such as data sparsity and the inability to capture long-range dependencies. As n-gram models scaled up to higher values of n, the computational complexity and data requirements increased significantly, leading to diminishing returns in performance.

The advent of machine learning marked a significant shift in the development of language models. Unlike rule-based systems, machine learning models learn patterns and structures from large datasets, enabling them to generalize and adapt to new data. Early machine learning approaches to NLP involved methods such as decision trees, support vector machines, and hidden Markov models. These methods allowed for more sophisticated handling of linguistic phenomena compared to their rule-based predecessors, although they still faced challenges in capturing the deeper syntactic and semantic relationships within text.

The transition to neural networks marked a transformative phase in the evolution of language models. Neural networks, with their ability to learn hierarchical representations and capture complex patterns, offered a new paradigm for processing language data. Early neural network models, such as feedforward neural networks, introduced the concept of learning from data without explicit feature engineering. However, these models were limited by their inability to handle sequential dependencies and context over long spans of text.

The introduction of Recurrent Neural Networks (RNNs) brought significant advancements by addressing the limitations of feedforward networks in processing sequential data. RNNs are designed to handle sequences by maintaining a hidden state that is updated with each new input, allowing them to capture temporal dependencies and context over varying lengths of text. Despite their advantages, RNNs faced challenges such as vanishing and exploding gradients, which hindered their ability to model long-range dependencies effectively.

To overcome these challenges, Long Short-Term Memory (LSTM) networks were developed. LSTMs introduced mechanisms such as gates and memory cells to manage and retain long-term dependencies, addressing the gradient issues encountered in traditional RNNs. This advancement enabled LSTMs to model complex sequences with greater accuracy, making them a popular choice for tasks such as machine translation, speech recognition, and text generation.

The next major leap in language modeling came with the introduction of transformer models. Transformers, proposed in the seminal paper "Attention is All You Need," revolutionized the field by employing self-attention mechanisms to process sequences in parallel rather than sequentially. This innovation allowed transformers to capture dependencies across entire sequences without the limitations imposed by RNNs. Self-attention mechanisms enable models to weigh the importance of different words in a sequence relative to each other, facilitating a more nuanced understanding of context and relationships.

The success of transformer models led to the development of advanced architectures such as BERT (Bidirectional Encoder Representations from Transformers) and GPT (Generative Pre-trained Transformer). BERT introduced bidirectional training, allowing the model to consider context from both the left and right of a word, thereby enhancing its understanding of meaning and context. GPT, on the other hand, focused on generative capabilities, using a unidirectional approach to generate coherent and contextually relevant text.

The impact of these advancements on the field of NLP has been profound. Modern language models, built upon the transformer architecture, have set new benchmarks in various NLP tasks, including text classification, sentiment analysis, and language translation. These models have achieved remarkable levels of performance and have been widely adopted in both research and industry, driving innovations across a range of applications.

As we explore the evolution of language models, it becomes evident that each stage of development has contributed to the current state-of-the-art technologies. From the early days of statistical models to the sophisticated deep learning architectures of today, the journey reflects a continuous effort to enhance the ability of machines to understand and generate human language. Understanding this historical context provides a crucial foundation for appreciating the capabilities and limitations of current language models and sets the stage for delving into their practical applications and future developments.

Recurrent Neural Networks (RNNs) marked a pivotal advancement in the field of language modeling by introducing the capability to handle sequences and maintain context over varying lengths of text. Unlike feedforward neural networks, RNNs have connections that form directed cycles, enabling them to maintain a form of memory. This memory allows RNNs to use information from previous steps in a sequence to influence current predictions, thus addressing the issue of sequential dependencies.

Despite their advantages, traditional RNNs struggled with long-range dependencies due to the vanishing and exploding gradient problems. These issues occur when gradients, which are used to update the model's weights during training, either diminish to zero or grow exponentially, making it difficult for the model to learn from distant parts of the sequence. This limitation prompted the development of specialized RNN architectures designed to mitigate these problems.

Long Short-Term Memory (LSTM) networks and Gated Recurrent Units (GRUs) are two such architectures that emerged to address the challenges faced by standard RNNs. LSTMs, introduced by Hochreiter and Schmidhuber in 1997, incorporate memory cells and gating mechanisms to regulate the flow of information. The memory cells allow LSTMs to maintain information over extended periods, while the gates control the addition and removal of information, making it easier for the network to retain relevant data and forget irrelevant details.

Similarly, GRUs, introduced by Cho et al. in 2014, streamline the LSTM architecture by combining the input and forget gates into a single update gate, simplifying the network while still providing the capability to manage long-term dependencies effectively. Both LSTMs and GRUs have been instrumental in improving the performance of various NLP tasks, including language modeling, machine translation, and speech recognition.

The development of neural network models continued to advance with the introduction of attention mechanisms. Attention mechanisms allow models to focus on different parts of a sequence with varying degrees of emphasis, dynamically adjusting the weight of each component based on its relevance to the current task. This capability proved particularly valuable in tasks that require understanding and generating sequences, such as machine translation.

The transformer model, introduced by Vaswani et al. in 2017, revolutionized the field of NLP by leveraging attention mechanisms to replace recurrent structures entirely. The transformer architecture uses self-attention mechanisms to process sequences in parallel, rather than sequentially. This parallelization significantly improves computational efficiency and scalability, allowing the model to handle longer sequences and capture complex dependencies more effectively.

Transformers consist of encoder and decoder layers, each containing multiple self-attention and feedforward sub-layers. The self-attention mechanism within the encoder layer enables the model to weigh different parts of the input sequence, allowing it to understand context and relationships between words more comprehensively. The decoder layer, equipped with similar attention mechanisms, generates output sequences by attending to both the encoded input and previously generated tokens.

The success of the transformer model led to the development of various pre-trained language models, such as BERT (Bidirectional Encoder Representations from Transformers) and GPT (Generative Pre-trained Transformer). BERT, introduced by Devlin et al. in 2018, focuses on bidirectional context by training on masked language modeling and next sentence prediction tasks. This approach allows BERT to capture context from both directions in a sentence, improving its ability to understand nuanced meanings and relationships.

GPT, introduced by OpenAI, represents a different approach by leveraging autoregressive language modeling. GPT is trained to predict the next word in a sequence based on the preceding context, allowing it to generate coherent and contextually relevant text. The successive versions of GPT, including GPT-2 and GPT-3, have demonstrated remarkable capabilities in text generation, comprehension, and various NLP applications, thanks to their large-scale training on diverse datasets.

The advancements in language modeling have had profound implications for the field of NLP. Modern models, built upon the principles of neural networks and attention mechanisms, have achieved state-of-the-art performance in a range of tasks, from machine translation and text summarization to question answering and conversational agents. These developments have enabled significant progress in automating and enhancing human-computer interactions, making language technologies more accessible and effective.

As we continue to explore the evolution of language models, it is essential to recognize the ongoing research and innovations shaping the future of NLP. The field remains dynamic, with new techniques and models constantly emerging to address the evolving challenges and demands of natural language understanding. By understanding the historical context and foundational advancements in language modeling, we can better appreciate the current state-of-the-art technologies and their potential impact on the future of artificial intelligence and language processing.

The advent of the transformer model marked a transformative moment in the evolution of language models. By eliminating the need for recurrent connections, transformers introduced a new paradigm for processing sequences through self-attention mechanisms. Self-attention allows the model to weigh the significance of each word in a sequence relative to every other word, regardless of their positional distance. This capability addresses one of the key limitations of RNNs and LSTMs, which struggle with efficiently managing dependencies over long sequences.

Transformers use a multi-head attention mechanism to capture various aspects of relationships between words. Each head in the multi-head attention mechanism processes the sequence from a different perspective, allowing the model to gather a richer understanding of the text. The outputs from these multiple heads are then combined and transformed through feedforward networks, enabling the model to integrate different aspects of the information before producing the final representation.

In addition to the attention mechanism, transformers incorporate positional encoding to account for the order of words in a sequence. Unlike RNNs, which process words sequentially and inherently capture positional information through their architecture, transformers process all words in parallel. Positional encodings are added to the input embeddings to provide the model with information about the relative or absolute position of words in a sequence. This encoding ensures that the model can maintain a sense of word order, which is crucial for understanding the structure and meaning of sentences.

The success of the transformer architecture paved the way for the development of large-scale pre-trained language models, which have since become foundational in the field of NLP. Models such as BERT (Bidirectional Encoder Representations from Transformers) and GPT (Generative Pre-trained Transformer) exemplify the impact of pre-training on language understanding. BERT, introduced by Devlin et al. in 2018, utilizes a bidirectional approach to training, allowing the model to consider both the left and right context of a word simultaneously. This bidirectional training enables BERT to achieve a deeper understanding of context and semantics compared to earlier models that processed text unidirectionally.

GPT, developed by OpenAI, represents another major milestone in language modeling. GPT-1, introduced in 2018, employed a unidirectional approach, generating text by predicting the next word in a sequence based on the preceding context. GPT-2 and GPT-3 further expanded on this concept by scaling up the model size and training data, resulting in models with billions of parameters capable of generating highly coherent and contextually relevant text. The GPT series demonstrates the potential of large-scale pre-trained models to perform a wide range of NLP tasks with minimal task-specific fine-tuning.

The integration of pre-trained language models into practical applications has revolutionized the capabilities of NLP systems. Fine-tuning these models on specific tasks, such as text classification, named entity recognition, and machine translation, has become a standard practice. The pre-training phase allows models to learn general language patterns and structures, while fine-tuning adapts them to specialized tasks, optimizing their performance based on domain-specific data.

The evolution of language models also highlights the growing importance of model scalability and efficiency. As language models become increasingly large and complex, the computational resources required for training and inference have risen correspondingly. Researchers and practitioners are continually exploring ways to balance model performance with computational efficiency. Techniques such as model pruning, quantization, and knowledge distillation are being developed to reduce the size and complexity of models while maintaining their effectiveness.

Furthermore, the ethical considerations surrounding language models have become a focal point of discussion. As these models gain the ability to generate human-like text, concerns about misuse, bias, and the potential impact on society have emerged. Addressing these challenges involves ongoing research into ensuring that language models are trained on diverse and representative datasets, implementing safeguards against harmful outputs, and fostering transparency in the development and deployment of these technologies.

The progression from simple statistical methods to sophisticated neural networks and transformers illustrates the remarkable advancements in language modeling. Each phase in this evolution has contributed to our ability to understand and generate human language with increasing accuracy and relevance. As we continue to develop and refine language models, the focus will increasingly shift towards enhancing their efficiency, addressing ethical concerns, and exploring new frontiers in language understanding and generation.

CHAPTER 3: BASICS OF TEXT PREPROCESSING

Text preprocessing is a fundamental step in natural language processing (NLP) that prepares raw text data for analysis and modeling. This process involves several techniques designed to clean, structure, and normalize text, ensuring that it is suitable for further computational tasks. Effective preprocessing is crucial because raw text data can be messy and unstructured, containing various inconsistencies, redundancies, and irrelevant information that can hinder analysis. By applying preprocessing techniques, we can transform this raw data into a more manageable and interpretable format.

The first technique in text preprocessing is tokenization, which involves breaking down text into smaller units called tokens. Tokens can be words, phrases, or characters, depending on the granularity required for the analysis. The primary goal of tokenization is to simplify the text into discrete elements that can be individually analyzed. For instance, the sentence "Text preprocessing is essential for NLP" can be tokenized into the following word tokens: "Text," "preprocessing," "is," "essential," "for," and "NLP." Tokenization is typically the first step in preprocessing, as it lays the foundation for subsequent processes.

Following tokenization, the text often undergoes normalization to standardize its format. Normalization includes several sub-processes such as converting text to lowercase, removing punctuation, and correcting misspellings. Converting text to lowercase helps in ensuring uniformity, as it eliminates case sensitivity. For example, "NLP" and "nlp" would be treated as different tokens without this step. Removing punctuation, such as commas and periods, further simplifies the text and eliminates potential noise that might interfere with analysis. Additionally, correcting misspellings helps in consolidating similar words and improving the accuracy of downstream tasks.

Stemming and lemmatization are techniques used to reduce words to their base or root forms, thus standardizing variations of a word. Stemming involves cutting off prefixes or suffixes to obtain a root form. For instance, the words "running," "runner," and "ran" might all be reduced to "run." Stemming is generally faster and more straightforward but can sometimes produce non-dictionary words. Lemmatization, on the other hand, is a more sophisticated process that involves mapping words to their base or dictionary forms. For example, "running" would be lemmatized to "run," and "better" would be lemmatized to "good." Although lemmatization is more accurate, it is computationally more intensive compared to stemming.

Removing stop words is another crucial preprocessing step. Stop words are common words such as "and," "the," "is," and "in" that frequently appear in text but carry little meaning in the context of analysis. These words are often removed to reduce the dimensionality of the text data and to focus on more meaningful words. The removal of stop words can improve the efficiency and effectiveness of text analysis by eliminating noise and highlighting the significant terms. For instance, the phrase "The quick brown fox jumps over the lazy dog" would be simplified to "quick brown fox jumps lazy dog" after stop words are removed.

Another important preprocessing technique is dealing with

special characters and formatting issues. Text data may contain special characters, HTML tags, or other formatting artifacts that are not relevant to the analysis. Removing or replacing these characters ensures that the text is clean and free from extraneous information. For example, text extracted from web pages might contain HTML tags like "<p>" and "</p>" that need to be removed before further processing.

Handling text normalization and expansion is also vital, particularly when dealing with informal or abbreviated language, such as text from social media. Expanding abbreviations and contractions (e.g., "don't" to "do not" and "U" to "you") helps in standardizing the text and improving its consistency. This normalization process makes the text more comparable and easier to analyze, especially in tasks such as sentiment analysis and machine learning.

In addition to these techniques, text preprocessing may involve more specialized processes depending on the nature of the data and the specific requirements of the analysis. For instance, entity recognition might be employed to identify and categorize proper nouns and other significant terms within the text. Named entity recognition (NER) systems can detect entities such as names of people, organizations, and locations, which can be particularly useful for applications like information extraction and question answering.

As we progress through the text preprocessing techniques, it becomes evident that each step plays a critical role in transforming raw text into a format that is suitable for analysis and modeling. Tokenization, normalization, stemming, lemmatization, stop word removal, and other preprocessing techniques collectively contribute to the preparation of text data, making it more structured and amenable to computational methods. Understanding and applying these techniques effectively is essential for anyone involved in natural language processing, as they lay the groundwork for building robust and accurate language models.

Another vital step in text preprocessing is the removal of stop words. Stop words are common words such as "and," "the," "in," and "on" that frequently occur in text but carry little meaningful information for many analytical tasks. The presence of these words can often overshadow the more significant terms in a text, leading to skewed results. Removing stop words helps in focusing on the more relevant words that contribute to the semantic content of the text. For example, in the sentence 'The cat sat on the mat," removing the stop words "the" and "on" leaves us with 'cat," "sat," and "mat," which are more indicative of the sentence's core meaning.

The process of stop word removal involves using predefined lists of common words that are considered stop words. These lists can vary depending on the language and the specific needs of the analysis. While removing stop words is a common practice, it's essential to consider the context in which stop words are used. In some cases, such as sentiment analysis or document classification, stop words might hold important contextual information and should be retained.

In addition to tokenization, normalization, stemming, lemmatization, and stop word removal, text preprocessing often includes techniques for dealing with specific text features, such as handling case sensitivity and addressing text length. Case sensitivity is particularly relevant when dealing with text data where the meaning might change based on capitalization. For instance, "Python" (the programming language) and "python" (the snake) have different meanings. Deciding whether to preserve case sensitivity or convert all text to lowercase depends on the specific goals of the analysis.

Text length normalization is another consideration in preprocessing, especially when dealing with tasks like document classification or clustering. Texts of varying lengths can impact the performance of certain algorithms, which may be sensitive to the length of the input data. Techniques such as padding (adding additional tokens to ensure uniform text length) or truncation (cutting off text that exceeds a certain length) are employed to standardize text lengths and ensure consistency across the dataset.

The handling of special characters and symbols is also a crucial aspect of text preprocessing. Special characters, such as emojis, hashtags, and URLs, can introduce additional complexity and noise into the text. Depending on the analysis, it may be necessary to remove, replace, or retain these special characters. For instance, in social media text analysis, hashtags and mentions might be valuable for understanding user interactions and sentiments, while URLs might be removed if they do not contribute to the semantic content.

The next step in text preprocessing often involves transforming text into numerical representations that can be processed by machine learning algorithms. One common method for this transformation is the use of bag-of-words (BoW) models. The BoW approach represents text as a collection of words with associated frequencies or counts, disregarding the order in which words appear. This method simplifies the text into a matrix of word counts, which can be used as input for various machine learning models. Although BoW is straightforward and effective for many tasks, it does not capture the semantic relationships between words or the context in which they occur.

To address the limitations of BoW, more advanced techniques such as term frequency-inverse document frequency (TF-IDF) and word embeddings have been developed. TF-IDF enhances the BoW model by weighting words based on their importance within a document relative to a collection of documents. This method helps to highlight terms that are unique to a particular document while downplaying common terms that occur frequently across all documents. TF-IDF provides a more nuanced representation of text by considering the significance of words in context.

Word embeddings, as mentioned earlier, represent words as dense vectors in a continuous space, capturing semantic relationships between words. Techniques such as Word2Vec and GloVe generate these embeddings by analyzing large corpora of text and learning to represent words based on their co-occurrence patterns. Word embeddings enable models to understand synonyms and related terms more effectively, as words with similar meanings are positioned closer together in the vector space.

In summary, text preprocessing involves a series of essential techniques that transform raw text into a structured and analyzable format. Tokenization, normalization, stemming, lemmatization, stop word removal, and special character handling are foundational processes that prepare text data for further analysis. Advanced methods such as BoW, TF-IDF, and word embeddings provide additional layers of representation, enabling more sophisticated modeling and analysis. Mastery of these preprocessing techniques is crucial for effective natural language processing, laying the groundwork for building and interpreting more advanced NLP models.

Another essential aspect of text preprocessing involves the handling of numerical and categorical data within text. In many cases, text data contains numerical values, dates, or categorical labels that need to be processed appropriately. For instance, when analyzing financial reports or scientific articles, numbers and dates often carry significant meaning. Numerical data might be normalized or scaled, while dates might be converted into a consistent format or extracted into separate features. Similarly, categorical labels, such as tags or categories, need to be encoded into a format that can be utilized by machine learning algorithms. This often involves converting categorical text into numerical values through techniques such as one-hot encoding or label encoding.

Additionally, text preprocessing may require handling text in different languages or dealing with multilingual datasets. Preprocessing techniques must be adapted to account for the linguistic differences and unique characteristics of each language. For example, languages like Chinese or Japanese do not use spaces between words, necessitating specialized tokenization approaches. Similarly, languages with rich morphology, such as Finnish or Turkish, may require more advanced lemmatization techniques to accurately capture word forms and meanings.

Dealing with slang, colloquialisms, and domain-specific jargon is another important consideration. Text data often includes informal language, abbreviations, and terminology specific to certain fields or communities. Preprocessing must address these variations to ensure that the text is accurately represented. This might involve expanding abbreviations, normalizing slang terms, or incorporating domain-specific knowledge into the preprocessing pipeline.

Finally, ensuring consistency and addressing potential biases in text data are critical steps in preprocessing. Consistency involves maintaining uniformity in the preprocessing approach across the entire dataset to ensure that all text is treated equally. Biases, on the other hand, can arise from imbalances in the data, such as overrepresentation of certain topics or viewpoints. Addressing these biases may involve techniques such as data augmentation or balancing, where additional samples are added to underrepresented classes to create a more representative dataset.

As the field of NLP continues to evolve, text preprocessing techniques are increasingly becoming more sophisticated and integrated into end-to-end pipelines. Advances in machine learning and deep learning have led to the development of models that can learn directly from raw text, reducing the need for extensive preprocessing. However, understanding and applying fundamental preprocessing techniques remains crucial for creating high-quality data that can effectively support analysis and model training.

By mastering the basics of text preprocessing, you will lay a solid foundation for tackling more complex tasks in NLP. These preprocessing steps are essential for transforming raw, unstructured text into a structured format that is conducive to analysis and modeling. Whether you are working on sentiment analysis, topic modeling, or text classification, the ability to preprocess text effectively will greatly enhance the quality and accuracy of your results.

In summary, text preprocessing involves a range of techniques designed to clean, structure, and normalize text data. From tokenization and normalization to stemming, lemmatization, and stop word removal, each step plays a vital role in preparing text for further analysis. Handling numerical and categorical data, addressing multilingual and domain-specific challenges, and ensuring consistency and fairness are also key aspects of preprocessing. As you continue your journey in NLP, these foundational techniques will be instrumental in developing robust and effective models capable of understanding and generating human language.

CHAPTER 4: FEATURE EXTRACTION AND REPRESENTATION

The transformation of text data into a format that can be effectively utilized by machine learning models is a crucial step in natural language processing. This process, known as feature extraction, involves converting raw text into numerical representations that capture the essential information for analysis. In this section, we will explore several key methods of feature extraction, including Bag of Words, Term Frequency-Inverse Document Frequency (TF-IDF), and word embeddings such as Word2Vec and GloVe. Each method offers distinct advantages and is suited to different types of tasks and models.

The Bag of Words (BoW) model is one of the most straightforward and widely used techniques for feature extraction. The BoW approach represents a text document as a collection of words, disregarding the order and grammar but focusing on the frequency of each word. To implement this model, one first creates a vocabulary of all unique words in the corpus. Each document is then represented as a vector in which each dimension corresponds to a word in the vocabulary, and the value in each dimension represents the frequency of the word in the document.

For instance, consider a small corpus consisting of three documents: "The cat sat on the mat," "The dog barked at the cat," and "The mat was on the floor." The vocabulary derived from this corpus would include words such as "the," "cat," "sat," "on," "mat," "dog," "barked," and "floor." The BoW representation for the first document might be a vector like [2, 1, 1, 1, 1, 0, 0, 0], where the values correspond to the counts of the words in the order of the vocabulary.

While the BoW model is simple and effective, it has certain limitations. One major drawback is its inability to capture the semantic meaning of words or their context within the document. To address this, the Term Frequency-Inverse Document Frequency (TF-IDF) model was developed. TF-IDF builds upon the BoW model by adding a weighting scheme that adjusts the importance of each word based on its frequency across the entire corpus.

In TF-IDF, the Term Frequency (TF) component measures how frequently a term appears in a document, reflecting its significance within that particular document. The Inverse Document Frequency (IDF) component, on the other hand, measures how important a term is across the entire corpus by penalizing common terms that appear in many documents. The TF-IDF score for a term is calculated by multiplying the TF and IDF values, resulting in a weight that represents the term's importance relative to other terms.

For example, in the corpus mentioned earlier, the term "mat" appears in two out of three documents. Its TF-IDF weight would be higher in documents where it appears more frequently compared to less frequent terms. This approach helps in highlighting terms that are more relevant to specific documents while reducing the influence of common but less informative terms.

Advancements in feature extraction continued with the introduction of word embeddings, which represent words in a continuous vector space. Unlike BoW and TF-IDF, word embeddings capture semantic relationships between words by placing similar words closer together in the vector space. This allows for a richer representation of text that can capture context and meaning more effectively.

Word2Vec, introduced by Mikolov et al. in 2013, is a popular method for generating word embeddings. Word2Vec employs two primary architectures: Continuous Bag of Words (CBOW) and Skip-gram. CBOW predicts a target word based on its surrounding context words, while Skip-gram does the reverse, predicting context words based on a given target word. Both architectures aim to learn word vectors that reflect the syntactic and semantic relationships between words.

For instance, in the Skip-gram model, if the target word is "cat," the context words might include "the," "sat," "on," and "mat." The model adjusts the word vectors to maximize the probability of these context words given the target word. As a result, words with similar meanings or usage patterns, such as "cat" and "dog," will have similar embeddings in the vector space.

Another influential word embedding technique is GloVe (Global Vectors for Word Representation), introduced by Pennington et al. in 2014. GloVe is based on matrix factorization techniques applied to word co-occurrence statistics. It constructs a word co-occurrence matrix from the corpus, capturing how often words appear together. By factorizing this matrix, GloVe generates word vectors that encode the global statistical properties of the corpus, allowing it to capture semantic similarities between words based on their co-occurrence patterns.

In summary, feature extraction and representation are crucial steps in preparing text data for machine learning models. The Bag of Words and TF-IDF models offer fundamental approaches for converting text into numerical features, each with its strengths and limitations. Word embeddings, such as those generated by Word2Vec and GloVe, provide more sophisticated representations that capture semantic relationships and contextual information. Understanding and applying these techniques will enable you to effectively prepare text data for various NLP tasks and models.

The Term Frequency-Inverse Document Frequency (TF-IDF) model enhances the Bag of Words approach by incorporating a weighting mechanism that accounts for the relative importance of words across a corpus. While Term Frequency (TF) measures how often a word appears in a document, Inverse Document Frequency (IDF) assesses how important a word is across the entire corpus. The IDF component is designed to diminish the weight of common words that appear in many documents and increase the weight of rare words that are more specific to particular documents.

The IDF value for a word is computed using the formula:
$$\text{IDF}(w) \log\left(\frac{N}{1 + \text{DF}(w)}\right)$$
where N represents the total number of documents in the corpus, and $\text{DF}(w)$ is the number of documents containing the word w. The addition of 1 to the denominator prevents division by zero for words that appear in all documents.

The TF-IDF weight of a term in a document is then calculated by multiplying the Term Frequency (TF) of the word by its IDF score:
$$\text{TF-IDF}(w, d) \text{TF}(w, d) \times \text{IDF}(w)$$
where $\text{TF}(w, d)$ is the frequency of word w in document d. This weighting mechanism provides a more nuanced representation of the text by emphasizing words that are unique to specific documents while downplaying words that are universally common.

TF-IDF is particularly useful for tasks such as information retrieval and text classification, where distinguishing between important and unimportant words can significantly impact performance. However, while TF-IDF improves on the BoW model by incorporating the relative importance of terms, it still lacks the ability to capture the semantic relationships between words.

To address this limitation, word embeddings such as Word2Vec and GloVe were developed. These methods represent words in a continuous vector space where semantically similar words are positioned closer together. Unlike TF-IDF and BoW, which rely on sparse vectors and word counts, word embeddings provide dense and low-dimensional representations of words, capturing their meanings based on their context within a large corpus.

Word2Vec, introduced by Mikolov et al., employs neural network models to learn word representations. The two main architectures used in Word2Vec are the Continuous Bag of Words (CBOW) model and the Skip-gram model. The CBOW model predicts the target word based on its surrounding context words, while the Skip-gram model performs the inverse, predicting context words given a target word. Both models utilize a large corpus to train the neural network, resulting in word vectors that capture semantic relationships such as word similarity and analogy.

For example, in a well-trained Word2Vec model, the vector representation for the word "king" might be close to "queen," "prince," and "monarch," reflecting their semantic relationships. Similarly, vector arithmetic can reveal analogies, such as "king - man + woman ≈ queen," by performing vector operations in the embedding space.

GloVe (Global Vectors for Word Representation), developed by Pennington et al., provides another approach to learning word embeddings. Unlike Word2Vec, which learns embeddings through local context windows, GloVe leverages global statistical information from the entire corpus. It constructs a word-word co-occurrence matrix and factorizes this matrix to learn word vectors that capture both local and global semantic information.

The GloVe model involves training on the co-occurrence matrix to optimize a cost function that ensures the dot product of word vectors approximates the logarithm of the co-occurrence probability. This method allows GloVe to capture meaningful word relationships and produce high-quality embeddings that reflect the overall structure of the corpus.

Both Word2Vec and GloVe have significantly advanced the field of NLP by providing rich, continuous representations of words that capture their meanings and relationships. These embeddings have become foundational in many NLP applications, including machine translation, sentiment analysis, and text generation.

In summary, feature extraction and representation are critical components of text preprocessing that transform raw text into formats suitable for machine learning models. The Bag of Words and TF-IDF models offer initial methods for representing text based on word counts and importance, while word embeddings such as Word2Vec and GloVe provide deeper, semantic representations that capture complex relationships between words. Each method has its strengths and applications, and understanding their principles and implementation is essential for leveraging text data effectively in various NLP tasks.

Word embeddings, such as Word2Vec and GloVe, represent a significant advancement in feature extraction by embedding words into continuous vector spaces that capture semantic relationships. Unlike traditional methods that treat words as discrete entities, embeddings leverage the context in which words appear to infer meaning.

Word2Vec, introduced by Tomas Mikolov and his team at Google, is a neural network-based approach that learns vector representations of words through their contextual usage. Word2Vec offers two primary models: Continuous Bag of Words

(CBOW) and Skip-gram. The CBOW model predicts a target word from its surrounding context words, while the Skip-gram model does the reverse, predicting the surrounding context from a given target word. These models utilize large corpora of text to learn dense, high-dimensional vectors for each word, with the goal of capturing syntactic and semantic similarities.

For example, in the Skip-gram model, if the word "king" is used in the context of "the king of the country," the model learns to place "king" close to other contextually relevant words like "queen," "royal," and "monarch" in the vector space. As a result, these words will have similar vector representations, reflecting their semantic relatedness. This contextual learning allows Word2Vec to capture nuanced word relationships, such as analogies, where "king" is to "queen" as "man" is to "woman."

GloVe, or Global Vectors for Word Representation, developed by Stanford researchers, takes a slightly different approach. Instead of learning word vectors from context windows, GloVe constructs word representations based on word co-occurrence statistics across the entire corpus. The core idea is to factorize the word co-occurrence matrix into lower-dimensional vectors, which are designed to capture the global statistical information of the corpus.

GloVe generates a co-occurrence matrix where each entry represents the frequency of a word appearing in the context of another word. The model then performs matrix factorization to derive word vectors that preserve the ratios of co-occurrence probabilities. This approach ensures that the resulting word vectors reflect both local and global relationships in the text, making them suitable for a variety of downstream tasks, including word similarity and analogy tasks.

Both Word2Vec and GloVe have significantly advanced the field of NLP by providing dense vector representations that capture rich semantic information. These embeddings are often pre-trained on large corpora and can be fine-tuned for specific tasks or used directly in applications such as sentiment analysis, named entity recognition, and machine translation.

Despite their strengths, word embeddings also have limitations. One challenge is the handling of out-of-vocabulary words—words that were not seen during the training of the embeddings. To address this issue, subword-level embeddings, such as FastText, extend the idea of word embeddings by representing words as bags of character n-grams. This approach allows the model to generate embeddings for rare or unseen words by leveraging the subword information.

In addition, embeddings learned from large corpora may inadvertently capture and perpetuate biases present in the data. For instance, word embeddings might reflect stereotypes or societal biases, such as gender or ethnic biases. Addressing these biases requires ongoing research and the development of techniques for mitigating unwanted biases in word representations.

As we progress in the field of NLP, the techniques for feature extraction and representation will continue to evolve. Modern approaches increasingly incorporate contextualized embeddings, such as BERT (Bidirectional Encoder Representations from Transformers) and its variants, which generate dynamic word representations based on the surrounding context of the entire sentence. These advancements further enhance the ability to capture complex linguistic phenomena and improve the performance of NLP models across a wide range of applications.

Understanding and applying these feature extraction methods is fundamental for transforming text data into meaningful numerical representations. Mastery of techniques such as Bag of Words, TF-IDF, and word embeddings equips practitioners with the tools to effectively analyze and model text data, paving the way for more sophisticated and accurate NLP solutions.

CHAPTER 5: UNDERSTANDING SENTIMENT ANALYSIS

Sentiment analysis is a pivotal task in natural language processing, aimed at deciphering the emotional tone behind a piece of text. This technique is widely employed to understand and quantify sentiments expressed in various forms of communication, from customer reviews to social media posts. The goal of sentiment analysis is to classify text into categories such as positive, negative, or neutral, and to gauge the intensity of these sentiments. In this exploration, we will delve into both lexicon-based methods and machine learning approaches, providing a comprehensive overview of how sentiment analysis is conducted and the challenges it entails.

Lexicon-based sentiment analysis relies on predefined lists of words and phrases, known as sentiment lexicons, to evaluate the sentiment of text. These lexicons assign sentiment scores to words based on their inherent emotional connotations. One common lexicon-based method is to use a sentiment dictionary where words are categorized as positive or negative, with associated scores indicating their strength. For example, words like "happy" or "excellent" might have high positive scores, while words like "sad" or "terrible" would have high negative scores.

To perform sentiment analysis using a lexicon-based approach, the text is first tokenized into individual words. Each word is then matched with its corresponding sentiment score from the lexicon. The overall sentiment of the text is determined by aggregating these scores, often using methods such as averaging or summing the individual word scores. For instance, if a review contains the words "good" (positive score) and "bad" (negative score), the overall sentiment might be calculated based on the balance of these scores.

While lexicon-based methods are relatively straightforward and easy to implement, they have limitations. They often struggle with context-dependent meanings, where the sentiment of a word can change based on its usage. For example, the word "sick" could be positive in the context of "That was a sick performance" but negative in "I feel sick today." Additionally, these methods might not capture the sentiment of phrases or sentences effectively, as they primarily focus on individual words.

Machine learning approaches offer a more dynamic and context-aware alternative to lexicon-based methods. These techniques involve training models to learn sentiment patterns from labeled text data. The process begins with collecting a dataset containing text samples annotated with sentiment labels, such as positive, negative, or neutral. This labeled data is then used to train a machine learning model, which learns to associate features of the text with specific sentiment categories.

One common machine learning approach for sentiment analysis is to use supervised learning algorithms, such as logistic regression, support vector machines (SVM), or decision trees. These models are trained on features extracted from the text, such as n-grams, part-of-speech tags, or syntactic structures. For instance, a logistic regression model might learn that the presence of certain words or phrases, along with their contextual usage, can predict whether a text expresses positive or negative sentiment.

In recent years, deep learning techniques have gained

prominence in sentiment analysis due to their ability to capture complex patterns in text data. Recurrent neural networks (RNNs), particularly long short-term memory (LSTM) networks, are commonly used for sentiment analysis because they are well-suited for processing sequential data and capturing long-range dependencies. These models can learn intricate relationships between words and their contexts, improving the accuracy of sentiment classification.

Another advanced technique involves the use of transformer-based models, such as BERT (Bidirectional Encoder Representations from Transformers), which have revolutionized sentiment analysis. BERT leverages attention mechanisms to understand the context of each word in relation to others in a sentence. By pre-training on large corpora and fine-tuning on specific sentiment analysis tasks, BERT models achieve state-of-the-art performance in various sentiment analysis benchmarks.

Despite the advancements in sentiment analysis techniques, several challenges remain. One major challenge is dealing with ambiguity and sarcasm in text. Sentiment analysis models can struggle with detecting sarcasm, where the sentiment expressed is opposite to the literal meaning of the words used. For example, the statement "Oh great, another delay" might be interpreted as positive if taken literally but is actually negative due to the sarcastic tone.

Another challenge is the handling of domain-specific language and jargon. Sentiment analysis models trained on general text corpora might not perform well on specialized domains, such as medical or financial texts, where specific terminology and context play a significant role in determining sentiment. Fine-tuning models on domain-specific data or incorporating domain knowledge can help address this issue.

Overall, sentiment analysis is a multifaceted field with a

range of techniques and applications. By understanding both lexicon-based and machine learning approaches, as well as the challenges involved, we can better harness the power of sentiment analysis to gain valuable insights from text data.

Machine learning approaches to sentiment analysis are often more effective at capturing the nuances and complexities of language compared to lexicon-based methods. These techniques leverage statistical models and algorithms to identify patterns and relationships in text data, making them more adaptable to diverse linguistic contexts. The process typically involves several stages, including data preprocessing, feature extraction, model training, and evaluation.

Initially, a labeled dataset is required, where each piece of text is annotated with a sentiment label, such as positive, negative, or neutral. This dataset is used to train machine learning models by providing examples of how different texts correlate with specific sentiments. Commonly used algorithms for sentiment analysis include Logistic Regression, Support Vector Machines (SVM), and Naive Bayes, each with its strengths and limitations.

Logistic Regression, a widely used classification algorithm, models the probability of a text belonging to a particular sentiment category. It does so by learning a set of weights associated with each feature in the text, which are then used to compute the likelihood of the text's sentiment. Support Vector Machines, on the other hand, find the hyperplane that best separates different sentiment classes in the feature space. This approach is particularly effective in high-dimensional spaces and can handle complex relationships between features.

Naive Bayes, based on Bayes' theorem, assumes that the presence of a particular feature in a text is independent of the presence of any other feature. Despite this simplifying assumption, Naive Bayes performs well in many practical applications due to its simplicity and efficiency. It calculates the probability of a text belonging to a particular sentiment class by considering the likelihood of individual features and the prior probability of each class.

The choice of features is crucial in machine learning-based sentiment analysis. Features can be derived from text using techniques such as Bag of Words or TF-IDF, which we discussed earlier. More advanced techniques include word embeddings like Word2Vec and GloVe, which capture semantic relationships and contextual meanings. By representing words as dense vectors, these embeddings provide richer feature representations that can improve the performance of sentiment analysis models.

Once the model is trained, it is evaluated using metrics such as accuracy, precision, recall, and F1 score. Accuracy measures the proportion of correctly classified texts out of the total number of texts. Precision and recall provide insights into the model's performance in identifying positive or negative sentiments specifically, with precision indicating the proportion of true positives among the predicted positives, and recall indicating the proportion of true positives among the actual positives. The F1 score, the harmonic mean of precision and recall, offers a balanced measure of a model's overall performance.

Despite the advancements in machine learning approaches, sentiment analysis still faces several challenges. One significant challenge is dealing with the ambiguity and variability of natural language. Words can have different meanings depending on their context, and sentiment can be expressed in subtle ways, such as through irony or sarcasm. For instance, the phrase "I couldn't be happier" could be interpreted as positive in a literal sense but might imply the opposite if spoken sarcastically. Training models to recognize and correctly interpret such nuances remains a complex task.

Another challenge is the diversity of language and the presence of domain-specific jargon. Sentiment analysis models trained on general datasets may not perform well on texts from specialized domains such as finance or medical literature, where terminology and expressions differ significantly from everyday language. To address this issue, domain-specific models or additional training data may be required.

Finally, the cultural and contextual factors influencing sentiment expression cannot be overlooked. Sentiment analysis models developed in one cultural or linguistic context may not transfer well to others. For example, expressions of politeness or formality can vary across cultures, affecting how sentiments are conveyed and interpreted. Models must be adapted or retrained to account for these variations to ensure accurate sentiment analysis in different contexts.

In conclusion, sentiment analysis is a powerful tool for understanding and interpreting the emotional tone of text. While lexicon-based methods offer simplicity and ease of implementation, machine learning approaches provide greater flexibility and context sensitivity. By leveraging a combination of feature extraction techniques and advanced algorithms, we can better capture the complexities of sentiment and apply this understanding to various domains. Nevertheless, challenges such as ambiguity, domain-specific language, and cultural differences highlight the need for ongoing research and refinement in sentiment analysis methodologies.

The practical applications of sentiment analysis span a wide range of domains, each benefiting from insights into public sentiment and emotional trends. In the business world, companies use sentiment analysis to monitor customer feedback, assess brand perception, and improve products and services. By analyzing customer reviews, social media posts, and other forms of feedback, businesses can gain valuable insights into their customers' experiences and sentiments. For instance, a company may track sentiment trends over time to understand how changes in their product or marketing strategies impact customer satisfaction.

In the realm of politics, sentiment analysis is employed to gauge public opinion and track shifts in voter sentiment. During election cycles, analysts use sentiment analysis to analyze speeches, debate transcripts, and social media discussions to understand public attitudes toward candidates and their policies. This information can be crucial for campaign strategies, helping political teams tailor their messages to resonate with voters' concerns and preferences.

The entertainment industry also leverages sentiment analysis to understand audience reactions to movies, television shows, and other media. By analyzing reviews and social media discussions, producers and studios can gauge the reception of their content, identify potential issues, and make data-driven decisions about future projects. For example, a film studio might use sentiment analysis to determine which aspects of a movie received the most positive or negative feedback, influencing their decisions on marketing and production.

Despite its many applications, sentiment analysis is not without its challenges. One of the primary difficulties is handling the subtleties of language, such as sarcasm, irony, and ambiguous expressions. Sentiments expressed sarcastically or ironically can be challenging for models to detect accurately, as the literal meaning of the text often contrasts with the intended sentiment. For example, the statement "Oh great, another traffic jam" could be interpreted as positive if taken literally but is actually negative in context.

Contextual understanding is another significant challenge. The sentiment of a word or phrase can vary depending on its surrounding context. For instance, the word "bank" can refer to a financial institution or the side of a river, and its sentiment can change based on the context in which it appears. Advanced techniques such as deep learning and context-aware models, like those based on transformer architectures, have shown promise in addressing these challenges by considering the broader context and dependencies within text.

Multilingual sentiment analysis presents additional difficulties, as sentiment lexicons and models often need to be adapted or retrained for different languages. The nuances of sentiment expression can vary significantly across languages and cultures, making it essential to develop language-specific resources and techniques. Machine learning models trained on data in one language may not perform well when applied to another language without appropriate adaptation and fine-tuning.

Moreover, sentiment analysis models can be biased based on the data they are trained on. If a model is trained on data that predominantly reflects certain viewpoints or demographics, it may produce skewed results when analyzing texts from different sources. Ensuring diversity and representativeness in training data is crucial for developing robust and fair sentiment analysis models. Regular evaluation and updates to models are necessary to address biases and maintain their accuracy over time.

In conclusion, sentiment analysis is a powerful tool for extracting emotional insights from text data, with applications ranging from business and politics to entertainment. Both lexicon-based and machine learning approaches offer valuable methods for performing sentiment analysis, each with its strengths and limitations. While challenges such as handling sarcasm, context, and language differences persist, advancements in natural language processing continue to improve the accuracy and applicability of sentiment analysis techniques. By understanding and addressing these challenges, we can harness the full potential of sentiment analysis to gain deeper insights into human emotions and behaviors.

CHAPTER 6: INTRODUCTION TO NAMED ENTITY RECOGNITION

Named Entity Recognition (NER) stands as a fundamental technique in natural language processing, pivotal for extracting structured information from unstructured text. NER involves the identification and classification of entities within a text, such as people's names, locations, dates, and other specific information. This capability is crucial for a variety of applications, including information retrieval, content extraction, and automated knowledge management. In this discussion, I will delve into both rule-based and machine learning-based methods of NER, illustrating their principles and implementations through practical examples.

At its core, NER aims to tag segments of text with predefined entity types. For example, in the sentence "Apple Inc. was founded in Cupertino on April 1, 1976," an NER system would identify "Apple Inc." as an organization, "Cupertino" as a location, and "April 1, 1976" as a date. This tagging process helps transform raw text into a structured format that is easier to analyze and query.

Rule-based NER methods utilize handcrafted rules and patterns to identify entities. These rules are typically based on linguistic patterns, such as specific sequences of words, capitalization, and the presence of certain keywords. For instance, a rule-based system might use patterns like "Mr. [Name]" to identify personal names or "on [Date]" to recognize dates. These rules are often crafted by experts who have a deep understanding of the text domain and the types of entities that are relevant.

One of the advantages of rule-based methods is their interpretability and precision in well-defined contexts. If the rules are carefully designed, they can perform well in specific domains where the entity types and contexts are predictable. However, the effectiveness of rule-based approaches often diminishes when dealing with diverse or unpredictable text. The rules may not generalize well across different domains or languages, and creating and maintaining these rules can be labor-intensive.

Machine learning-based NER methods offer a more flexible and scalable alternative to rule-based systems. These methods involve training models to recognize entities based on annotated training data. The training data consists of text where entities have been manually labeled, and the model learns to generalize from these examples to identify entities in unseen text.

A common approach in machine learning-based NER is to use sequence labeling techniques, where the goal is to predict a label for each token in a sequence of text. For instance, given the sentence "Barack Obama was born in Honolulu," the model would label "Barack Obama" as a person, "Honolulu" as a location, and the remaining tokens as not part of any entity. Sequence labeling can be achieved using various algorithms, including Hidden Markov Models (HMMs) and Conditional Random Fields (CRFs).

Hidden Markov Models are statistical models that assume each token's label depends on the previous token's label and the observed token. CRFs, on the other hand, provide a more flexible framework by modeling the dependencies between labels more explicitly and allowing for features from the entire sequence to influence label predictions. CRFs can incorporate a wide range of features, such as word shapes, surrounding context, and orthographic patterns, which helps improve the accuracy of entity recognition.

Deep learning has further advanced NER by employing neural network architectures that can capture complex patterns in text. Recurrent Neural Networks (RNNs) and their more advanced variants, such as Long Short-Term Memory (LSTM) networks and Gated Recurrent Units (GRUs), are particularly well-suited for sequence labeling tasks due to their ability to maintain context over long sequences. Additionally, the introduction of attention mechanisms and transformers has significantly improved NER performance by enabling models to focus on relevant parts of the text and handle long-range dependencies more effectively.

A prominent example of a deep learning model for NER is the BERT (Bidirectional Encoder Representations from Transformers) model, which leverages bidirectional context to understand the meaning of words based on their surrounding text. BERT and similar models have set new benchmarks in NER by achieving state-of-the-art performance on various datasets.

To implement NER in practice, one often begins by selecting a suitable method based on the requirements of the application. For rule-based systems, creating comprehensive rules and patterns is crucial, while for machine learning-based systems, curating a high-quality annotated dataset and choosing appropriate algorithms are key steps. In either case, evaluating and refining the NER system through metrics such as precision, recall, and F1 score helps ensure its effectiveness and accuracy.

NER plays a vital role in numerous applications beyond basic entity extraction. In information retrieval, NER helps improve search relevance by tagging and indexing entities within documents. In content extraction, it enables the automated extraction of key information from large volumes of text. By understanding and applying NER techniques, one can harness the power of structured information to enhance data-driven insights and decision-making processes.

In machine learning-based Named Entity Recognition, sequence labeling techniques are central. These techniques involve predicting a label for each token in a sequence of text. One of the most widely used methods for sequence labeling is the Conditional Random Field (CRF), which models the conditional probability of a sequence of labels given a sequence of observations. CRFs are particularly effective in NER tasks because they take into account the dependencies between neighboring labels, improving the accuracy of entity recognition by considering the context in which an entity appears.

For instance, in the sentence "Barack Obama was born in Honolulu," a CRF model would recognize "Barack Obama" as a person and "Honolulu" as a location, taking into account the surrounding words and their possible roles in the sentence. The CRF framework allows for the incorporation of various features, such as word shape, capitalization, and part-of-speech tags, which help in distinguishing entities from other text elements.

Another significant advancement in NER is the application of deep learning techniques, particularly neural networks. One notable approach is the use of Recurrent Neural Networks (RNNs) with Long Short-Term Memory (LSTM) units. LSTMs address the issue of vanishing gradients in traditional RNNs, allowing the model to learn long-range dependencies in text. By incorporating LSTMs, NER systems can better capture the context and relationships between tokens over long distances, improving entity recognition accuracy.

A more recent development in deep learning for NER is the advent of transformer-based models. The Transformer architecture, introduced in the paper "Attention Is All You Need," relies on self-attention mechanisms to process text data. Transformer-based models, such as BERT (Bidirectional Encoder Representations from Transformers), have achieved state-of-the-art performance in many NLP tasks, including NER. BERT's bidirectional approach allows it to consider both preceding and following words in a sentence, providing a more nuanced understanding of context and meaning. By fine-tuning BERT on annotated NER data, the model learns to recognize entities with high accuracy, leveraging its deep contextual representations.

The practical implementation of NER often involves several steps beyond just selecting the appropriate model. Data preparation is a critical aspect, as the quality and quantity of annotated training data directly impact the performance of the NER system. Creating a high-quality annotated dataset involves manually labeling entities in a large corpus of text, which can be time-consuming and resource-intensive. However, this annotated data is essential for training and evaluating NER models effectively.

In addition to model training, evaluating the performance of an NER system is crucial. Common evaluation metrics include precision, recall, and F1-score. Precision measures the proportion of correctly identified entities out of all entities identified by the model, while recall measures the proportion of correctly identified entities out of all actual entities in the text. The F1-score provides a balanced measure of precision and recall, which is particularly useful when dealing with imbalanced datasets where some entities are more frequent than others.

In practice, NER systems are often integrated into larger NLP pipelines to support various applications. For example, in information retrieval systems, NER can enhance search capabilities by tagging and indexing entities within documents. This tagging allows for more accurate and relevant search results when users query specific entities. Similarly, in content extraction applications, NER helps in structuring and summarizing information by identifying and categorizing key entities, facilitating more efficient data processing and retrieval.

Another application of NER is in relation extraction, where the goal is to identify and categorize relationships between entities. For instance, in a text discussing scientific research, NER can identify entities such as genes, diseases, and drugs, and relation extraction can determine how these entities are related, such as identifying which drugs are used to treat specific diseases.

Despite the advancements in NER, there are ongoing challenges and areas for improvement. One challenge is handling ambiguous or context-dependent entities, where the same word or phrase may refer to different entities based on context. For example, the term "Apple" can refer to the technology company or the fruit, depending on the context. Advanced NER systems must incorporate contextual information and disambiguation techniques to address such challenges effectively.

Additionally, multilingual NER presents its own set of challenges, as models need to be trained on text in multiple languages, each with its own linguistic nuances and entity types. Transfer learning techniques, where models pre-trained on one language are adapted to other languages, have shown promise in addressing these challenges by leveraging shared knowledge across languages.

In summary, Named Entity Recognition is a vital component of NLP systems, facilitating the extraction and classification of key information from text. By understanding both rule-based and machine learning-based methods, as well as the practical applications and challenges of NER, you will be better equipped to implement and utilize this technology in various domains. Whether for enhancing search capabilities, structuring information, or extracting relationships, NER continues to be a powerful tool in the field of natural language processing.

Creating a high-quality annotated dataset is pivotal for training effective NER models. The annotation process involves marking entities within text and assigning them appropriate labels, such as "PERSON," "LOCATION," or "DATE." This process is labor-intensive and requires a deep understanding of the context in which entities occur. Manual annotation is often performed by domain experts who can ensure that the labeled data accurately reflects the nuances of the language and the specific entity types of interest.

For many applications, domain-specific annotated datasets are necessary. For instance, in the medical domain, entities such as drug names, diseases, and medical procedures need to be recognized. Consequently, domain experts must annotate texts with medical terminology and concepts. These datasets help train models to understand and classify medical entities accurately, which is crucial for applications like clinical information extraction or biomedical literature analysis.

Once the annotated data is prepared, it must be divided into training, validation, and test sets. The training set is used to teach the model how to recognize and classify entities. The validation set helps in tuning hyperparameters and evaluating the model's performance during training, while the test set is used to assess the final model's performance on unseen data. This split ensures that the model is evaluated on its ability to generalize to new, unannotated texts, which is essential for its real-world application.

Evaluation metrics for NER systems are crucial for understanding their effectiveness. Common metrics include precision, recall, and F1-score. Precision measures the proportion of correctly identified entities among all entities identified by the model. Recall assesses the proportion of correctly identified entities among all actual entities in the text. The F1-score is the harmonic mean of precision and recall, providing a single metric that balances both aspects. These metrics help gauge how well the NER system performs and where improvements are needed.

Another critical aspect of implementing NER systems is handling ambiguous or complex entity types. Some entities, such as "Washington," could refer to a person, a location, or even a state. Resolving these ambiguities often requires additional contextual information or sophisticated disambiguation algorithms. Advanced NER systems leverage context, such as surrounding words and sentences, to disambiguate entities effectively. For instance, a model might use the context of "George Washington" to determine that "Washington" refers to a person rather than a location or state.

The integration of NER systems into broader applications is another important consideration. For example, in information retrieval systems, NER can be used to enhance search capabilities by indexing and retrieving documents based on recognized entities. In content extraction applications, NER helps in identifying and extracting relevant information from large volumes of text, such as extracting company names and financial data from news articles for financial analysis.

In addition to these practical considerations, ethical and privacy issues must be addressed when deploying NER systems. The use of personal data for training NER models raises concerns about data privacy and consent. Ensuring that sensitive information is handled appropriately and that models do not inadvertently disclose or misuse personal data is essential for maintaining ethical standards in NLP applications.

Overall, Named Entity Recognition represents a crucial aspect of natural language processing, bridging the gap between unstructured text and structured information. By leveraging both traditional rule-based methods and modern machine learning approaches, NER systems can accurately identify and classify entities in diverse contexts. The ongoing advancements in NER technology continue to enhance its capabilities, making it an indispensable tool in information retrieval, content extraction, and numerous other applications. Understanding and effectively implementing NER techniques is essential for harnessing the power of text data and driving innovation in various fields.

CHAPTER 7: PART-OF-SPEECH TAGGING AND PARSING

Understanding the syntactic structure of sentences is essential for numerous applications in natural language processing (NLP). Part-of-Speech (POS) tagging and parsing are foundational techniques that help us achieve this understanding by assigning grammatical categories to words and analyzing the relationships between them. To effectively leverage these techniques, it is crucial to grasp their underlying principles, algorithms, and tools.

Part-of-Speech tagging involves the process of assigning a grammatical category to each word in a sentence. These categories include, but are not limited to, nouns, verbs, adjectives, adverbs, and prepositions. POS tagging helps in identifying the role of each word within a sentence, which is vital for many NLP tasks such as named entity recognition, information retrieval, and sentiment analysis.

There are several approaches to POS tagging, including rule-based, stochastic, and hybrid methods. Rule-based POS tagging relies on a set of predefined linguistic rules that dictate how words should be tagged based on their context. For example, a rule might specify that if a word follows a determiner, it is likely to be a noun. While rule-based systems can be precise, they often require extensive manual effort to develop and maintain.

Stochastic methods, on the other hand, use probabilistic models to assign POS tags based on statistical patterns observed in large annotated corpora. The Hidden Markov Model (HMM) is a classic example of such a method. In an HMM, the sequence of POS tags is modeled as a hidden process, where the observed words provide evidence for estimating the most probable sequence of tags. This approach is data-driven and can adapt to various language patterns, but it may struggle with rare or unseen words.

Hybrid methods combine rule-based and stochastic approaches to leverage the strengths of both. For instance, a system might use rules to handle well-defined contexts and probabilistic models to address more ambiguous cases. This combination can lead to improved accuracy and robustness in POS tagging.

Parsing involves analyzing the grammatical structure of sentences to understand how words relate to each other. The goal of parsing is to generate a syntactic representation of the sentence, often in the form of a parse tree. This tree illustrates the hierarchical structure of the sentence, showing how phrases and clauses are organized and how they relate to one another.

There are different types of parsing techniques, including constituency parsing and dependency parsing. Constituency parsing breaks a sentence into nested constituents, such as noun phrases and verb phrases, and arranges them into a hierarchical tree structure. Each node in the tree represents a constituent, and the branches indicate the relationships between them. Constituency parsers are useful for tasks that require a detailed syntactic analysis, such as syntactic ambiguity resolution and machine translation.

Dependency parsing, in contrast, focuses on the relationships between individual words in a sentence, representing these relationships as a directed graph. Each word is a node, and the edges denote syntactic dependencies, such as subject-verb or object-verb relationships. Dependency parsing is particularly valuable for applications that require an understanding of how words influence each other, such as information extraction and question answering.

To perform parsing, various algorithms and tools are available. Earley's algorithm and CYK (Cocke-Younger-Kasami) algorithm are examples of algorithms used for constituency parsing. Earley's algorithm is particularly useful for parsing ambiguous grammars and can handle both context-free and context-sensitive grammars. The CYK algorithm, on the other hand, is efficient for parsing context-free grammars and works well with dynamic programming techniques.

For dependency parsing, algorithms such as the Eisner algorithm and the Chu-Liu/Edmonds algorithm are commonly used. The Eisner algorithm is known for its efficiency in parsing projective dependency structures, while the Chu-Liu/Edmonds algorithm is used for non-projective structures and handles more complex dependencies. These algorithms enable the generation of accurate dependency trees and facilitate tasks that require a nuanced understanding of syntactic relationships.

In practice, several tools and libraries are available to facilitate POS tagging and parsing. For instance, the Natural Language Toolkit (NLTK) and spaCy provide robust implementations of POS tagging and parsing algorithms. These tools offer pre-trained models, easy-to-use interfaces, and support for various languages, making them accessible for both research and application purposes.

Integrating POS tagging and parsing into NLP pipelines can significantly enhance the ability to process and understand natural language. By accurately tagging parts of speech and parsing sentence structures, NLP systems can achieve a deeper comprehension of text, leading to improved performance in tasks such as text classification, machine translation, and automated summarization.

Understanding and implementing POS tagging and parsing techniques are essential for developing sophisticated NLP applications. By exploring the principles, algorithms, and tools associated with these tasks, you will gain a solid foundation in syntactic analysis and be well-equipped to tackle complex linguistic challenges in your NLP endeavors.

The methodologies employed in parsing are diverse and cater to various linguistic theories and practical needs. Among the most notable are constituency parsing and dependency parsing. Constituency parsing, rooted in phrase structure grammar, seeks to decompose sentences into nested constituents or phrases. Each constituent is a subpart of the sentence that functions as a single unit in the syntactic hierarchy. For instance, in the sentence "The cat sat on the mat," the noun phrase 'The cat" and the prepositional phrase "on the mat" are constituents of the sentence. Constituency parsers use grammar rules to generate a parse tree where each node represents a constituent, and the edges denote the syntactic relationships between these constituents.

Dependency parsing, in contrast, focuses on the relationships between individual words rather than phrases. This approach is grounded in dependency grammar, which posits that the syntactic structure of a sentence is defined by the dependencies between words. In dependency parsing, each word is linked to its syntactic governor, forming a tree structure where nodes represent words, and directed edges indicate grammatical dependencies. For example, in the sentence "The cat sat on the mat," "sat" is the root of the sentence, and it governs "cat," "on," and "mat," which in turn govern their respective elements. Dependency parsing is particularly useful for languages with flexible word orders and for tasks that require fine-grained syntactic analysis.

To achieve effective parsing, various algorithms and tools

are utilized. One of the earliest and most straightforward parsing algorithms is the Earley parser, which is a dynamic programming parser that can handle all context-free grammars. It builds parse trees incrementally and can be particularly useful for dealing with ambiguous grammars. The CYK (Cocke-Younger-Kasami) algorithm is another approach, specifically designed for parsing context-free grammars. The CYK algorithm uses a chart parsing method where a matrix is populated with possible parse trees for substrings of the sentence, ultimately yielding the complete parse tree for the entire sentence.

More recent advances have seen the adoption of probabilistic parsing methods, such as those based on probabilistic context-free grammars (PCFGs). These methods enhance parsing by incorporating probabilistic information about grammar rules, which helps in choosing the most likely parse tree when multiple trees are possible. This probabilistic approach is often employed in modern NLP systems to improve parsing accuracy, especially when dealing with noisy or ambiguous input.

In addition to these classical algorithms, machine learning-based approaches have revolutionized parsing in recent years. Statistical models, such as the maximum entropy models and support vector machines, have been applied to parsing, leveraging annotated corpora to learn probabilistic models of syntax. More recently, neural network-based models have taken center stage, with approaches such as sequence-to-sequence models and attention mechanisms significantly advancing the state of the art in parsing. These models benefit from their ability to learn complex, high-dimensional representations of language and to capture nuanced syntactic relationships.

The application of part-of-speech tagging and parsing extends beyond linguistic analysis into practical NLP applications. For example, in information retrieval, understanding the syntactic structure of queries can improve the relevance of search results by enabling more accurate matching of query terms with document content. In machine translation, syntactic parsing helps in generating grammatically correct translations by maintaining the syntactic structure of the source language in the target language. Furthermore, in question answering systems, POS tagging and parsing facilitate the extraction of meaningful information from text, enabling systems to provide precise and contextually relevant answers.

Despite their importance, POS tagging and parsing present several challenges. Ambiguity in language, where a word or phrase can have multiple grammatical roles, complicates the process of assigning correct tags or constructing accurate parse trees. Moreover, languages with complex syntactic structures or free word orders can pose difficulties for parsing algorithms. Addressing these challenges often requires combining multiple techniques, such as integrating linguistic rules with statistical models or using large annotated corpora to train machine learning models.

In summary, part-of-speech tagging and parsing are pivotal for understanding and processing natural language. These techniques provide essential insights into the grammatical structure of text, facilitating a range of NLP applications. By exploring both traditional algorithms and modern machine learning methods, we can develop robust systems capable of handling the complexities and nuances of human language.

Moving beyond traditional methods, modern approaches to parsing increasingly leverage neural networks and machine learning models. These techniques offer significant improvements in accuracy and adaptability over rule-based and probabilistic methods. The advent of deep learning has introduced models such as Recurrent Neural Networks (RNNs) and Transformer-based architectures, which have transformed both POS tagging and parsing tasks.

Neural network-based POS tagging employs architectures that can capture complex patterns in text data. For instance,

Bidirectional Long Short-Term Memory (BiLSTM) networks, a type of RNN, have proven particularly effective for this purpose. By processing text in both forward and backward directions, BiLSTMs can leverage contextual information from both the preceding and following words, which enhances the accuracy of POS tagging. These models are typically trained on large annotated corpora, allowing them to learn subtle linguistic patterns that rule-based systems might miss.

The integration of word embeddings into these neural models further improves performance. Word embeddings, such as those generated by Word2Vec or GloVe, provide dense, continuous vector representations of words that capture semantic similarities. When used in conjunction with BiLSTMs, these embeddings enrich the model's understanding of context, leading to more precise tagging results. For example, the embedding for the word "bank" would vary depending on whether it appears in a financial context or a riverbank context, aiding the model in disambiguating such terms.

Parsing, too, has benefited from advancements in neural network architectures. Transformer models, exemplified by BERT (Bidirectional Encoder Representations from Transformers), have set new benchmarks in syntactic analysis. Transformers utilize self-attention mechanisms to weigh the importance of each word relative to every other word in the sentence, allowing the model to capture intricate syntactic and semantic relationships. This approach is particularly useful for dependency parsing, where understanding the relationships between words is crucial.

Graph-based neural models represent another leap forward in parsing technology. These models frame parsing as a graph-based optimization problem, where nodes correspond to words and edges represent dependencies. Using graph neural networks (GNNs), these models learn to predict the most likely syntactic dependencies by exploring the structure of the graph, which improves parsing accuracy and robustness.

Despite these advancements, several challenges persist in both POS tagging and parsing. One notable issue is handling the syntactic and semantic ambiguities present in natural language. For instance, the sentence "He saw the man with the telescope" can be interpreted in multiple ways depending on whether the prepositional phrase "with the telescope" modifies "man" or "saw." Such ambiguities require sophisticated models that can weigh context and infer the most probable interpretation.

Another challenge is the variability and richness of languages. While English and other major languages benefit from extensive annotated corpora, less-resourced languages pose difficulties due to limited data. This scarcity can hinder the performance of machine learning models, which rely on large datasets for training. Techniques such as transfer learning, where models trained on resource-rich languages are adapted to less-resourced ones, are being explored to address this issue.

Moreover, the integration of POS tagging and parsing with other NLP tasks, such as Named Entity Recognition (NER) and sentiment analysis, introduces additional complexity. For example, correctly identifying entities in a sentence often relies on understanding its syntactic structure, making accurate parsing essential for effective NER. Similarly, sentiment analysis can benefit from syntactic information to discern the sentiment expressed in various parts of a sentence.

In summary, while traditional POS tagging and parsing methods laid the groundwork for understanding sentence structure, contemporary techniques leveraging deep learning and neural networks have significantly advanced these tasks. The use of BiLSTMs and Transformer models has enhanced the accuracy and flexibility of POS tagging and parsing, allowing for more nuanced and context-aware analysis. However, challenges remain, particularly in dealing with ambiguity, language variability, and integrating these tasks with other NLP processes. As the field continues to evolve, ongoing research and technological advancements will likely address these challenges, further refining our ability to analyze and understand natural language.

CHAPTER 8: BUILDING AND TRAINING LANGUAGE MODELS

The construction and training of language models represent a critical phase in natural language processing, wherein raw data is transformed into systems capable of understanding and generating human language. This process begins with the selection of an appropriate modeling approach, followed by the preparation of data, implementation of algorithms, and thorough evaluation of model performance. Here, we will explore these steps in detail, starting with an overview of traditional and modern techniques, and moving towards practical considerations in model training and evaluation.

Traditional statistical models, such as n-grams, have been fundamental in early language modeling. An n-gram model predicts the probability of a word given the preceding \(n-1\) words, utilizing historical counts of word sequences in training data. For instance, a bigram model uses the previous word to predict the current word, while a trigram model uses the previous two words. The simplicity of n-grams makes them computationally straightforward, but they suffer from limitations such as sparsity of data and inability to capture long-range dependencies. To address these issues, smoothing techniques, such as Laplace smoothing, are employed to adjust probability estimates for unseen word sequences.

In contrast, modern language modeling predominantly relies on deep learning techniques. Recurrent Neural Networks (RNNs) were among the first to address the limitations of statistical models by maintaining a hidden state that captures information from previous words in a sequence. However, RNNs, including their advanced variant Long Short-Term Memory (LSTM) networks, face challenges related to long-term dependencies and computational efficiency. LSTMs introduce mechanisms like gates to control the flow of information, thereby mitigating issues of vanishing and exploding gradients.

The introduction of Transformers marked a significant advancement in language modeling. Unlike RNNs, Transformers leverage self-attention mechanisms to weigh the importance of each word in relation to every other word in the sequence. This approach allows Transformers to process words in parallel, significantly improving efficiency and enabling the capture of complex dependencies across long sequences. Notable models based on this architecture, such as BERT (Bidirectional Encoder Representations from Transformers) and GPT (Generative Pre-trained Transformer), have set new benchmarks in various NLP tasks.

When building a language model, the first step is data collection and preprocessing. For statistical models, this involves compiling a large corpus of text and performing tasks such as tokenization, normalization, and removal of stop words. In deep learning contexts, data preparation also includes the creation of word embeddings or token representations that capture semantic meanings. This preprocessing ensures that the text data is in a suitable format for the training algorithms.

Training a language model involves defining and optimizing the model's parameters to best fit the training data. For statistical models, training entails counting occurrences of word sequences and applying smoothing techniques. In deep learning, this process is more complex and involves setting up neural network architectures, initializing weights, and iteratively adjusting them through backpropagation. The training process for deep learning models is computationally intensive and often requires specialized hardware such as GPUs or TPUs to handle the large volumes of data and complex calculations.

A key component of training is hyperparameter tuning. Hyperparameters are configuration settings that are not learned from the data but are crucial for model performance. These include the learning rate, batch size, and the number of layers or units in the model. Techniques such as grid search or random search are used to explore different hyperparameter settings, while more sophisticated methods like Bayesian optimization can also be employed to find optimal configurations.

Evaluating the performance of a language model is essential to ensure its effectiveness and generalizability. Common metrics for evaluation include perplexity, which measures how well the model predicts a sample, and accuracy for classification tasks. For models like BERT or GPT, performance is often assessed using specific benchmarks or datasets that reflect real-world applications. Cross-validation is another technique used to assess model performance by splitting the data into training and validation sets, thereby reducing the risk of overfitting.

Once trained, a language model must be validated to ensure that it performs well on unseen data. This involves testing the model on a separate dataset to evaluate its accuracy, robustness, and ability to generalize. Performance metrics are analyzed, and any discrepancies between training and validation results are addressed. This iterative process helps refine the model and improve its capabilities.

In addition to evaluation, deployment and fine-tuning are critical stages in the lifecycle of a language model. Fine-tuning involves adapting a pre-trained model to specific tasks or domains by continuing training on task-specific data. This approach leverages the knowledge acquired during pre-training and tailors the model to perform optimally in specialized contexts.

Throughout this process, it is crucial to remain aware of potential ethical considerations, such as bias in training data and the implications of model decisions. Ensuring transparency, fairness, and accountability in model development and application is essential to building trustworthy and effective language systems.

In summary, the journey of building and training language models involves a careful blend of statistical methods, deep learning techniques, and rigorous evaluation. By understanding these processes and applying best practices, one can develop powerful models capable of addressing a wide array of natural language processing tasks.

Building and training language models requires a comprehensive approach that integrates both theoretical understanding and practical skills. After the data collection and preprocessing phases, we proceed to the core tasks of model design, training, and evaluation. The choice of modeling technique significantly impacts these tasks, and we must carefully consider whether to employ traditional statistical models or to leverage modern deep learning architectures.

For traditional statistical models, once the data is preprocessed, we construct features based on word sequences. This involves determining the n-gram size and constructing frequency tables to capture the statistical properties of the data. In practice, this means creating a vocabulary of all unique words or word pairs (in the case of bigrams) from the training corpus and counting their occurrences. These counts are used to compute probabilities, which are fundamental for predicting the likelihood of sequences.

The training process for statistical models is relatively straightforward. For example, in a bigram model, the probability of a word given the previous word is estimated by dividing the count of the bigram by the count of the preceding word. This process is computationally efficient, though it can become impractical for large corpora due to the combinatorial explosion of possible n-grams.

In contrast, training deep learning models involves more complex procedures. For neural network-based models, such as those utilizing RNNs or Transformers, the process starts with defining the architecture of the model. In an RNN, this involves specifying the number of hidden layers, the size of each layer, and the type of activation functions. For LSTMs and GRUs (Gated Recurrent Units), additional parameters related to gating mechanisms must be configured.

The training of deep learning models relies on backpropagation, a technique used to minimize the loss function by adjusting the model's weights. The loss function quantifies the discrepancy between the predicted and actual outcomes, and optimization algorithms like Adam or SGD (Stochastic Gradient Descent) are employed to iteratively adjust the weights to reduce this loss. Training deep learning models requires a substantial amount of computational power and memory, particularly when dealing with large datasets and complex architectures.

Once a model is trained, it must be evaluated to determine its performance. For statistical models, evaluation typically involves assessing the likelihood of held-out test data and checking the model's generalization capability. Metrics such as perplexity, which measures how well a probability model predicts a sample, are commonly used. Lower perplexity indicates better predictive performance.

For deep learning models, evaluation often includes a range of metrics depending on the task. For language generation tasks, metrics like BLEU (Bilingual Evaluation Understudy) score or ROUGE (Recall-Oriented Understudy for Gisting Evaluation) score may be employed to assess the quality of generated text compared to human reference texts. For classification tasks, accuracy, precision, recall, and F1 score are used to evaluate the model's performance.

The evaluation process also involves analyzing errors to understand the model's limitations. For instance, in sequence-to-sequence models, it is crucial to examine how well the model handles long-term dependencies and whether it generates coherent and contextually appropriate outputs. Error analysis may reveal common patterns or issues, such as overfitting, where the model performs well on training data but poorly on unseen data.

Additionally, hyperparameter tuning is an essential step in improving model performance. Hyperparameters are settings that are not learned from the data but are specified before training, such as learning rate, batch size, and number of epochs. Techniques like grid search or random search, and more advanced methods like Bayesian optimization, are used to systematically explore different combinations of hyperparameters to find the optimal configuration.

Implementing and training language models also involves leveraging frameworks and libraries that simplify these processes. Tools like TensorFlow, PyTorch, and Hugging Face's Transformers provide robust support for building and training deep learning models, offering pre-built architectures, optimized implementations, and extensive documentation. These libraries facilitate the creation of custom models and experimentation with state-of-the-art techniques.

Finally, deploying trained models for real-world applications requires careful consideration of scalability and efficiency. For large-scale applications, models may need to be optimized for inference speed and memory usage. Techniques such as model quantization, pruning, and distillation can be applied to reduce the model size and improve its performance on resource-constrained devices.

In summary, building and training language models is a multifaceted process that involves selecting appropriate modeling techniques, preparing data, training the model, and evaluating its performance. By understanding the intricacies of both traditional and modern approaches, and by utilizing advanced tools and techniques, we can develop effective models that contribute to various NLP applications, from text classification to language generation.

When it comes to evaluating deep learning models, we employ different metrics and techniques compared to traditional statistical models. Accuracy, precision, recall, and F1 score are commonly used to assess the performance of models, especially in classification tasks. For language models, perplexity is a crucial metric, measuring how well a model predicts a sample. Lower perplexity indicates that the model is better at predicting the test data.

One of the significant advantages of deep learning models, particularly those based on the Transformer architecture, is their ability to handle vast amounts of data and learn complex patterns that traditional models might miss. Transformers, such as BERT (Bidirectional Encoder Representations from Transformers) and GPT (Generative Pre-trained Transformer), utilize self-attention mechanisms to capture long-range dependencies within the text, which significantly enhances their performance in various NLP tasks.

Training these advanced models involves a two-step process: pre-training and fine-tuning. During pre-training, the model learns general language patterns from a large corpus of text data without any specific task in mind. This phase is computationally intensive and requires considerable resources.

After pre-training, the model is fine-tuned on a smaller, task-specific dataset to adapt it to particular requirements, such as sentiment analysis or named entity recognition.

Fine-tuning typically involves adjusting the model's weights based on the specific dataset and task. This process often employs transfer learning, where the knowledge gained during pre-training is leveraged to improve performance on the new task. This method helps in achieving high accuracy even with relatively smaller datasets compared to those required for training models from scratch.

For practical implementation, libraries such as Hugging Face's Transformers provide pre-built models and tools that simplify the training and fine-tuning processes. These libraries offer pre-trained models that can be readily adapted to various NLP tasks, making it easier to build state-of-the-art language models without needing extensive computational resources.

In addition to training and fine-tuning, model evaluation also involves validating the model's robustness and generalization ability. Techniques like cross-validation, where the dataset is split into training and validation subsets multiple times, help in assessing how well the model performs on unseen data. This process is crucial in preventing overfitting, where the model performs well on training data but poorly on new data.

Moreover, it is important to consider the model's interpretability and explainability. While deep learning models achieve impressive performance, they often operate as "black boxes," making it challenging to understand how they arrive at specific predictions. Techniques such as attention visualization, saliency maps, and SHAP (SHapley Additive exPlanations) values can provide insights into the model's decision-making process, aiding in interpreting and trusting the results.

In conclusion, building and training language models involves selecting the appropriate techniques based on the task and data available. Traditional statistical models, while simpler and less resource-intensive, are often limited by their inability to capture complex patterns in large datasets. Modern deep learning models, with their sophisticated architectures and training processes, offer significant improvements in performance but come with higher computational demands.

Whether using statistical methods or advanced neural networks, understanding the intricacies of model training, evaluation, and interpretation is essential for developing effective language models. The choice of techniques and tools will depend on the specific requirements of the task, the available resources, and the desired performance outcomes. As the field of NLP continues to evolve, staying informed about the latest advancements and best practices will be crucial for building state-of-the-art models capable of tackling a wide range of language processing challenges.

CHAPTER 9: ADVANCED TECHNIQUES IN TEXT CLASSIFICATION

Text classification, an essential component of natural language processing (NLP), encompasses various sophisticated techniques that go beyond traditional methods to address the complexities of modern data. While basic approaches such as bag-of-words and term frequency-inverse document frequency (TF-IDF) have established a solid foundation, recent advancements in deep learning have significantly enhanced the capabilities and performance of text classification systems. In this exploration, we will investigate advanced techniques, focusing on Convolutional Neural Networks (CNNs) and Recurrent Neural Networks (RNNs), examining their strengths, limitations, and practical applications.

To understand how deep learning models have transformed text classification, we first need to appreciate their underlying mechanisms. CNNs, originally designed for image processing, have shown remarkable efficacy in text classification tasks. Their strength lies in their ability to capture local features and patterns within text data. By applying convolutional filters to word embeddings or token representations, CNNs can identify and learn n-gram features, which are critical for tasks such as sentiment analysis and topic categorization.

The core concept of a CNN involves a series of convolutional layers, pooling layers, and fully connected layers. Convolutional layers apply filters to input data, creating feature maps that highlight specific patterns. Pooling layers, typically max pooling, reduce the dimensionality of the feature maps, focusing on the most prominent features. Finally, fully connected layers interpret these features to produce classification results. This architecture enables CNNs to handle variable-length inputs and effectively recognize patterns, making them suitable for tasks that require the identification of specific phrases or terms.

In contrast to CNNs, Recurrent Neural Networks (RNNs) are designed to handle sequential data, which is inherent in text. RNNs maintain a form of memory through their recurrent connections, allowing them to capture temporal dependencies and context over sequences. This characteristic is particularly valuable for tasks such as text generation, machine translation, and sentiment analysis, where understanding the sequential nature of text is crucial.

A key limitation of traditional RNNs is their struggle with long-range dependencies due to issues like vanishing and exploding gradients. To address these challenges, advanced variants such as Long Short-Term Memory (LSTM) networks and Gated Recurrent Units (GRUs) have been developed. LSTMs and GRUs incorporate gating mechanisms that regulate the flow of information, enabling the network to maintain relevant context over longer sequences. This enhancement improves the model's ability to capture intricate relationships and dependencies in text.

When applying RNNs to text classification, the input text is typically represented as a sequence of word embeddings, which are processed through recurrent layers to generate context-aware representations. These representations are then used for classification tasks, with the model learning to associate certain patterns or sequences with specific categories.

Combining CNNs and RNNs can leverage the strengths of both architectures, resulting in models that can capture both local features and sequential dependencies. Hybrid models often utilize CNNs to extract features from word embeddings or token sequences, followed by RNN layers to process these features in sequence. This approach is particularly effective for complex classification tasks where both local patterns and contextual information are essential.

Another advanced technique in text classification involves attention mechanisms, which enhance the model's ability to focus on relevant parts of the input sequence. Attention mechanisms assign different weights to different parts of the input, allowing the model to concentrate on more important words or phrases. This capability is particularly beneficial for handling variable-length sequences and improving the interpretability of the model's predictions.

The implementation of advanced text classification techniques requires careful consideration of various factors, including model architecture, training data, and computational resources. For instance, deep learning models often require large amounts of labeled data to achieve optimal performance. Transfer learning, where pre-trained models are adapted to specific tasks, can mitigate this challenge by leveraging knowledge from related domains.

In addition to model selection and data considerations, evaluation metrics play a crucial role in assessing the performance of text classification systems. Metrics such as accuracy, precision, recall, and F1 score provide insights into how well the model performs across different classes and how effectively it handles imbalanced datasets.

As we explore these advanced techniques, it is also essential to consider their practical implications and limitations. While deep learning models offer significant advantages in terms of performance and flexibility, they also come with challenges related to computational complexity, interpretability, and the need for extensive labeled data. Balancing these factors and selecting the most appropriate approach for a given task requires a thorough understanding of both the models and the specific requirements of the application.

In summary, advanced techniques in text classification, including CNNs, RNNs, and attention mechanisms, represent significant strides in the field of NLP. These methods offer powerful tools for tackling complex classification tasks, leveraging deep learning's ability to capture intricate patterns and dependencies in text data. By carefully considering model architecture, data requirements, and evaluation metrics, practitioners can harness these techniques to develop robust and effective text classification systems.

As we delve further into deep learning techniques for text classification, it is essential to examine how Convolutional Neural Networks (CNNs) and Recurrent Neural Networks (RNNs) are implemented and optimized for various tasks. Each model type has its strengths and use cases, but also comes with limitations that must be addressed.

Convolutional Neural Networks, initially tailored for image analysis, have been adapted to text classification by leveraging their capacity to detect patterns and features. In text classification, CNNs operate by transforming text into a fixed-length vector using word embeddings such as Word2Vec or GloVe. These embeddings are then processed through convolutional layers that apply multiple filters of varying sizes. Each filter detects specific patterns, such as n-grams or key phrases, within the input text. The pooling layers that follow aggregate the most relevant features detected by these filters, reducing dimensionality and emphasizing important patterns. This process allows CNNs to capture local dependencies in the text efficiently.

The strength of CNNs lies in their ability to identify hierarchical patterns and learn from local features. For example, in sentiment analysis, CNNs can detect sentiment-indicative phrases like "excellent service" or "poor quality" by recognizing patterns in the embeddings. However, CNNs have limitations in capturing sequential dependencies due to their fixed-size context window. They are less adept at understanding the relationships between distant words or phrases within a document.

On the other hand, Recurrent Neural Networks (RNNs) are specifically designed to handle sequential data, making them well-suited for tasks that require an understanding of context over time. RNNs process input sequences one step at a time, maintaining a hidden state that is updated at each time step. This hidden state acts as a form of memory, enabling the network to retain information about previous words or tokens. Consequently, RNNs are particularly effective for tasks such as text generation and sequence labeling, where understanding the flow and context of the text is crucial.

Despite their advantages, traditional RNNs face challenges when dealing with long sequences due to problems like vanishing and exploding gradients. To overcome these issues, variants such as Long Short-Term Memory (LSTM) networks and Gated Recurrent Units (GRUs) have been developed. LSTMs and GRUs introduce gating mechanisms that control the flow of information, allowing the network to maintain long-range dependencies more effectively. These mechanisms enable LSTMs and GRUs to remember relevant information across long sequences, which is especially useful in applications like machine translation and sentiment analysis.

For instance, in a sentiment analysis task where the sentiment of a sentence may depend on the context provided by several preceding words, LSTMs and GRUs can capture these dependencies more accurately than standard RNNs. By maintaining a memory of past information and selectively updating this memory, these models can discern nuanced sentiment patterns that are not immediately apparent.

In addition to LSTMs and GRUs, Transformer-based models represent a significant advancement in sequence processing. Transformers use self-attention mechanisms to weigh the importance of different tokens in a sequence, allowing them to capture dependencies across long distances more effectively than RNNs. Although Transformer models like BERT and GPT have largely supplanted RNNs in many text classification tasks, understanding RNNs and their variants remains valuable for grasping the evolution of sequence modeling in NLP.

Another critical aspect of building effective text classification models is model evaluation and tuning. For deep learning models, this involves monitoring performance metrics such as accuracy, precision, recall, and F1-score, and applying techniques like hyperparameter tuning, dropout, and regularization to improve generalization. Cross-validation is often employed to assess model performance on different subsets of the data, ensuring robustness and reducing overfitting.

In practical applications, combining different approaches can enhance text classification performance. For instance, integrating CNNs and RNNs in a hybrid model can leverage the strengths of both architectures, capturing both local features and sequential dependencies. Additionally, transfer learning, where a pre-trained model is fine-tuned on a specific task, has become a common strategy to achieve high performance with limited training data. Models like BERT and GPT, pre-trained on vast corpora, can be adapted to specific text classification tasks with relatively little additional training.

In summary, advanced techniques in text classification, particularly CNNs and RNNs, offer powerful tools for analyzing and interpreting text data. While CNNs excel at identifying local patterns, RNNs and their variants are better suited for capturing sequential relationships and context. Understanding these techniques, along with model evaluation and tuning strategies, equips practitioners with the knowledge to build and refine effective text classification systems.

Expanding on the advanced techniques in text classification, it is imperative to address how modern architectures build upon the foundational concepts of Convolutional Neural Networks (CNNs) and Recurrent Neural Networks (RNNs). In recent years, attention mechanisms and transformer-based models have emerged as powerful tools, revolutionizing the field of NLP.

Attention mechanisms were introduced to tackle the limitations of RNNs and their difficulty with long-range dependencies. In essence, attention mechanisms allow models to focus on different parts of the input sequence dynamically. Rather than treating all input tokens with equal importance, attention mechanisms assign varying levels of importance to different tokens based on their relevance to the current context. This capability significantly enhances the model's ability to capture relationships between words that are far apart in the sequence, addressing one of the primary shortcomings of RNNs.

The Transformer architecture, which incorporates attention mechanisms, represents a substantial advancement in NLP. Transformers rely entirely on self-attention mechanisms and dispense with recurrence entirely. The self-attention mechanism computes a set of attention scores, which determine how each token in the input sequence should weigh other tokens when producing its representation. This process enables transformers to handle long-range dependencies effectively and facilitates parallel processing of tokens, leading to improved efficiency and scalability.

Transformers have paved the way for pre-trained language models such as BERT (Bidirectional Encoder Representations from Transformers) and GPT (Generative Pre-trained Transformer). BERT utilizes a bidirectional approach to pre-train language representations, meaning it considers both the left and right context of each token, providing a more nuanced understanding of text. This bidirectional context enables BERT to excel in a variety of NLP tasks, including text classification, where understanding the context of each token is crucial.

Conversely, GPT models adopt a unidirectional approach, focusing on generating text by predicting the next token in the sequence given the preceding context. While GPT models are particularly effective for text generation tasks, they also perform exceptionally well in classification tasks when fine-tuned on specific datasets. The pre-training on vast amounts of text data allows these models to capture rich language patterns and generalize well to various classification scenarios.

The deployment of these advanced models involves a few critical steps. Initially, a pre-trained model like BERT or GPT is fine-tuned on a task-specific dataset. Fine-tuning adjusts the model's weights to better align with the nuances of the target task. This process involves adding task-specific layers, such as classification heads, to the pre-trained model and training it on labeled data. The fine-tuning process often includes techniques such as dropout and regularization to prevent overfitting and ensure robust performance.

Moreover, hyperparameter tuning plays a crucial role in optimizing model performance. Parameters such as learning rate, batch size, and the number of training epochs can significantly influence the effectiveness of the fine-tuning process. Grid search and random search are common strategies for exploring different hyperparameter configurations, although more sophisticated techniques like Bayesian optimization can provide more efficient and effective results.

Evaluating the performance of advanced text classification models involves metrics such as accuracy, precision, recall, and F1-score. These metrics provide insights into how well the model distinguishes between different classes and handles imbalanced datasets. Confusion matrices are also valuable tools for visualizing model performance and identifying areas where the model may be making systematic errors.

In practice, integrating advanced text classification models into applications involves several considerations. The computational resources required for training and deploying transformer-based models can be substantial, necessitating the use of specialized hardware such as GPUs or TPUs. Additionally, the handling of large-scale datasets and the management of model versions and updates are crucial for maintaining the effectiveness and relevance of the deployed models.

Overall, the advancements in text classification through deep learning models have greatly enhanced the capability to tackle complex NLP tasks. By leveraging CNNs, RNNs, and transformer-based models, we can achieve significant improvements in accuracy and efficiency, ultimately enabling more sophisticated and reliable text classification systems. The continued evolution of these technologies promises further innovations and enhancements in the field, underscoring the importance of staying abreast of the latest developments and best practices.

CHAPTER 10: GENERATING TEXT WITH LANGUAGE MODELS

Text generation stands as one of the most fascinating applications within the field of natural language processing (NLP), offering the capability to produce human-like text based on input prompts. The evolution of language models has brought forth sophisticated methods for generating coherent, contextually relevant, and diverse text. To delve into these techniques, I will explore various models, starting with Recurrent Neural Networks (RNNs) and progressing to Transformer-based models such as GPT (Generative Pre-trained Transformer).

Recurrent Neural Networks, which represent an earlier but fundamental approach to text generation, excel in modeling sequential data. RNNs are designed to handle input sequences where the current output depends not only on the current input but also on previous inputs, effectively capturing the temporal dynamics of sequences. For text generation, RNNs process text one token at a time while maintaining a hidden state that reflects information about the sequence processed so far. This hidden state acts as a form of memory, enabling the model to generate text that is contextually relevant to preceding tokens.

However, despite their advantages, traditional RNNs face significant limitations, particularly with longer sequences. They often struggle with vanishing and exploding gradient problems, which hinder their ability to capture long-range dependencies in text. This challenge was partially addressed by the development of Long Short-Term Memory (LSTM) networks and Gated Recurrent Units (GRUs). LSTMs incorporate mechanisms to regulate the flow of information, allowing the network to retain important information over longer sequences and mitigate issues related to gradient decay. Similarly, GRUs simplify the LSTM architecture by combining the forget and input gates into a single update gate, achieving comparable performance with fewer parameters.

Despite these advancements, RNNs, including their LSTM and GRU variants, are not without their drawbacks. The sequential nature of RNNs inherently limits their ability to leverage parallelism, which is crucial for efficient processing of large-scale data. This limitation becomes particularly apparent when dealing with extensive text corpora or complex generation tasks.

The advent of Transformer-based models marks a transformative leap in text generation technology. Unlike RNNs, Transformers rely on self-attention mechanisms that allow the model to weigh the importance of different tokens in a sequence dynamically, irrespective of their positions. This approach overcomes the limitations of sequential processing by enabling parallelization and more efficient handling of long-range dependencies.

The core innovation behind Transformers is the self-attention mechanism, which computes attention scores to determine how much focus each token should receive relative to other tokens in the input sequence. This mechanism produces contextual embeddings for each token, capturing its meaning based on its relationship with all other tokens. The result is a model capable of generating highly coherent text, as it can consider the entire sequence when producing each token.

One of the most influential Transformer-based models is GPT, which operates as a generative model designed to predict the next token in a sequence given a prompt. GPT's training involves predicting tokens across large-scale datasets, learning rich language representations that capture syntactic and semantic patterns. When generating text, GPT samples from this learned distribution to produce tokens that follow the prompt contextually. The model can be fine-tuned for specific tasks or domains to enhance its performance and relevance to particular applications.

For text generation tasks, GPT excels in producing coherent and contextually appropriate text by leveraging its extensive training on diverse data sources. However, despite its strengths, GPT is not without limitations. Generated text may sometimes lack factual accuracy or coherence, particularly in longer sequences where maintaining context becomes challenging. Additionally, the quality of generated text can be influenced by the prompt provided and the sampling strategy used during generation.

To address these challenges, several techniques have been developed to refine and control text generation. For instance, temperature settings can adjust the creativity and diversity of generated text. A higher temperature value results in more varied and unpredictable text, while a lower temperature favors more conservative and coherent outputs. Another method, known as beam search, explores multiple potential sequences during generation to select the most promising one based on predefined criteria.

In conclusion, text generation using language models has evolved significantly, with RNNs and Transformer-based models each offering distinct advantages and limitations. While RNNs laid the groundwork for sequential text processing, Transformer models have revolutionized the field with their ability to handle long-range dependencies and parallel processing. By understanding and leveraging these models, one can effectively tackle various text generation tasks, from creative writing to automated content creation. The challenges associated with text generation underscore the need for continuous advancements in model architectures and training methodologies to achieve even higher levels of coherence and relevance in generated text.

The Transformer architecture, introduced in the landmark paper "Attention is All You Need," represents a significant departure from traditional sequential models like RNNs. At the heart of the Transformer model is the self-attention mechanism, which enables the model to consider all tokens in the input sequence simultaneously. This parallelism greatly enhances the efficiency of training and allows for the processing of long-range dependencies more effectively.

Self-attention operates by computing a set of attention scores for each token in the input sequence. These scores are used to weight the importance of different tokens when generating each output token. Specifically, self-attention calculates three vectors for each token: the query vector, the key vector, and the value vector. The attention score is derived from the interaction between the query and key vectors, determining how much focus each token should receive. The resulting weighted sum of the value vectors produces the output representation for each token. This mechanism enables the model to capture complex relationships between tokens, regardless of their distance in the sequence.

Transformers are typically structured with multiple layers of self-attention and feed-forward networks. The model's architecture is divided into an encoder and a decoder, each consisting of several such layers. In the context of text generation, the decoder plays a crucial role. It generates text by attending to the input sequence and producing one token at a time, using previously generated tokens as context. This autoregressive generation process ensures that the output is coherent and contextually aligned with the input.

One of the most prominent implementations of the Transformer model is the Generative Pre-trained Transformer (GPT). GPT models, particularly in their more advanced iterations like GPT-2 and GPT-3, have demonstrated remarkable capabilities in generating human-like text. These models are pre-trained on vast amounts of text data in an unsupervised manner, learning to predict the next word in a sequence given the preceding context. This pre-training enables GPT models to generate text that is not only contextually relevant but also stylistically diverse.

GPT's autoregressive nature allows it to generate long passages of text by repeatedly sampling from the model's predictions. The model uses its learned representations to predict the probability distribution of the next token, from which a token is sampled. This process continues until the desired length of text is generated or a stopping criterion is met. While GPT models exhibit impressive fluency and coherence, they also face challenges such as maintaining consistency over longer passages and generating content that aligns with specific user prompts.

Another notable Transformer-based model is BERT (Bidirectional Encoder Representations from Transformers), which, unlike GPT, is designed for tasks requiring a deep understanding of context in both directions. BERT's bidirectional attention mechanism enables it to consider the full context of a token, rather than just preceding or succeeding tokens. While BERT is primarily used for understanding tasks such as question answering and sentiment analysis, its underlying architecture has influenced various text generation models, particularly those focusing on contextual comprehension.

When applying these models to text generation tasks, several challenges arise. One key issue is ensuring the quality and relevance of the generated text. Despite the impressive capabilities of models like GPT-3, they can sometimes produce outputs that are nonsensical or inconsistent. This is often due to the model's reliance on statistical patterns learned during training, which may not always align with coherent narrative structures or factual accuracy. Fine-tuning and prompt engineering are essential strategies to address these issues. Fine-tuning involves training the model further on a specific dataset related to the desired application, allowing it to adapt its responses to particular contexts. Prompt engineering, on the other hand, involves crafting input prompts that guide the model towards producing more relevant and coherent outputs.

Ethical considerations also play a significant role in text generation. Models that can generate convincing and coherent text raise concerns about the potential misuse of such technology. Issues such as generating misleading information, creating harmful content, or manipulating public opinion highlight the need for responsible use and oversight of text generation capabilities.

Overall, the advancement in language models and text generation techniques has opened up new possibilities for creating sophisticated and contextually aware text. The combination of self-attention mechanisms in Transformers and the autoregressive capabilities of models like GPT enables the generation of high-quality text across various domains. As these technologies continue to evolve, ongoing research and development will be crucial in addressing their limitations and ethical implications, ensuring that they are used in ways that benefit society and advance the field of natural language processing.

Despite the impressive capabilities of models like GPT, generating high-quality text remains fraught with challenges. One of the primary concerns is ensuring coherence and relevance over long passages. While Transformer models excel in capturing short-term dependencies, maintaining coherence across extended texts requires managing the balance between diversity and consistency. If a model becomes too creative, it may produce text that deviates from the intended topic or context. Conversely, overly conservative models might generate repetitive or uninspired content.

Another challenge in text generation is handling the trade-off between creativity and factual accuracy. Language models, especially those trained on diverse datasets, can generate text that sounds plausible but is factually incorrect or misleading. This issue arises because these models generate text based on learned patterns and statistical associations rather than an understanding of truth. Therefore, it is crucial to implement mechanisms to verify and validate the generated content to ensure it aligns with factual information.

To address these issues, researchers have developed several strategies. One approach is the use of fine-tuning, where a pre-trained model is further trained on a specific dataset that reflects the desired style or content domain. This method helps the model adapt its generative capabilities to produce text that is more relevant to the target domain. Fine-tuning can improve the model's ability to generate content that is not only coherent but also contextually appropriate for specific applications, such as legal documents, technical reports, or creative writing.

Another technique is the incorporation of human feedback during the generation process. Methods such as reinforcement learning with human feedback (RLHF) involve training the model with feedback from human evaluators who assess the quality of generated text. This feedback helps guide the model towards producing more accurate and contextually appropriate outputs. By iteratively refining the model based on human evaluations, it is possible to enhance the overall quality and reliability of the generated text.

Moreover, techniques such as controlled text generation have gained prominence. These methods involve conditioning the model on specific attributes or constraints to guide the generation process. For example, models can be conditioned to generate text in a particular style, tone, or length, which helps in aligning the output with predefined criteria. Control codes or prompts can be used to specify these attributes, allowing for more targeted and relevant text generation.

Despite these advancements, ethical considerations in text generation are paramount. Language models can inadvertently generate biased or harmful content due to biases present in the training data. Addressing these issues involves employing techniques for bias detection and mitigation, as well as implementing ethical guidelines for responsible AI use. It is essential to ensure that the models are trained and evaluated in ways that minimize the risk of perpetuating harmful stereotypes or generating inappropriate content.

Evaluating the quality of generated text is another critical aspect. Traditional metrics such as perplexity, which measures the model's ability to predict the next word, provide limited insight into the text's coherence and relevance. Consequently, researchers have developed more sophisticated evaluation methods, including human evaluations and automated metrics like BLEU (Bilingual Evaluation Understudy) and ROUGE (Recall-Oriented Understudy for Gisting Evaluation). These metrics assess various aspects of text quality, such as fluency, informativeness, and alignment with reference outputs.

In practical applications, generating high-quality text also involves considering the specific requirements of the task at hand. For instance, in conversational AI, generating responses that are contextually relevant and engaging is crucial. In contrast, for content creation tasks like article writing or story generation, maintaining a consistent narrative flow and stylistic coherence is more important. Tailoring the text generation approach to the specific needs of the application ensures that the outputs are both effective and suitable for their intended purpose.

Ultimately, text generation with language models represents a dynamic and rapidly evolving field. Continued research and innovation are necessary to address the ongoing challenges and harness the full potential of these models. By integrating advancements in model architecture, training techniques, and evaluation methods, we can strive towards generating text that is not only coherent and contextually relevant but also ethically sound and aligned with user expectations.

CHAPTER 11: EVALUATING NLP MODELS

To develop effective NLP systems, it is essential to accurately evaluate the performance of models. This involves understanding and applying various evaluation metrics and techniques to assess how well a model performs its intended tasks. Evaluating NLP models is not merely about determining their effectiveness but also about gaining insights into their strengths and weaknesses, which can guide improvements and refinements.

One of the fundamental metrics used in NLP evaluation is precision. Precision measures the proportion of true positive predictions among all positive predictions made by the model. For example, in a text classification task where the goal is to identify spam emails, precision indicates how many of the emails flagged as spam are actually spam. High precision is desirable when the cost of false positives is high, such as in medical diagnosis or legal document classification, where incorrectly classifying a benign instance as positive can have serious consequences.

Complementing precision is recall, which measures the proportion of true positive predictions among all actual positive instances. Recall is crucial in scenarios where missing a positive instance has significant implications. For instance, in a sentiment analysis task aimed at identifying negative reviews, high recall ensures that most negative reviews are captured by the model, even if it means some non-negative reviews are mistakenly classified as negative. High recall is especially important in situations where the consequences of false negatives are severe, such as in disease detection where failing to identify a positive case can be detrimental.

To provide a balanced evaluation, precision and recall are often combined into a single metric known as the F1 score. The F1 score is the harmonic mean of precision and recall, offering a more comprehensive measure of a model's performance, especially when dealing with imbalanced datasets. The F1 score balances the trade-off between precision and recall, providing a unified metric that reflects both the accuracy and completeness of the model's predictions. It is particularly useful in tasks where both false positives and false negatives have significant implications and a balanced approach is necessary.

In addition to these classification metrics, perplexity is a metric widely used in evaluating language models, particularly for tasks involving text generation and language modeling. Perplexity measures how well a probability distribution or model predicts a sample. It is the inverse probability of the test set normalized by the number of words. In simpler terms, perplexity quantifies how well the model predicts the next word in a sequence. Lower perplexity indicates that the model is more confident in its predictions and performs better in terms of generating coherent and contextually relevant text.

Another crucial aspect of evaluation involves analyzing errors and understanding the model's limitations. Error analysis helps in identifying specific cases where the model underperforms, providing insights into potential areas for improvement. By examining the types of errors made, such as false positives, false negatives, or incorrect classifications, developers can refine the model, adjust hyperparameters, or enhance the training data to address these issues.

Cross-validation is a technique used to assess the generalizability of a model by partitioning the dataset into multiple subsets or folds. The model is trained on some folds and tested on the remaining ones, with this process repeated several times to ensure that each subset serves as a test set at least once. Cross-validation helps in evaluating how well the model performs across different subsets of data and can provide a more robust estimate of its performance, reducing the risk of overfitting to a particular subset of the data.

Moreover, evaluating NLP models also involves considering the interpretability and fairness of the model's predictions. Interpretability refers to the model's ability to explain its predictions in a comprehensible manner, which is particularly important in applications where transparency is crucial. Fairness involves ensuring that the model does not exhibit bias against certain groups or individuals. Techniques such as model explainability tools and fairness audits are used to assess and improve these aspects, ensuring that the model's predictions are not only accurate but also ethical and equitable.

Finally, performance evaluation is an ongoing process. As new data becomes available and models are updated or retrained, continuous evaluation is necessary to ensure that the model maintains its effectiveness over time. Regularly monitoring performance metrics and conducting periodic reviews help in identifying any degradation in model performance or emerging issues, allowing for timely adjustments and improvements.

In summary, evaluating NLP models involves a comprehensive approach that includes using precision, recall, F1 score, and perplexity to measure performance, conducting error analysis, and ensuring interpretability and fairness. By employing these techniques, developers can gain valuable insights into their models, refine their approaches, and build more effective and reliable NLP systems.

Evaluating the performance of NLP models involves not only calculating metrics like precision, recall, F1 score, and perplexity but also understanding their implications in different contexts. Each metric provides valuable insights into specific aspects of a model's performance, but they must be interpreted carefully to draw meaningful conclusions and guide improvements.

Precision is a metric that provides a measure of the exactness of the model. It answers the question: Of all the instances that the model identified as positive, how many were actually positive? High precision means that the model has a low false positive rate, which is particularly important in scenarios where false positives can lead to undesirable outcomes. For instance, in an email filtering system designed to detect spam, high precision ensures that legitimate emails are not wrongly classified as spam, avoiding unnecessary confusion or loss of important communication. However, focusing solely on precision might come at the cost of missing some positive instances, which is where recall comes into play.

Recall, on the other hand, measures the completeness of the model. It answers the question: Of all the actual positive instances, how many did the model successfully identify? High recall indicates that the model has a low false negative rate, which is crucial in scenarios where failing to identify positive instances has significant consequences. For instance, in a medical diagnostic model, high recall ensures that most cases of a disease are detected, even if it means some non-disease cases are incorrectly flagged. Balancing precision and recall is often necessary, especially when dealing with imbalanced datasets where one class is significantly more prevalent than the other.

The F1 score, which combines precision and recall into a single metric, is particularly useful when you need to balance the trade-offs between precision and recall. The F1 score provides a harmonic mean of the two metrics, offering a more nuanced view of the model's performance. It is especially valuable in situations where both false positives and false negatives have important implications and you need a metric that reflects overall performance rather than just one aspect. For example, in sentiment analysis where both missing negative reviews (false negatives) and incorrectly labeling positive reviews as negative (false positives) can have substantial effects, the F1 score helps to gauge the model's overall effectiveness.

Perplexity, a metric often used in evaluating language models, measures how well a model predicts a sample of text. It quantifies the model's uncertainty in predicting the next word in a sequence. A lower perplexity indicates that the model is better at predicting the next word, suggesting a more effective language model. In text generation tasks, perplexity helps in assessing how well the model captures the structure and nuances of the language. However, while perplexity is a useful measure of a model's performance in generating coherent text, it is not always a perfect indicator of text quality. For instance, a model might have low perplexity but still generate text that lacks fluency or coherence due to issues such as overfitting or lack of contextual understanding.

To thoroughly evaluate NLP models, it is also important to consider additional aspects such as robustness, fairness, and interpretability. Robustness refers to the model's ability to handle variations in input data, including noise or adversarial examples. Evaluating robustness involves testing the model against a range of inputs that it might encounter in real-world scenarios to ensure consistent performance. Fairness involves assessing whether the model's predictions are biased against certain groups or individuals, which is crucial in applications like hiring, lending, or legal decisions. Interpretability refers to the extent to which the model's decisions can be understood and explained, which is important for building trust and transparency in NLP systems.

In practice, evaluating NLP models requires a combination of metrics and techniques to gain a comprehensive understanding of their performance. Metrics like precision, recall, F1 score, and perplexity provide quantitative assessments, but qualitative evaluation through human judgment and domain expertise is also essential. For example, in tasks involving creative text generation, human evaluators can assess the coherence, relevance, and fluency of generated text, providing insights that metrics alone may not capture. Combining these evaluations with quantitative metrics helps in developing more effective and reliable NLP systems.

Furthermore, continuous evaluation and iteration are key to improving model performance. As models are exposed to new data and use cases, their performance may evolve, necessitating ongoing assessment and refinement. Regular evaluation helps in identifying areas for improvement, adapting to changes in data distribution, and ensuring that the model remains effective and reliable over time.

In summary, evaluating NLP models involves a multifaceted approach that includes calculating and interpreting various metrics, understanding their implications in different contexts, and considering additional factors such as robustness, fairness, and interpretability. By employing a comprehensive evaluation strategy, we can gain valuable insights into model performance, guide improvements, and develop more effective NLP systems.

Perplexity is particularly pertinent in evaluating probabilistic language models. It measures how well a model predicts a sequence of words by computing the inverse probability of the test set normalized by the number of words. Specifically, perplexity quantifies the uncertainty or "confusion" the model experiences when predicting the next word in a sequence. A lower perplexity indicates that the model is more confident and accurate in its predictions, while a higher perplexity suggests greater uncertainty and less accuracy. This metric is crucial for models like n-grams and more advanced language models, as it provides insight into how well the model understands and generates coherent text.

Understanding how to interpret these metrics requires a nuanced approach. For instance, in cases where precision and recall cannot be equally maximized, understanding the specific needs of the application can guide which metric should be prioritized. In a spam detection system, where false positives (legitimate emails marked as spam) are less acceptable than false negatives (spam emails that are missed), precision may be more critical. Conversely, in a medical diagnosis scenario, recall might take precedence to ensure that as many cases as possible are identified, even if it means a higher false positive rate.

The selection of evaluation metrics should also align with the model's intended use and the nature of the data. For instance, in natural language generation tasks, metrics like BLEU score (for machine translation) or ROUGE score (for summarization) are used alongside perplexity to assess the quality of generated text against reference outputs. These metrics evaluate factors such as fluency, adequacy, and content overlap, providing a more comprehensive view of the model's performance.

Furthermore, evaluating models in real-world settings often requires more than just applying standard metrics. Practical evaluation involves assessing model performance on diverse datasets that reflect different contexts and usage scenarios. This ensures that the model is not only accurate in controlled environments but also robust and reliable in practice. For example, a sentiment analysis model trained on movie reviews may perform well on similar data but struggle with user reviews on social media, where language use and context can differ significantly.

Cross-validation and holdout testing are additional techniques that can be employed to ensure that model evaluations are not biased by the particularities of the training data. Cross-validation involves dividing the data into multiple subsets, training the model on some subsets while validating it on others, and averaging the results to get a more reliable estimate of performance. Holdout testing involves reserving a portion of the data for testing purposes, ensuring that the model is evaluated on completely unseen data. Both methods help to assess how well the model generalizes to new data and reduces the risk of overfitting.

Finally, understanding the limitations of each metric and approach is crucial for a well-rounded evaluation. Metrics such as precision, recall, F1 score, and perplexity provide valuable insights but do not capture every aspect of model performance. For instance, these metrics may not fully account for the model's behavior in edge cases or its ability to handle adversarial inputs. Therefore, combining quantitative metrics with qualitative assessments, such as user studies or expert evaluations, can provide a more holistic view of the model's effectiveness and usability in real-world applications.

In conclusion, evaluating NLP models is a multi-faceted process that requires careful consideration of various metrics, techniques, and real-world factors. By employing a range of evaluation methods and understanding their implications, we can develop more accurate, reliable, and effective NLP systems. This comprehensive approach not only helps in assessing model performance but also in guiding improvements and ensuring that models meet the needs of their intended applications.

CHAPTER 12: PART-OF-SPEECH TAGGING

Part-of-Speech (POS) tagging is a foundational task in Natural Language Processing (NLP), crucial for understanding and analyzing the syntactic structure of text. By assigning grammatical categories such as nouns, verbs, adjectives, and adverbs to each word in a sentence, POS tagging enables deeper linguistic analysis and supports various downstream applications, including parsing, named entity recognition, and information retrieval. This section will explore the key techniques used for POS tagging, including rule-based methods, Hidden Markov Models (HMMs), and modern neural network approaches, and discuss their significance in the broader context of NLP.

Rule-based methods for POS tagging represent one of the earliest approaches to this task. These methods rely on hand-crafted rules and lexical resources to determine the POS tags of words. A typical rule-based tagger operates by examining the context in which a word appears and applying predefined rules that reflect syntactic and semantic patterns. For example, a rule might specify that if a word appears between an article and a noun, it is likely to be an adjective. Rule-based methods often utilize extensive linguistic resources such as dictionaries and grammar rules to make decisions. While effective in many cases, these approaches can be limited by their reliance on handcrafted rules, which may not capture all linguistic nuances or adapt well to new or unseen contexts.

Hidden Markov Models (HMMs) represent a statistical approach to POS tagging. HMMs are probabilistic models that use the principles of Markov processes to determine the most likely sequence of POS tags given a sequence of words. In this approach, each word in a sentence is assigned a tag based on the probabilities of tag sequences and the likelihood of each tag given the word. HMMs are trained on annotated corpora, where the model learns to predict POS tags based on observed patterns in the training data. The key advantage of HMMs is their ability to model sequential dependencies between tags, which allows them to capture context and make more informed tagging decisions. However, HMMs rely heavily on the assumption that the probability of a tag depends only on the previous tag (the Markov assumption), which can limit their ability to capture more complex dependencies.

In recent years, modern neural network approaches have become increasingly popular for POS tagging. These methods leverage deep learning techniques to learn contextual representations of words and their tags from large datasets. Recurrent Neural Networks (RNNs), particularly Long Short-Term Memory (LSTM) networks and their variants, have proven effective in handling sequential data and capturing long-range dependencies. LSTMs can remember information over long sequences, making them well-suited for POS tagging, where the context provided by preceding and following words is crucial for accurate tagging. Furthermore, Conditional Random Fields (CRFs) can be combined with LSTMs to model the dependencies between tags more explicitly, improving the overall performance of the tagger.

Another significant advancement in neural network-based POS tagging is the use of Transformer models, such as BERT (Bidirectional Encoder Representations from Transformers). Transformers leverage self-attention mechanisms to capture contextual relationships between words more effectively than traditional RNNs. BERT, for instance, pre-trains on large text corpora using masked language modeling and then fine-tunes on specific tasks, including POS tagging. This approach has demonstrated remarkable performance improvements over previous methods by providing richer contextual embeddings for words and allowing for more accurate and nuanced tagging.

The importance of POS tagging extends beyond mere categorization; it plays a vital role in understanding the syntactic structure of text. By accurately identifying grammatical categories, POS tagging helps in parsing sentences, identifying phrases and clauses, and understanding the grammatical relationships between words. This information is essential for more complex NLP tasks, such as syntactic parsing, machine translation, and question answering. For instance, in syntactic parsing, POS tags provide the necessary information to build parse trees that represent the hierarchical structure of sentences, facilitating the analysis of sentence structure and meaning.

In practical applications, POS tagging is used to enhance the performance of various NLP systems. In information retrieval, POS tagging helps in indexing and retrieving documents by improving the accuracy of keyword matching and query expansion. In named entity recognition, POS tags provide valuable features that aid in distinguishing between different types of entities, such as people, organizations, and locations. Additionally, POS tagging supports text-to-speech systems by enabling accurate pronunciation and intonation based on the grammatical structure of the text.

Despite the advances in POS tagging techniques, several challenges remain. One challenge is dealing with ambiguity, as many words can serve multiple grammatical functions depending on their context. For example, the word "bank" can be a noun referring to a financial institution or a verb meaning to tilt. Effective POS tagging requires disambiguating these cases based on contextual information. Another challenge is handling out-of-vocabulary words, which are words not seen during training. Robust POS tagging systems must generalize well to new and unseen words while maintaining high accuracy.

Overall, Part-of-Speech tagging remains a critical task in NLP, providing the foundation for many advanced linguistic analyses and applications. As techniques continue to evolve, incorporating neural network approaches and leveraging large-scale data, the accuracy and utility of POS tagging systems are expected to improve, further enhancing their role in understanding and processing natural language.

In the realm of neural network approaches to POS tagging, various architectures have demonstrated substantial improvements over traditional methods. One prominent example is the use of Recurrent Neural Networks (RNNs), particularly Long Short-Term Memory (LSTM) networks. RNNs are well-suited to sequence data due to their inherent ability to maintain context over time, which is crucial for tasks like POS tagging where the meaning of a word often depends on its surrounding context. LSTMs, a type of RNN designed to mitigate the vanishing gradient problem, excel in capturing long-range dependencies in sequences. By leveraging LSTMs, we can enhance the accuracy of POS tagging by considering the entire context in which a word appears, rather than just its immediate surroundings.

The introduction of bidirectional LSTMs (BiLSTMs) further refines this approach by processing sequences in both forward and backward directions. This bidirectional context allows the model to gain a more comprehensive understanding of the surrounding words, which is particularly useful for disambiguating words that could belong to different POS categories depending on their context. For instance, the word "bank" can be a noun or a verb depending on whether it appears in the context of a financial institution or the act of banking. A

BiLSTM can leverage context from both before and after "bank" to determine its correct POS tag.

Another significant advancement in neural POS tagging is the application of Transformer-based models, such as BERT (Bidirectional Encoder Representations from Transformers). Transformers use self-attention mechanisms to weigh the importance of different words in a sentence relative to each other, which allows them to capture intricate dependencies and contextual relationships. Unlike RNNs, Transformers do not process data sequentially but rather attend to all positions in the input sequence simultaneously. This ability to consider the entire context at once makes Transformers highly effective at capturing the nuances of language, leading to superior performance in POS tagging tasks.

Transformers also benefit from pre-training on large corpora followed by fine-tuning on specific tasks. For instance, a model like BERT is pre-trained on a vast amount of text data to learn general language patterns and then fine-tuned on POS tagging datasets to specialize in this task. This transfer learning approach allows Transformers to leverage broad language knowledge and adapt it to the specific requirements of POS tagging, resulting in high accuracy and robustness.

Despite the advancements offered by neural network approaches, it is essential to recognize that these models require substantial computational resources and large annotated datasets for training. The computational demands of training deep learning models can be a limiting factor for some applications, particularly in resource-constrained environments. Moreover, while neural models achieve impressive performance, they may still struggle with certain linguistic phenomena or out-of-domain texts where training data is sparse or not representative of the target distribution.

Evaluating POS tagging systems involves assessing the

accuracy of the tags assigned to each word against a gold standard annotated corpus. Common evaluation metrics include precision, recall, and F1 score, which collectively provide insights into the model's performance. Precision measures the proportion of correctly assigned POS tags among all assigned tags, while recall evaluates the proportion of correctly assigned tags out of all actual tags in the data. The F1 score, which is the harmonic mean of precision and recall, provides a balanced view of performance by considering both the accuracy and completeness of the tagging.

Another important metric is accuracy, which measures the overall proportion of correctly tagged words in the dataset. While accuracy provides a straightforward measure of performance, precision, recall, and F1 score offer more nuanced insights, particularly in cases where class imbalances or specific error types need to be addressed. For example, if a model is particularly good at identifying nouns but struggles with adjectives, precision and recall for each POS category can help pinpoint these strengths and weaknesses.

In addition to these metrics, error analysis plays a critical role in improving POS tagging systems. By examining the types of errors made by the model, such as incorrect tag assignments or frequent confusion between similar POS categories, researchers and practitioners can identify areas for improvement. This analysis may lead to refinements in the model architecture, adjustments to training data, or the incorporation of additional features to enhance tagging accuracy.

In summary, POS tagging is a pivotal task in NLP that underpins many advanced applications and models. The evolution from rule-based methods to statistical models like HMMs and the advent of deep learning techniques such as RNNs and Transformers have significantly advanced the field. Each approach offers distinct advantages and challenges, and selecting the appropriate method often depends on the specific requirements of the task and available resources. As the field continues to evolve, ongoing advancements in model architectures and training techniques will likely further enhance the accuracy and applicability of POS tagging systems.

The practical implementation of part-of-speech (POS) tagging, whether through rule-based methods, Hidden Markov Models (HMMs), or advanced neural network approaches, presents unique challenges and opportunities for enhancing text analysis and understanding.

In practice, implementing POS tagging begins with the preprocessing phase, where text data is prepared for analysis. This involves tokenizing the text into individual words or tokens and normalizing these tokens by lowercasing, stemming, or lemmatization. For neural network approaches, additional steps include embedding the tokens into dense vector representations. These embeddings capture semantic relationships between words and are crucial for models like LSTMs and Transformers to understand context.

Once the text is prepared, the choice of tagging method significantly impacts the accuracy and efficiency of the process. Rule-based POS taggers operate on a set of predefined rules that reflect grammatical principles. These rules can be handcrafted based on linguistic expertise or generated from annotated corpora. While rule-based systems offer high precision and interpretability, they may struggle with the variability and complexity of natural language. This is where statistical and machine learning-based approaches, such as HMMs and neural networks, become advantageous.

Hidden Markov Models, for example, use a probabilistic approach to POS tagging by modeling sequences of words as sequences of states, where each state corresponds to a POS tag. The model learns transition probabilities between tags and emission probabilities of words given a tag from training data. HMMs can capture context to some extent but are limited by their linear nature and the need for large annotated corpora to perform effectively. Despite these limitations, HMMs remain a cornerstone of statistical NLP due to their simplicity and effectiveness in many scenarios.

In contrast, modern neural network models offer greater flexibility and accuracy. Recurrent Neural Networks (RNNs), and more specifically Long Short-Term Memory (LSTM) networks, address some of the limitations of traditional methods by maintaining a memory of previous words in a sequence, which helps in understanding context over longer spans. This memory is particularly useful for disambiguating words whose POS depends on their surrounding words. LSTMs manage to retain long-range dependencies better than simple RNNs, thanks to their gating mechanisms that control the flow of information.

Bidirectional LSTMs (BiLSTMs) enhance this capability by processing text in both forward and backward directions. This bidirectional approach provides a more comprehensive understanding of context, which is particularly useful for ambiguous words or phrases whose meaning can only be inferred from surrounding text. For instance, understanding the context of "playing" in "playing piano" versus "playing a role" benefits from the ability to consider the entire sentence.

The introduction of Transformer-based models represents a paradigm shift in POS tagging and other NLP tasks. Transformers, particularly models like BERT, utilize self-attention mechanisms to weigh the importance of each word in relation to others within a sequence. This attention mechanism enables the model to capture complex dependencies and contextual relationships without the sequential processing constraints of RNNs. Transformers leverage large-scale pre-training on diverse text data, allowing them to learn nuanced language patterns and apply this knowledge to specific tasks like POS tagging.

BERT, for example, is pre-trained using a masked language model approach, where parts of the input text are masked, and the model learns to predict these masked parts. This pre-training allows BERT to develop a deep understanding of language, which is then fine-tuned on task-specific data. For POS tagging, this means that BERT can adapt its general language understanding to the specific patterns and requirements of tagging tasks, often resulting in superior performance compared to traditional models.

The evaluation of POS tagging systems involves assessing their accuracy and effectiveness using various metrics. Precision, recall, and F1 score are commonly used to measure the performance of tagging systems. Precision quantifies the proportion of correctly assigned tags among all assigned tags, while recall measures the proportion of correctly assigned tags among all true tags. The F1 score, the harmonic mean of precision and recall, provides a balanced measure of a model's performance. Additionally, accuracy, which measures the proportion of correctly assigned tags out of all tags, is a straightforward metric that offers an overall view of performance.

Perplexity is another metric that, while more commonly associated with language modeling, can provide insights into the quality of POS tagging when combined with other evaluations. Lower perplexity indicates better model performance in predicting the next word or tag in a sequence, reflecting a more coherent understanding of language structure.

In summary, the choice of POS tagging method and evaluation metrics greatly influences the effectiveness of NLP systems. Rule-based methods offer simplicity and interpretability but may lack adaptability. Statistical models like HMMs provide a balance of accuracy and practicality but can be limited by their probabilistic nature. Neural network approaches, including LSTMs, BiLSTMs, and Transformers, offer advanced capabilities in capturing contextual dependencies and complex language patterns, resulting in higher accuracy and flexibility. By carefully selecting and evaluating these methods, we can enhance our ability to understand and process natural language, leading to more robust and effective NLP applications.

CHAPTER 13: PARSING AND SYNTAX TREES

Parsing, a fundamental process in natural language processing (NLP), is concerned with analyzing the syntactic structure of sentences to understand their grammatical relationships and hierarchical organization. The ability to parse text effectively enables a deeper comprehension of how words and phrases interact within a sentence, providing insights into the syntactic and semantic nuances of language. This chapter will explore various parsing techniques, focusing on constituency parsing and dependency parsing, and examine how syntax trees are employed to represent sentence structures.

To begin with, parsing techniques are crucial for transforming raw text into a structured format that captures the syntactic relationships among words. Constituency parsing, also known as phrase structure parsing, involves breaking down a sentence into nested constituents or phrases. Each constituent represents a group of words that function as a single unit within the sentence. For instance, in the sentence "The quick brown fox jumps over the lazy dog," the constituency parser identifies "The quick brown fox" as a noun phrase and "jumps over the lazy dog" as a verb phrase. This hierarchical structure reflects the grammatical organization of the sentence and can be represented using a syntax tree.

A syntax tree, or parse tree, is a visual representation of the syntactic structure of a sentence. It illustrates how different constituents combine to form larger units, ultimately leading to the complete sentence. Each node in the tree represents a grammatical category, such as a noun phrase, verb phrase, or sentence, and the branches depict the relationships between these categories. Syntax trees provide a clear view of how words are grouped and how phrases are organized, making them valuable for understanding sentence structure and for further linguistic analysis.

On the other hand, dependency parsing focuses on the relationships between individual words in a sentence. Unlike constituency parsing, which emphasizes phrase structure, dependency parsing highlights how words are connected to one another through dependencies. In dependency parsing, each word is considered a node in a directed graph, with arrows representing syntactic dependencies between words. For example, in the sentence "She writes a letter," "writes" is the root word, and "She" and "letter" are dependent on it. Dependency parsing captures the grammatical relations, such as subject-verb and verb-object connections, which are essential for understanding sentence meaning and structure.

Dependency parsing is particularly useful for tasks that require understanding the roles of individual words and their relationships, such as information extraction and question answering. It provides a more granular view of sentence structure compared to constituency parsing, which can be advantageous for certain applications. Dependency trees offer insights into the functional roles of words, such as identifying the subject and object of a verb or determining the grammatical function of a modifier.

The choice between constituency parsing and dependency parsing depends on the specific requirements of the application and the type of linguistic analysis needed. Constituency parsing is often employed in applications that require a detailed understanding of phrase structure, such as machine translation and syntactic grammar checking. Dependency parsing, on the other hand, is frequently used in tasks that involve semantic analysis and extraction of relational information, such as semantic role labeling and relationship extraction.

To illustrate the impact of parsing on language understanding, consider a practical example of machine translation. In translating a sentence from one language to another, it is essential to capture not only the individual words but also their syntactic relationships. Constituency parsing can help ensure that phrases are correctly translated and restructured according to the target language's grammar. Similarly, dependency parsing can aid in aligning syntactic dependencies between languages, facilitating accurate translation of complex sentences with intricate relationships.

Another example is in the field of information retrieval, where parsing plays a crucial role in extracting relevant information from text. By analyzing the syntactic structure of queries and documents, parsers can help identify key entities and relationships, improving the accuracy of search results and retrieval systems. Dependency parsing, in particular, can enhance the extraction of specific pieces of information by understanding how different words in a query are related to each other.

In summary, parsing and syntax trees are essential tools for understanding the syntactic structure of sentences. Constituency parsing provides a hierarchical view of sentence structure through phrase-based trees, while dependency parsing focuses on the relationships between individual words through directed graphs. Both techniques offer valuable insights into grammatical organization and play a significant role in various NLP applications. By employing parsing methods effectively, we can enhance our ability to analyze and interpret language, leading to more accurate and meaningful linguistic analysis.

Continuing with parsing techniques, let us delve deeper into the implementation and practical applications of both constituency parsing and dependency parsing. These techniques not only provide structural insights but also serve as the foundation for various advanced NLP tasks.

In the realm of constituency parsing, there are several methodologies used to generate syntax trees. One of the traditional methods is based on context-free grammars (CFGs). CFGs consist of a set of production rules that define how symbols can be replaced with other symbols or groups of symbols. The Earley parser and the CYK (Cocke-Younger-Kasami) parser are two notable algorithms for parsing sentences based on CFGs. The Earley parser is particularly versatile, capable of handling ambiguous grammars and non-context-free languages, making it suitable for a wide range of linguistic applications. The CYK parser, on the other hand, is more efficient with a fixed grammar but is restricted to context-free grammars, which limits its applicability to more complex linguistic structures.

With the advent of statistical models and machine learning, the field of parsing has been revolutionized by probabilistic context-free grammars (PCFGs). PCFGs extend CFGs by associating probabilities with each production rule, enabling parsers to select the most likely parse tree given the probabilistic information. This approach enhances the parser's ability to handle ambiguities and improve accuracy by leveraging statistical data from large corpora.

Moving on to dependency parsing, this technique involves the use of dependency grammars, where the focus is on the relationships between words rather than their groupings into phrases. Dependency parsing can be performed using various methods, including graph-based and transition-based approaches. Graph-based dependency parsing constructs a global graph representation of the sentence and then uses algorithms to find the optimal set of dependencies that form a valid parse tree. One common algorithm in this category is the maximum spanning tree algorithm, which finds the most probable dependency tree based on the graph's weights.

Transition-based dependency parsing, conversely, operates by building the parse tree incrementally through a series of transitions. This approach uses a sequence of actions to process the input sentence, progressively constructing the dependency structure. Algorithms such as the arc-standard and arc-eager parsing algorithms are commonly used in this approach. Transition-based parsers are typically more efficient than graph-based parsers, making them suitable for real-time applications and large-scale parsing tasks.

Modern dependency parsers often utilize neural network models to enhance performance. Neural network-based parsers leverage deep learning techniques to learn complex patterns in syntactic structures from large annotated corpora. Recurrent Neural Networks (RNNs), particularly those with Long Short-Term Memory (LSTM) units, and Transformer-based models have shown significant improvements in parsing accuracy and efficiency. These models are capable of capturing long-range dependencies and nuanced syntactic relationships that traditional parsers may struggle with.

The application of parsing techniques extends beyond syntactic analysis to a variety of NLP tasks. For instance, parsing is instrumental in information extraction, where it helps identify and categorize entities, relationships, and events within text. In machine translation, parsing contributes to syntactic alignment between source and target languages, facilitating more accurate translations. Additionally, parsing supports text summarization by identifying and preserving the most relevant syntactic structures in condensed summaries.

Another notable application of parsing is in question answering systems. By analyzing the syntactic structure of questions and their corresponding contexts, parsing enables these systems to understand and retrieve accurate answers. For example, in a reading comprehension task, a parser can identify the key components of a question and match them with relevant information in the text, thereby enhancing the system's ability to provide precise responses.

Despite its advancements, parsing still faces several challenges. Ambiguity remains a significant issue, as sentences can often be parsed in multiple valid ways. The task of disambiguating between these options requires sophisticated algorithms and large annotated datasets to train accurate models. Additionally, parsing performance can be influenced by linguistic phenomena such as syntactic variations, language-specific features, and domain-specific jargon, which necessitates ongoing research and development to address these limitations.

In summary, parsing and syntax trees play a crucial role in understanding and processing natural language. By exploring both constituency and dependency parsing techniques, we gain valuable insights into the structural and relational aspects of sentences. The application of advanced algorithms, including statistical models and neural network-based approaches, enhances parsing accuracy and efficiency, enabling more effective NLP systems across various domains.

Parsing techniques offer valuable insights into the structure of sentences, revealing both grammatical relationships and hierarchical organization. To fully grasp the implications of parsing in natural language processing, it is crucial to understand how these structures are used to inform language models and applications.

In practical applications, parsing results are often leveraged for a range of NLP tasks. For instance, in machine translation, understanding the syntactic structure of sentences in both the source and target languages is essential for generating accurate translations. Parsing helps in aligning syntactic structures between languages, ensuring that translations preserve grammatical correctness and meaning. Similarly, in information extraction, parsing allows systems to identify and categorize entities and relationships within text, facilitating tasks such as summarization and question answering.

The accuracy and effectiveness of parsing techniques are highly dependent on the quality of the linguistic resources and models used. Training data, for instance, plays a pivotal role in shaping the performance of parsers. High-quality annotated corpora with detailed syntactic information are essential for training robust parsing models. For constituency parsing, treebanks such as the Penn Treebank provide extensive annotated examples of syntactic structures, aiding the development of effective CFG-based and PCFG-based parsers. For dependency parsing, resources like the Universal Dependencies corpus offer annotated data for training and evaluating dependency parsers across different languages.

Additionally, parsing models can be evaluated using various metrics to gauge their performance. Common evaluation metrics include accuracy, which measures the proportion of correctly identified syntactic relations or structures, and the F1 score, which balances precision and recall in parsing tasks. For dependency parsing, the labeled attachment score (LAS) and unlabeled attachment score (UAS) are specific metrics used to assess the correctness of dependency relations and labels. These metrics help in comparing different parsing approaches and in refining models for better performance.

Another important aspect of parsing is its integration with other NLP components. For example, parsing can be combined with named entity recognition (NER) to enhance entity extraction tasks. By understanding the syntactic context in which entities appear, systems can improve the accuracy of entity identification and classification. Similarly, in sentiment analysis, parsing provides insights into sentence structure that can aid in understanding the sentiment conveyed by different parts of a sentence, leading to more nuanced sentiment classification.

Recent advancements in parsing have also been driven by deep learning techniques. Neural network-based models, such as those employing bidirectional LSTMs (Long Short-Term Memory networks) and transformers, have demonstrated significant improvements over traditional parsing approaches. These models leverage large-scale datasets and sophisticated architectures to capture complex syntactic patterns and dependencies. For instance, the use of attention mechanisms in transformers has enabled more accurate parsing by allowing the model to focus on relevant parts of the input sentence when predicting syntactic structures.

Despite these advancements, challenges remain in parsing. For example, parsing ambiguous or noisy text, such as user-generated content or informal language, can be particularly difficult. Ambiguities in language, such as polysemy and syntactic ambiguity, often require sophisticated handling to ensure accurate parsing. Additionally, the scalability of parsing systems to handle large corpora and real-time applications remains a critical consideration.

In summary, parsing and syntax trees are foundational to understanding sentence structure in natural language processing. By employing various parsing techniques, from traditional rule-based methods to advanced neural network approaches, we can gain deeper insights into language and enhance the performance of a wide array of NLP applications. The choice of parsing technique and the quality of resources used directly impact the effectiveness of parsing models, underscoring the importance of continued research and development in this area. As NLP technologies evolve, parsing will continue to play a vital role in advancing our ability to analyze and understand human language.

CHAPTER 14: COREFERENCE RESOLUTION

Coreference resolution is a critical aspect of natural language understanding that involves identifying when different expressions within a text refer to the same entity. This task is essential for ensuring coherence and context in text analysis, as it helps to link pronouns, names, and other referring expressions to their antecedents, thereby enabling a deeper comprehension of the text.

The coreference resolution process can be approached through various methods, including rule-based systems, machine learning techniques, and a combination of both. Rule-based systems rely on handcrafted rules and heuristics to identify coreferent expressions based on syntactic and semantic cues. These systems often use patterns and linguistic knowledge to make decisions about coreference. For example, a rule-based system might use patterns such as "the [Noun] and his [Pronoun]" to infer that the pronoun refers to the noun.

However, rule-based systems have limitations, primarily due to their reliance on predefined rules that may not cover all possible scenarios or variations in language. As a result, machine learning approaches have gained prominence in coreference resolution. These approaches leverage statistical models and algorithms to learn patterns from annotated training data, allowing for more flexible and scalable solutions.

One of the most common machine learning techniques for coreference resolution is the use of supervised learning models. These models are trained on large annotated corpora, where coreferent mentions are explicitly labeled. The training process involves learning features that are indicative of coreference relationships, such as the similarity between mentions, their grammatical roles, and their contextual information. Popular machine learning algorithms for coreference resolution include decision trees, support vector machines (SVMs), and conditional random fields (CRFs).

Conditional random fields, in particular, have been widely used in coreference resolution due to their ability to model complex dependencies between mentions and capture contextual information. CRFs can incorporate a range of features, including syntactic, semantic, and lexical cues, to make predictions about coreference relationships. These features are extracted from the text and used to train the model to recognize patterns that indicate when two mentions refer to the same entity.

Recent advancements in coreference resolution have been driven by neural network-based models, which have shown significant improvements over traditional approaches. Neural networks, particularly those employing deep learning techniques, can automatically learn features from raw text without requiring extensive feature engineering. Models such as bidirectional LSTM (Long Short-Term Memory) networks and attention-based mechanisms have been used to capture complex relationships between mentions and their context.

Bidirectional LSTM networks process text in both forward and backward directions, allowing them to capture dependencies that span across the entire text. This bidirectional approach enhances the model's ability to understand the context surrounding each mention and improve coreference resolution accuracy. Attention mechanisms, on the other hand, enable models to focus on specific parts of the text that are most relevant for resolving coreferences, further enhancing performance.

In addition to these neural network-based approaches, transformer models have also made a significant impact on coreference resolution. Transformer architectures, such as BERT (Bidirectional Encoder Representations from Transformers), have been pre-trained on large corpora and fine-tuned for specific tasks, including coreference resolution. The self-attention mechanism in transformers allows these models to capture long-range dependencies and contextual relationships between mentions, resulting in improved resolution of coreferences.

Coreference resolution is not only important for improving the coherence of individual texts but also for enhancing various NLP applications. For instance, in information extraction, accurately resolving coreferences helps in identifying and linking entities across documents, enabling more effective extraction of relevant information. In question answering systems, coreference resolution ensures that the system correctly interprets pronouns and references in the user's query and the documents being searched, leading to more accurate answers.

Furthermore, coreference resolution plays a crucial role in summarization tasks. By resolving coreferences, summarization systems can produce coherent and concise summaries that accurately reflect the relationships between entities mentioned in the original text. This is particularly important for generating summaries that are easy to read and understand, as it ensures that the relationships between entities are clearly conveyed.

Despite the advancements in coreference resolution techniques, challenges remain, particularly when dealing with complex texts and ambiguous references. For example, resolving coreferences in texts with multiple entities or those involving vague or ambiguous pronouns can be difficult. To address these challenges, ongoing research continues to explore new methods and improve existing models, incorporating more sophisticated features and leveraging larger datasets to enhance coreference resolution accuracy.

In summary, coreference resolution is a fundamental task in NLP that enhances text coherence and context by identifying when different expressions refer to the same entity. From rule-based systems to machine learning and deep learning approaches, a variety of techniques have been developed to tackle this task. Understanding and implementing effective coreference resolution methods is essential for improving the performance of various NLP applications, ensuring that they produce accurate and contextually relevant results.

Building on the foundational methods of coreference resolution, neural network-based models have transformed this task by leveraging sophisticated representations of text. These models, particularly those based on deep learning architectures, have greatly advanced the accuracy and flexibility of coreference resolution systems.

Neural network models for coreference resolution often use embeddings to represent words and phrases. Word embeddings, such as Word2Vec or GloVe, capture semantic relationships between words by mapping them into continuous vector spaces. However, more recent models employ contextual embeddings, like those produced by BERT (Bidirectional Encoder Representations from Transformers), which take into account the context in which words appear. This context-sensitive approach allows the model to better understand nuanced meanings and relationships between words in varying contexts.

For instance, BERT's transformer-based architecture enables the model to consider both the left and right contexts of a word simultaneously. This bidirectional approach helps in accurately predicting coreference relationships by providing a more holistic view of the text. When applied to coreference resolution, BERT can generate contextual embeddings for each mention and use these embeddings to determine whether two mentions refer to the same entity. The model does this by computing similarity scores between embeddings, which indicate the likelihood of coreference.

Moreover, end-to-end neural network models have emerged, integrating coreference resolution into a unified framework. These models typically use sequence-to-sequence architectures or other advanced deep learning techniques to process text and make coreference predictions. For example, a common approach involves using a neural network to encode the entire text and then predict coreference links between all pairs of mentions. This end-to-end approach simplifies the resolution process by treating it as a single optimization problem, where the model learns to make global decisions about coreference based on the overall text.

Another significant advancement in neural network-based coreference resolution is the use of graph-based methods. In these approaches, the text is represented as a graph where nodes correspond to mentions and edges represent potential coreference relationships. Graph neural networks (GNNs) are then used to process this graph, allowing the model to capture complex dependencies and interactions between mentions. GNNs can effectively leverage the structural information of the graph to enhance coreference prediction accuracy.

Despite the significant progress with neural models, coreference resolution remains a challenging task due to several factors. One major challenge is the handling of ambiguous mentions, where a single mention could refer to multiple entities depending on the context. For instance, in the sentence "Mary said she would call John if he was available," the pronouns "she" and "he" could refer to different individuals depending on the broader context, which may not always be explicitly provided.

Additionally, coreference resolution models must deal with variations in language usage, including different ways of referring to the same entity, such as using pronouns, names, or titles. These variations require models to be flexible and robust, capable of generalizing across different linguistic forms and contexts.

Evaluation of coreference resolution systems is also a critical aspect of developing effective models. Performance is typically assessed using metrics such as precision, recall, and F1 score, which measure the accuracy of the model's predictions compared to a gold standard. Precision reflects the proportion of correctly identified coreferent pairs among all identified pairs, while recall indicates the proportion of actual coreferent pairs that were correctly identified. The F1 score provides a balanced measure that combines both precision and recall.

To further improve coreference resolution, ongoing research focuses on integrating additional sources of information, such as knowledge bases and external world knowledge. For example, incorporating information about named entities and their relationships can enhance the model's ability to resolve coreferences, especially in cases where the text alone does not provide sufficient context.

In summary, the field of coreference resolution has evolved from rule-based methods to advanced neural network approaches, reflecting significant advancements in natural language processing. Neural models, particularly those leveraging contextual embeddings and deep learning techniques, have dramatically improved the accuracy and flexibility of coreference resolution systems. Nevertheless, challenges such as handling ambiguous mentions and language variations persist, driving continued research and development in this area.

In addressing the challenges faced in coreference resolution, especially with ambiguous mentions, it is crucial to consider the interplay between various linguistic cues. Ambiguous mentions can arise from pronouns with multiple potential antecedents or from entities that are mentioned in different ways throughout a text. For instance, the pronoun "he" could refer to any male character introduced in the text, and a proper noun like "John" might be referred to as "the doctor" in another mention. Accurately resolving these ambiguities often requires a model to integrate contextual information, syntactic cues, and even world knowledge.

To handle such complexities, many advanced coreference resolution systems incorporate a combination of features. These features might include syntactic parsing results, which provide structural information about the relationships between words in a sentence. For instance, if two mentions appear within the same noun phrase or subject-verb-object structure, they are more likely to be coreferent. Additionally, semantic similarity measures, which compare the meanings of different mentions, play a critical role. Neural network-based models that leverage embeddings capture these semantic relationships more effectively than traditional methods.

Another important aspect of modern coreference resolution systems is their ability to handle long-range dependencies. In lengthy documents or conversations, coreferential links may span multiple sentences or even paragraphs. Traditional rule-based systems often struggled with such long-range dependencies due to their limited scope of analysis. However, deep learning models, particularly those using attention mechanisms such as Transformers, excel in this area. Attention mechanisms allow models to focus on different parts of the text when making predictions, thereby improving their ability to resolve coreferences across longer spans.

Evaluation of coreference resolution systems is also a critical component of developing effective models. Common evaluation metrics include precision, recall, and F1 score, which assess how well the system identifies and links coreferent mentions. Precision measures the proportion of correctly identified coreference links out of all predicted links, while recall assesses the proportion of actual coreference links that were successfully identified. The F1 score provides a balanced measure by combining precision and recall, offering a more comprehensive view of a system's performance. Additionally, more nuanced metrics like MUC (Mention Understanding Conference), B3, and CEAF (Cross-Entity Alignment F1) are used to evaluate different aspects of coreference resolution, such as mention linking and entity-level performance.

In practice, coreference resolution has a wide range of applications. In information extraction, accurate coreference resolution enhances the quality of extracted entities by ensuring that mentions refer to the same real-world objects. For example, in news articles, identifying that "the President" and "Barack Obama" refer to the same person improves the clarity and usefulness of the extracted information. Similarly, in question answering systems, coreference resolution helps in understanding the context of questions and generating appropriate answers by linking pronouns and other references to their correct entities.

Moreover, coreference resolution is integral to text summarization. By resolving coreferences, summarization systems can generate more coherent and concise summaries by consolidating information about entities mentioned throughout the text. This not only improves the readability of summaries but also ensures that critical information is accurately represented.

In dialogue systems and chatbots, coreference resolution plays a crucial role in maintaining context over multiple turns of conversation. Without effective coreference handling, chatbots may struggle to keep track of the entities being discussed, leading to incoherent or irrelevant responses. By resolving coreferences, dialogue systems can maintain a coherent context and provide more relevant and engaging interactions.

Despite the advancements in coreference resolution, ongoing research continues to explore ways to improve these systems. Current research areas include enhancing the handling of complex linguistic phenomena such as ellipsis (where parts of sentences are omitted), exploring cross-lingual coreference resolution, and improving models' robustness to noisy or informal text. As these techniques evolve, they promise to further enhance the accuracy and applicability of coreference resolution across diverse linguistic and contextual settings.

In conclusion, coreference resolution is a vital task in natural language processing, with significant implications for understanding and generating coherent text. By employing a combination of traditional rule-based methods, machine learning approaches, and advanced neural network techniques, we can effectively resolve coreferences and improve various NLP applications. As research in this field progresses, we can anticipate even more sophisticated methods for handling the complexities of language and enhancing the overall performance of text analysis systems.

CHAPTER 15: MACHINE TRANSLATION FUNDAMENTALS

Machine translation (MT) is a fascinating field of study focused on automatically translating text from one language to another. This process involves a range of methodologies and technologies, each addressing the intricacies of language and context in unique ways. To understand the current landscape of machine translation, it is essential to grasp both its foundational concepts and the evolution of its techniques over time.

Historically, statistical machine translation (SMT) was one of the first significant advancements in the field. SMT models rely on statistical methods to translate text based on the analysis of large bilingual corpora. These corpora consist of parallel texts where the same content is available in multiple languages. By examining these texts, SMT systems estimate the likelihood of a particular translation based on statistical associations. Key components of SMT include phrase-based translation models and alignment models. Phrase-based models break down text into phrases and translate these units independently, while alignment models focus on mapping words or phrases in the source language to their counterparts in the target language.

Despite its advancements, SMT has notable limitations, particularly with regard to handling ambiguities and preserving the nuances of meaning across languages. SMT systems often struggle with context, leading to translations that may be grammatically correct but contextually inappropriate. For instance, idiomatic expressions and culturally specific references are challenging for SMT models, which may translate them literally rather than capturing their intended meaning.

The introduction of neural machine translation (NMT) marked a significant shift in addressing these challenges. NMT models use deep learning techniques to translate text, offering substantial improvements over SMT in terms of fluency and context. A fundamental component of NMT is the use of neural networks, specifically sequence-to-sequence (seq2seq) models. These models consist of an encoder and a decoder. The encoder processes the input text and transforms it into a contextually rich representation, while the decoder generates the translated text from this representation.

One of the key advancements in NMT is the attention mechanism, which allows the model to focus on different parts of the input sequence when generating each word in the output sequence. This capability significantly enhances the model's ability to capture long-range dependencies and contextual information. For example, when translating a complex sentence, the attention mechanism helps the model identify relevant words and phrases from the entire input sequence, leading to more coherent and accurate translations.

Further progress in NMT is exemplified by Transformer-based models, which build upon the attention mechanism. Transformers use self-attention to compute the importance of each word relative to others in the sequence, enabling the model to handle intricate syntactic and semantic relationships more effectively. The Transformer architecture has become the foundation for many state-of-the-art translation models, such as BERT (Bidirectional Encoder Representations from Transformers) and GPT (Generative Pre-trained Transformer), which push the boundaries of translation quality by leveraging vast amounts of data and advanced neural network techniques.

One of the major challenges in machine translation remains handling ambiguities, which can arise from multiple sources. Polysemy, where a single word has multiple meanings, can cause confusion in translation. For instance, the word "bank" could refer to a financial institution or the side of a river, and the correct translation depends on the context in which it is used. Similarly, syntactic ambiguities, such as the placement of adjectives or adverbs, can affect the interpretation of a sentence. Addressing these issues requires sophisticated modeling techniques that go beyond surface-level analysis to understand and generate contextually appropriate translations.

Another challenge is preserving meaning across languages, which involves accounting for differences in grammatical structures, cultural nuances, and idiomatic expressions. Languages often have unique ways of expressing ideas that may not have direct equivalents in other languages. For example, the Japanese phrase "いっしょうけんめい" (isshōkenmei) conveys a sense of putting one's utmost effort into something, a concept that may not translate easily into a single English word or phrase. Ensuring that such nuances are captured accurately in translation requires a deep understanding of both source and target languages, as well as advanced modeling techniques that can bridge these linguistic gaps.

To enhance translation quality, recent advancements focus on improving training data and model robustness. High-quality bilingual corpora, including diverse and representative samples, are crucial for training effective translation models. Additionally, techniques such as transfer learning and fine-tuning allow models to adapt to specific domains or languages by leveraging pre-trained models and domain-specific data. These approaches help address the limitations of general-purpose models and improve translation accuracy in specialized contexts.

As machine translation continues to evolve, ongoing research and development aim to address existing challenges and explore new possibilities. Innovations in neural network architectures, data augmentation techniques, and multilingual modeling contribute to the ongoing improvement of translation systems. By combining these advancements with a deeper understanding of language and context, the field of machine translation strives to achieve ever more accurate and contextually appropriate translations.

Neural machine translation (NMT) has significantly advanced the field of machine translation by leveraging deep learning techniques to achieve higher accuracy and fluency in translations. A major breakthrough in NMT is the development of transformer models, which have revolutionized how machine translation systems handle context and dependencies in text. Unlike previous models, transformers do not rely on sequential processing but instead use self-attention mechanisms to capture relationships between all words in a sentence simultaneously. This allows for a more comprehensive understanding of context and improves the model's ability to generate translations that are not only grammatically correct but also contextually appropriate.

Transformers are based on the concept of attention mechanisms, which enable the model to weigh the importance of different words when generating translations. For instance, in translating a complex sentence, the attention mechanism allows the model to focus on relevant parts of the input sequence, considering their importance relative to the current word being translated. This results in translations that better capture the meaning and nuance of the source text.

Additionally, transformers facilitate parallel processing, which speeds up training and inference compared to older sequential models.

The success of transformers has led to the development of several advanced models, such as BERT, GPT, and their variants. BERT (Bidirectional Encoder Representations from Transformers) is designed to understand context from both directions (left-to-right and right-to-left), which enhances its ability to grasp the nuances of language. GPT (Generative Pre-trained Transformer) models, on the other hand, are optimized for generating coherent and contextually relevant text based on large-scale pre-training and fine-tuning. These models have set new benchmarks for translation quality and fluency, demonstrating the effectiveness of transformer-based architectures in handling complex language tasks.

Despite these advancements, machine translation still faces several challenges. One significant issue is the handling of low-resource languages, where there is limited training data available. Models trained on large-scale datasets for high-resource languages, such as English and Spanish, often struggle to achieve similar performance for languages with fewer available resources. Addressing this issue requires innovative approaches, such as transfer learning, where models are pre-trained on high-resource languages and fine-tuned on low-resource languages, or leveraging multilingual models that can learn from multiple languages simultaneously.

Another challenge in machine translation is dealing with the ambiguity inherent in language. Words and phrases can have multiple meanings depending on their context, and resolving these ambiguities is crucial for accurate translation. Context-aware models, such as those using transformers, have improved the handling of ambiguity by considering broader context and leveraging attention mechanisms to disambiguate meanings. However, fine-tuning these models for specific domains or languages remains an ongoing area of research.

Additionally, preserving the meaning and style of the original text while translating is a complex task. Machine translation systems must balance literal accuracy with the need to convey the same tone and intent as the source text. This requires sophisticated models that can understand and replicate stylistic elements, cultural references, and idiomatic expressions. For example, translating idiomatic phrases requires not only translating the words but also understanding and conveying the underlying meaning in a way that is natural in the target language.

Recent advancements in machine translation have also explored the integration of external knowledge sources and linguistic resources to enhance translation quality. For instance, incorporating world knowledge or domain-specific information can improve the accuracy of translations in specialized fields such as medicine or law. Furthermore, leveraging bilingual dictionaries, parallel corpora, and other linguistic tools can aid in translating technical terms and phrases that may not have direct equivalents in the target language.

Overall, the evolution of machine translation technologies from statistical methods to sophisticated neural network models has significantly improved the quality and usability of automatic translations. The integration of transformers and advanced neural architectures has enabled models to handle complex language structures, context, and ambiguities more effectively. However, ongoing research and development are essential to address the remaining challenges, such as handling low-resource languages, managing linguistic ambiguity, and preserving stylistic elements. As the field continues to advance, machine translation will increasingly bridge language barriers, facilitating communication and understanding across diverse linguistic and cultural contexts.

The challenge of handling ambiguities in language is profound, as words or phrases may have multiple meanings depending on their context. This is particularly problematic in translation tasks where disambiguation is crucial for preserving the intended meaning of the source text. Traditional statistical machine translation models often struggled with this issue, as they relied on phrase tables and statistical probabilities derived from bilingual corpora, which were limited in their ability to capture subtle contextual nuances. Neural machine translation models, with their advanced contextual understanding capabilities, have made strides in addressing these ambiguities by leveraging large-scale datasets and sophisticated algorithms that model language more comprehensively.

One of the key advancements in neural machine translation is the development of context-aware mechanisms, such as self-attention, which allows models to consider the entire context of a sentence or paragraph when generating translations. This is particularly important in languages where word order and syntactic structures can vary significantly. For instance, in languages with flexible word order, such as German or Russian, context-aware models can better handle cases where the position of words affects their meaning, ensuring that the translation remains coherent and contextually accurate.

In addition to handling ambiguities, machine translation systems must also deal with the challenge of preserving meaning across languages with different syntactic and semantic structures. Languages may differ in their treatment of tense, aspect, modality, and other grammatical features, which can complicate the translation process. To address this, modern neural models employ techniques such as encoder-decoder architectures, where the encoder processes the input text and captures its semantic meaning, while the decoder generates the output text in the target language. This separation of encoding and decoding functions allows the model to better align the meaning of the source text with the grammatical and syntactic norms of the target language.

Moreover, recent advancements in transfer learning and multilingual models have further enhanced translation quality. Transfer learning enables models to leverage knowledge gained from high-resource languages to improve performance on low-resource languages. This approach can involve pre-training a model on a large corpus of high-resource language pairs and then fine-tuning it on specific low-resource language pairs, allowing the model to benefit from previously learned language patterns and structures. Multilingual models, such as mBERT (multilingual BERT) and mT5 (multilingual T5), are designed to handle multiple languages simultaneously, making them particularly effective in translating between languages with limited data availability. These models are trained on data from various languages, enabling them to learn cross-lingual representations that facilitate better translation across a wide range of language pairs.

Despite these advancements, evaluating the performance of machine translation systems remains a critical aspect of development. Traditional evaluation metrics, such as BLEU (Bilingual Evaluation Understudy), have been widely used to assess translation quality by comparing the generated translations to reference translations. However, BLEU and similar metrics have limitations, including their reliance on exact matches and their inability to fully capture the nuances of translation quality. To address these limitations, newer metrics, such as METEOR (Metric for Evaluation of Translation with Explicit ORdering) and TER (Translation Edit Rate), have been developed to provide a more comprehensive evaluation of translation quality by considering factors such as synonymy, paraphrasing, and word order.

In addition to automatic evaluation metrics, human evaluation remains an essential component of assessing translation quality. Human evaluators can provide insights into the fluency, adequacy, and overall quality of translations, which are often difficult to capture with automated metrics alone. Human evaluations involve assessing translations based on criteria such as grammatical correctness, adherence to the source text's meaning, and naturalness of expression. These evaluations are typically conducted through various methods, including expert assessments, crowdsourcing, and comparative evaluations, where multiple translations are compared to determine which best captures the intended meaning.

As machine translation technology continues to evolve, researchers and practitioners are exploring new approaches to further enhance translation quality and address existing challenges. For instance, the integration of external knowledge sources, such as knowledge graphs and domain-specific information, is being investigated to improve the handling of domain-specific terminology and context. Additionally, efforts are underway to develop models that can adapt to evolving language patterns and emerging language phenomena, ensuring that translation systems remain relevant and effective in dynamic linguistic environments.

The field of machine translation has come a long way from its early days of rule-based and statistical approaches to the sophisticated neural network-based models we have today. Each advancement has contributed to a better understanding of language translation, enabling systems to produce more accurate, fluent, and contextually appropriate translations. The ongoing research and development in this area promise to further improve the capabilities of machine translation systems, making them increasingly valuable tools for global communication and information exchange.

CHAPTER 16: TEXT GENERATION TECHNIQUES

Text generation involves creating coherent and contextually relevant text from a given input, and it plays a critical role in various applications such as chatbots, content creation, and automated responses. This process requires a nuanced understanding of language and context to produce text that is not only grammatically correct but also contextually appropriate and engaging. To achieve this, different techniques have been developed over the years, each offering distinct advantages and facing unique challenges.

Initially, text generation methods were predominantly rule-based. Rule-based systems rely on predefined sets of linguistic rules and templates. These methods involve crafting explicit rules for grammar, syntax, and even content to generate text. For example, a rule-based system might use templates such as "The [adjective] [noun] [verb] [adverb]" to generate sentences. While these systems can produce text that adheres to grammatical conventions, their major limitation is their rigidity. They often lack the ability to handle variability in language use and cannot easily adapt to new contexts or generate text that deviates from the predefined templates. Despite these limitations, rule-based methods can still be useful in scenarios where predictability and control are paramount, such as generating structured reports or simple responses in customer service applications.

As computational resources and data availability increased, statistical models began to supplement and eventually largely replace rule-based approaches. Statistical machine translation and n-gram models are early examples of statistical methods used for text generation. In statistical methods, the probability of a word or phrase occurring in a given context is determined by analyzing large corpora of text. For instance, an n-gram model predicts the probability of the next word in a sequence based on the previous n-1 words. This approach allows for more flexibility and variability in the generated text compared to rule-based systems. However, statistical models are still limited by their reliance on frequency counts and may struggle with generating coherent long-form text or understanding nuanced contexts.

The advent of neural network-based approaches marked a significant leap forward in text generation techniques. Neural networks, especially recurrent neural networks (RNNs) and their more advanced variants, such as long short-term memory (LSTM) networks, introduced a more dynamic way of modeling language. RNNs are designed to handle sequential data, making them well-suited for text generation tasks. They can maintain context across words in a sequence by passing information through their hidden states. LSTMs, a type of RNN, further enhance this capability by addressing the problem of vanishing gradients, allowing the network to maintain long-term dependencies and generate more coherent and contextually relevant text.

A major breakthrough in text generation came with the introduction of Transformer models, which leverage self-attention mechanisms to process sequences more effectively than RNNs. Transformers, as exemplified by models like BERT and GPT, can consider all words in a sequence simultaneously rather than sequentially, allowing them to capture complex dependencies and context more efficiently. The self-attention mechanism enables these models to weigh the importance of different words in relation to each other, providing a more nuanced understanding of context. For example, in generating a sentence, a Transformer model can effectively manage dependencies between words that are far apart in the text, resulting in more coherent and contextually appropriate output.

Generative Pre-trained Transformers (GPT) have been particularly influential in advancing text generation. GPT models are trained on vast amounts of text data using a pre-training and fine-tuning approach. During pre-training, the model learns general language patterns and structures from diverse text sources, while fine-tuning involves adapting the model to specific tasks or domains. This approach allows GPT models to generate text that is both coherent and contextually relevant, making them suitable for a wide range of applications, from conversational agents to creative writing.

Despite these advancements, generating human-like text remains a challenging task. One significant challenge is ensuring that the generated text is not only contextually appropriate but also free from biases and inaccuracies. Neural network models, particularly those trained on large datasets from the internet, can inadvertently learn and perpetuate biases present in the training data. Addressing these biases requires careful dataset curation and ongoing evaluation of the generated text. Additionally, maintaining coherence over long passages of text remains an area of active research, as current models may struggle with consistency and relevance in extended dialogues or narratives.

Another challenge is handling diverse and dynamic contexts. While models like GPT are highly capable, they can still struggle with generating text that aligns perfectly with specific user intentions or highly specialized topics. Ensuring that the generated text is relevant and engaging requires ongoing improvements in model training and fine-tuning techniques.

In summary, text generation techniques have evolved significantly from rule-based methods to sophisticated neural network models. Each approach offers distinct advantages and addresses different aspects of text generation. Understanding these techniques and their associated challenges is crucial for developing effective text generation systems that can produce coherent, contextually relevant, and human-like text across various applications.

Neural networks, particularly Long Short-Term Memory (LSTM) networks, revolutionized text generation by addressing some of the fundamental limitations of earlier models. LSTMs, a type of RNN, are designed to capture long-range dependencies in sequential data, making them more adept at maintaining context over longer stretches of text. Unlike basic RNNs, which suffer from issues such as vanishing gradients and difficulty remembering information over long sequences, LSTMs use gating mechanisms to regulate the flow of information. This allows them to remember relevant details across extended contexts and make more coherent and contextually accurate predictions.

Building on LSTMs, attention mechanisms further advanced text generation techniques by allowing models to focus on different parts of the input sequence as needed. The attention mechanism dynamically adjusts the model's focus, enabling it to consider various parts of the input text when generating each word of the output. This capability greatly enhances the model's ability to produce relevant and contextually appropriate text. The Transformer architecture, which relies heavily on attention mechanisms, represents one of the most significant advancements in text generation. Transformers are designed to handle sequences in parallel, significantly improving training efficiency and scalability compared to RNNs and LSTMs.

The introduction of models like GPT (Generative Pre-trained

Transformer) has demonstrated the power of Transformers in generating human-like text. GPT and its successors, including GPT-2 and GPT-3, are pre-trained on vast amounts of data and then fine-tuned for specific tasks. These models use unsupervised learning to understand language patterns and generate text that is often indistinguishable from that written by humans. The pre-training involves predicting the next word in a sentence, which helps the model learn a wide range of language structures and contexts. Fine-tuning then adapts the model to particular applications or domains, allowing it to generate text that is both relevant and tailored to specific needs.

Despite these advancements, generating human-like text remains a complex challenge. One major issue is managing the balance between creativity and coherence. While models like GPT can produce highly creative and varied text, they sometimes generate outputs that are inconsistent or lack coherence over longer passages. This problem arises because these models, while proficient at predicting the next word based on previous context, may not always maintain a logical progression or adhere to the specific nuances required by complex contexts.

Another challenge is handling ambiguity and ensuring that the generated text is contextually appropriate. Language is inherently ambiguous, and the same words or phrases can have different meanings depending on the context. Ensuring that generated text resolves these ambiguities correctly requires models to have a deep understanding of context, something that remains an area of active research. Advances in context-aware models and techniques for disambiguation continue to improve the accuracy and relevance of generated text, but achieving perfect contextual understanding remains an ongoing goal.

The ethical implications of text generation also warrant consideration. The ability to generate realistic text raises questions about authenticity, misinformation, and the potential for misuse. For example, text generation models can be used to create fake news, deceptive content, or misleading information, posing significant challenges for information integrity. Researchers and developers must therefore consider safeguards and ethical guidelines to mitigate these risks while leveraging the benefits of text generation technology.

In practical applications, text generation techniques have demonstrated their value across various domains. In chatbots and virtual assistants, for instance, these models can provide responsive and contextually relevant interactions, enhancing user experience and efficiency. Content creation tools powered by text generation can assist in drafting articles, creating marketing copy, or generating creative writing, streamlining processes and sparking creativity. Additionally, text generation has applications in automated translation, summarization, and data augmentation, where generating high-quality text can significantly impact effectiveness and performance.

Overall, the evolution of text generation techniques reflects significant advancements in natural language processing, driven by the development of sophisticated models and approaches. From rule-based systems to neural network-based methods, each technique has contributed to our understanding and capability in generating coherent and contextually relevant text. As technology continues to advance, the focus will likely shift towards improving the balance between creativity and coherence, enhancing contextual understanding, and addressing ethical concerns to maximize the benefits and minimize potential risks associated with text generation.

Handling the complexities of human language in text generation extends beyond merely creating grammatically correct sentences. One significant challenge is maintaining contextual relevance over extended interactions. This difficulty is particularly apparent in applications such as chatbots and interactive storytelling, where coherence must be sustained throughout a conversation or narrative. Models often struggle to preserve the thread of conversation or narrative context, leading to disjointed responses or deviations from the initial topic. Addressing this issue involves designing systems that can track and recall context effectively, integrating mechanisms to manage and utilize context dynamically.

Another area of concern is the prevention of biased or inappropriate content. As text generation models learn from vast datasets that include a wide array of human-generated text, they can inadvertently replicate or amplify existing biases present in the training data. This challenge necessitates the development of methods to detect and mitigate biases during both the training and generation phases. Techniques such as adversarial training, where models are trained to avoid producing biased content, and post-processing filters, which scan and adjust outputs for fairness, are essential for addressing these concerns.

Furthermore, ensuring that generated text is not only coherent but also accurate and informative is crucial, particularly in applications such as automated journalism or technical content creation. Models must be equipped to verify facts and avoid generating misleading or incorrect information. This requirement involves integrating mechanisms for information retrieval and fact-checking into the text generation process. Approaches such as knowledge graphs, which provide structured data about entities and their relationships, can be utilized to enhance the factual accuracy of generated content.

Evaluation of text generation systems also presents a set of unique challenges. Traditional metrics such as BLEU (Bilingual Evaluation Understudy) score, used primarily in machine translation, may not fully capture the quality of generated text in applications requiring more nuanced evaluations of coherence and creativity. Alternative evaluation strategies, such as human judgment and user satisfaction surveys, are often employed to assess how well the generated text meets specific requirements. Developing robust and reliable evaluation criteria remains an ongoing area of research, aiming to provide comprehensive assessments of generated text across different dimensions of quality.

The integration of text generation technology into real-world applications necessitates ongoing refinement and adaptation. For instance, in customer service applications, text generation systems must be continually updated to reflect new information and evolving customer expectations. Similarly, in content creation, models need to adapt to changing trends and preferences to remain relevant and engaging. This adaptability requires not only technical advancements but also a deep understanding of the domains in which these systems are applied.

Overall, the field of text generation continues to advance rapidly, driven by innovations in machine learning and natural language processing. As models become more sophisticated, their ability to produce high-quality, coherent, and contextually appropriate text improves, leading to increasingly effective applications in a variety of domains. However, challenges such as maintaining coherence, mitigating biases, and ensuring factual accuracy must be addressed to fully realize the potential of these technologies. Through ongoing research and development, the goal is to create text generation systems that not only perform well technically but also align with the ethical and practical needs of their users.

CHAPTER 17: LANGUAGE MODEL FINE-TUNING

The process of fine-tuning a pre-trained language model is a critical step in adapting general-purpose models to specialized tasks or domains. Fine-tuning involves taking a model that has already been trained on a large, diverse corpus and further training it on a smaller, task-specific dataset. This approach leverages the broad linguistic knowledge captured during the initial training phase while customizing the model's capabilities to address specific needs or improve performance in targeted areas.

To begin the fine-tuning process, selecting an appropriate pre-trained model is paramount. Pre-trained models such as GPT (Generative Pre-trained Transformer), BERT (Bidirectional Encoder Representations from Transformers), or their variants have been trained on extensive and varied datasets, making them robust in general language understanding. However, the choice of the model should align with the specific requirements of the task at hand. For example, GPT models are often favored for tasks involving text generation due to their autoregressive nature, whereas BERT models, with their bidirectional context understanding, are better suited for tasks requiring comprehension and classification.

Once a suitable model has been chosen, preparing domain-specific data for fine-tuning is the next crucial step. This data should be representative of the task or domain for which the model is being adapted. For instance, if the goal is to fine-tune a language model for legal document analysis, the training dataset should consist of legal texts, such as contracts or court rulings, to ensure that the model learns the relevant terminology and context. The data preparation process involves not only gathering and curating text but also preprocessing it to ensure consistency and relevance. This might include tokenization, normalization, and removal of irrelevant information.

During the fine-tuning phase, the model is further trained on the domain-specific dataset. This step adjusts the model's parameters to improve its performance on the particular task. Fine-tuning is typically performed using supervised learning, where the model is trained to minimize a loss function specific to the task, such as cross-entropy loss for classification or mean squared error for regression. The training process involves iterating over the dataset multiple times, updating the model's weights based on the gradients computed from the loss function.

One of the critical aspects of fine-tuning is the careful tuning of hyperparameters. These parameters, such as learning rate, batch size, and the number of training epochs, significantly influence the model's performance and training efficiency. An excessively high learning rate may lead to unstable training, while a very low learning rate might result in slow convergence. Therefore, hyperparameter optimization, often achieved through techniques like grid search or random search, is essential to strike a balance between model accuracy and training stability.

Evaluating the performance of the fine-tuned model involves assessing its effectiveness on task-specific metrics. For classification tasks, metrics such as accuracy, precision, recall, and F1 score are commonly used. In contrast, for tasks like text generation, measures such as BLEU score, ROUGE score, or even human evaluations might be more appropriate. It's important to use a validation set, which is separate from the training data, to gauge the model's performance and ensure it generalizes well to unseen examples.

Case studies of fine-tuning illustrate the practical benefits of this approach. For instance, fine-tuning BERT on a medical corpus significantly enhances its ability to understand and categorize medical terminologies, thereby improving its performance on tasks such as clinical note classification or medical question answering. Similarly, fine-tuning GPT models on conversational data enables them to generate responses that are more contextually relevant and coherent, making them more effective for applications in customer support or virtual assistants.

Fine-tuning also plays a crucial role in transferring knowledge across different domains. For example, a language model pre-trained on general news articles can be fine-tuned on financial reports to adapt its capabilities for financial text analysis. This transfer of knowledge enables the model to leverage its general language understanding while specializing in the nuances of the new domain.

The process of fine-tuning is iterative and may require multiple rounds of training and evaluation to achieve the desired performance. Continuous monitoring and adjustment are necessary to address issues such as overfitting, where the model becomes too specialized to the training data and performs poorly on new data. Regularly updating the fine-tuned model with new data and refining its parameters help maintain its relevance and effectiveness.

Overall, fine-tuning is a powerful technique that enables pre-trained language models to be adapted for specific tasks, improving their accuracy and applicability. By carefully selecting models, preparing relevant data, tuning hyperparameters, and evaluating performance, one can leverage the strengths of pre-trained models while tailoring them to meet the specific demands of various applications.

When engaging in the fine-tuning process, one must also address several practical considerations to ensure optimal outcomes. One key aspect is the management of overfitting. Since fine-tuning involves training a pre-trained model on a smaller, domain-specific dataset, there is a risk that the model might adapt too closely to the nuances of the fine-tuning data, thus diminishing its ability to generalize to new unseen examples. To mitigate overfitting, various strategies can be employed. Techniques such as regularization, dropout, and early stopping can help prevent the model from becoming overly specialized. Regularization methods add a penalty to the loss function to constrain the model's complexity, dropout randomly deactivates a subset of neurons during training to encourage robustness, and early stopping halts training when the model's performance on a validation set ceases to improve.

Another important consideration is the evaluation of model performance during and after the fine-tuning process. Evaluating the fine-tuned model requires a well-defined metric that aligns with the task's objectives. For example, in a text classification task, accuracy, precision, recall, and F1 score are commonly used metrics. In contrast, for generative tasks like text completion or generation, metrics such as BLEU (Bilingual Evaluation Understudy) or ROUGE (Recall-Oriented Understudy for Gisting Evaluation) might be more appropriate. These metrics provide insights into how well the model performs relative to the specific requirements of the task, helping to gauge its effectiveness and identify areas for further improvement.

The process of fine-tuning is not without its challenges. One significant challenge is the need for a large amount of labeled data, which is often not readily available for many specialized tasks. In such cases, semi-supervised or unsupervised methods might be employed to augment the training data. Techniques such as data augmentation, which involves generating additional training examples by modifying existing data, or transfer learning, where a model trained on a related task is adapted for the target task, can be beneficial in addressing the data scarcity issue.

Moreover, computational resources play a critical role in the fine-tuning process. Fine-tuning, especially with large models and extensive datasets, requires substantial computational power. This often necessitates the use of high-performance hardware such as GPUs (Graphics Processing Units) or TPUs (Tensor Processing Units) to handle the computational demands efficiently. Efficient management of computational resources, including the use of distributed training and cloud-based solutions, can significantly impact the feasibility and speed of the fine-tuning process.

Practical examples and case studies can illustrate the effectiveness and application of fine-tuning. For instance, in the domain of healthcare, fine-tuning a language model on medical literature and patient records can improve its ability to understand and generate text related to medical diagnoses, treatments, and patient interactions. This specialized model can then be used to assist healthcare professionals with tasks such as automated summarization of patient records or generating relevant responses to patient inquiries.

In the financial sector, fine-tuning a language model on financial news articles, market reports, and company filings can enhance its capability to analyze and interpret financial data. This adaptation allows the model to generate insightful summaries, identify key trends, and even assist in investment decision-making by providing contextually relevant recommendations.

The continuous advancement in fine-tuning techniques reflects the growing sophistication of natural language processing. Researchers and practitioners continually explore innovative approaches to enhance the performance of fine-tuned models. For example, recent developments include the use of multi-task learning, where a model is simultaneously fine-tuned on multiple related tasks to improve its versatility and generalization capabilities, and few-shot learning, which enables a model to perform well with limited task-specific data by leveraging its pre-trained knowledge.

In conclusion, the process of fine-tuning a pre-trained language model is a complex but rewarding endeavor that involves selecting the appropriate model, preparing domain-specific data, addressing challenges related to overfitting and data scarcity, and evaluating performance effectively. By leveraging these techniques and addressing the associated challenges, fine-tuning can significantly enhance a model's accuracy and relevance, leading to more effective and specialized applications in various fields. The practical examples and ongoing advancements underscore the importance of fine-tuning in advancing natural language processing capabilities and improving the practical utility of language models across diverse domains.

When implementing fine-tuning, attention must be paid to the specifics of how the pre-trained model is adapted to the new task. The first crucial step is selecting an appropriate pre-trained model. The choice largely depends on the nature of the target task and the domain. For instance, models like BERT (Bidirectional Encoder Representations from Transformers) are highly effective for tasks that require understanding context and semantics, such as sentiment analysis or named entity recognition. Conversely, GPT (Generative Pre-trained Transformer) models are often preferred for tasks involving text generation due to their strong performance in generating coherent and contextually relevant text.

Once the pre-trained model is chosen, preparing domain-specific data involves several key processes. First, it is essential to preprocess the data to ensure it is in a format that the model can effectively learn from. This includes tokenization, where text is split into manageable pieces, such as words or subwords, and normalization, which may involve converting text to lowercase or removing special characters. Proper preprocessing ensures that the data is clean and consistent, which is crucial for effective training.

Additionally, the creation of training and validation datasets is a vital step. The training dataset is used to adjust the model's weights, while the validation dataset helps in monitoring the model's performance and preventing overfitting. It is also important to perform data augmentation if the available data is limited. Techniques such as paraphrasing, back-translation, or the synthetic generation of data using models can help in creating more training examples and improving the model's robustness.

During the fine-tuning process, monitoring and adjusting hyperparameters is essential for optimizing model performance. Hyperparameters, such as learning rate, batch size, and number of training epochs, significantly impact how well the model adapts to the new task. The learning rate, for instance, controls how quickly the model adjusts its weights; too high a learning rate might lead to unstable training, while too low a learning rate might result in slow convergence. Therefore, it is often beneficial to employ techniques such as learning rate schedules or adaptive learning rates to balance these considerations.

Furthermore, evaluating the fine-tuned model involves assessing how well it performs on unseen data, which is critical for understanding its generalization capability. Besides standard metrics, it can be useful to conduct error analysis to identify and address specific weaknesses of the model. For instance, analyzing incorrect predictions or generating confusion matrices can provide insights into systematic errors or areas where the model might need additional fine-tuning or data augmentation.

Fine-tuning is not merely a technical exercise but also requires careful consideration of ethical and practical implications. For example, when adapting a model to a specific domain, it is important to ensure that the data used is representative and free from biases. Biases present in the training data can be learned and perpetuated by the model, potentially leading to unfair or discriminatory outcomes. Hence, ethical considerations should guide the selection of training data and the evaluation of model outputs.

To illustrate the practical application of fine-tuning, consider a scenario where a pre-trained language model is adapted for legal document analysis. A general language model may perform well on general text but might struggle with the specialized terminology and style of legal language. By fine-tuning the model on a corpus of legal documents, the model can learn the specific jargon, context, and structure of legal text, thus improving its ability to perform tasks such as document classification, information extraction, or summarization within the legal domain.

Similarly, in the realm of customer service, a general conversational model may be adapted to handle specific customer queries by fine-tuning it with data from customer interactions. This adaptation can help the model understand and respond to domain-specific questions, improving the relevance and accuracy of its responses and ultimately enhancing the customer experience.

In summary, fine-tuning a pre-trained language model involves a nuanced process of selecting an appropriate base model, preparing and processing domain-specific data, adjusting hyperparameters, and evaluating performance. Addressing the challenges of overfitting, computational requirements, and ethical considerations ensures that the fine-tuned model performs optimally and is applicable to the intended use case. Through careful implementation and ongoing evaluation, fine-tuning can significantly enhance the capabilities of language models, making them more effective and relevant for specialized tasks and domains.

CHAPTER 18: HANDLING MULTILINGUAL DATA

Navigating the complexities of multilingual data involves addressing several unique challenges that arise from the inherent diversity of languages. The initial challenge is the need for effective processing and analysis of text in multiple languages, which necessitates the development of robust techniques that can accommodate the vast range of linguistic structures, vocabularies, and syntactic rules.

Machine translation, a cornerstone of multilingual data processing, plays a crucial role in bridging the language gap. The foundational approach involves translating text from one language to another to facilitate consistent analysis. Early methods in machine translation relied heavily on statistical approaches, where translation was based on probabilities derived from large corpora of bilingual text. These systems were effective in many cases but often struggled with idiomatic expressions and context-specific nuances. The advent of neural machine translation (NMT) marked a significant improvement. NMT employs deep learning models to translate text more naturally and contextually. By using sequence-to-sequence models and attention mechanisms, NMT systems can handle long-range dependencies in text and provide more accurate translations that better capture the meaning of the source text.

Another vital technique in handling multilingual data is the use of cross-lingual embeddings. Cross-lingual embeddings involve mapping words or phrases from different languages into a shared vector space. This technique allows for the comparison and integration of semantic information across languages. Models like multilingual BERT (mBERT) and XLM-R (Cross-lingual RoBERTa) are designed to generate such embeddings. These models are trained on multiple languages simultaneously, enabling them to learn language-agnostic features that can be utilized for various NLP tasks. Cross-lingual embeddings are particularly useful for tasks such as information retrieval and question answering, where understanding the relationship between concepts in different languages is essential.

To address the challenge of language diversity, multilingual models have become increasingly important. These models are trained on data from various languages and are capable of performing NLP tasks across multiple languages without requiring separate models for each language. Multilingual models leverage transfer learning, where knowledge gained from one language can be applied to another. This approach not only reduces the computational resources required but also enhances the model's ability to generalize across languages. For instance, a multilingual model trained on English, Spanish, and Chinese can perform translation and text classification tasks in all three languages with high efficiency.

Ensuring consistency in analysis across different languages is another critical aspect of handling multilingual data. One challenge here is maintaining uniformity in the representation of entities, concepts, and relationships. For instance, named entity recognition (NER) models must be adapted to recognize entities in various languages and scripts. This often involves fine-tuning the models on language-specific data and developing language-specific rules to enhance performance. Additionally, integrating outputs from different language models requires careful consideration to ensure that the results are consistent and coherent when aggregated.

Handling multilingual data also involves addressing the issue of data sparsity. In many cases, there may be limited data available for less-resourced languages. To mitigate this, techniques such as transfer learning and data augmentation are employed. Transfer learning allows models to leverage knowledge from high-resource languages to improve performance in low-resource languages. Data augmentation methods, such as generating synthetic data through back-translation, can help in creating more training examples and improving model robustness.

Moreover, evaluating the performance of multilingual models requires specific metrics and methodologies. Traditional metrics used for monolingual tasks, such as accuracy and F1 score, need to be adapted to account for the challenges of multilingual data. Evaluation might include measuring the model's ability to maintain meaning across languages, its performance on language-specific nuances, and its effectiveness in handling multilingual inputs.

In summary, handling multilingual data requires a multifaceted approach that integrates machine translation, cross-lingual embeddings, and multilingual models. The effective processing and analysis of text across languages depend on sophisticated techniques that address the linguistic diversity and ensure consistency in interpretation. By leveraging advances in neural machine translation, cross-lingual embeddings, and multilingual modeling, one can navigate the complexities of multilingual data and enhance the overall quality and reliability of NLP systems.

When working with multilingual data, it is essential to address the inherent challenges of language diversity and ensure consistency in analysis. One key aspect is managing the varying degrees of resource availability across languages.

While languages such as English, Chinese, and Spanish benefit from extensive linguistic resources and large datasets, less widely spoken languages may suffer from data sparsity. This disparity can impact the performance of models trained on these languages. To mitigate this issue, researchers employ techniques such as data augmentation and synthetic data generation. By creating additional training examples or leveraging transfer learning from high-resource languages, it is possible to enhance the performance of models for low-resource languages.

Handling linguistic diversity also involves dealing with structural differences among languages. For instance, languages differ in terms of syntax, morphology, and semantics, which can complicate text processing tasks. For example, word order varies significantly between languages like English and Japanese. English typically follows a Subject-Verb-Object (SVO) order, while Japanese uses a Subject-Object-Verb (SOV) structure. This variation necessitates adaptive models that can understand and generate text according to the specific syntactic rules of each language. Techniques such as dependency parsing and part-of-speech tagging must be tailored to accommodate these differences.

Another significant challenge is ensuring consistency in text analysis across different languages. This involves aligning concepts and entities across languages to maintain coherent and comparable results. For instance, in sentiment analysis, sentiment expressions may differ across languages due to cultural and contextual variations. A phrase that conveys positive sentiment in one language may not have the same connotation in another. To address this, models must be trained to recognize and adapt to these nuances. Cross-lingual transfer learning can be employed to train models on multiple languages, allowing them to capture a broad spectrum of sentiment expressions and ensure consistent analysis.

Moreover, evaluating multilingual models requires careful consideration. Traditional evaluation metrics, such as accuracy and F1 score, may not fully capture the performance of models across different languages. Metrics need to be adapted to account for the specific linguistic characteristics and challenges of each language. For instance, BLEU (Bilingual Evaluation Understudy) score, commonly used for machine translation evaluation, may not be equally applicable to all languages due to differences in grammar and syntax. Instead, custom evaluation methods that take into account language-specific factors and align with the goals of the task should be employed.

Practical applications of multilingual data processing highlight the importance of these techniques. In customer support systems, multilingual capabilities enable businesses to serve a diverse clientele by providing support in multiple languages. Chatbots and virtual assistants that leverage multilingual models can understand and respond to user queries across various languages, enhancing user experience and accessibility. Similarly, in global content management, multilingual models can facilitate the translation and localization of content, ensuring that messages are consistent and contextually appropriate across different languages.

Furthermore, advancements in multilingual data handling have opened new opportunities for research and development. The integration of cross-lingual embeddings and multilingual models has led to significant improvements in tasks such as cross-lingual information retrieval and document classification. Researchers are exploring innovative approaches to further enhance these capabilities, such as incorporating domain-specific knowledge and leveraging recent developments in transformer architectures.

In summary, dealing with multilingual data requires a multifaceted approach that addresses the challenges of language diversity and ensures consistency in analysis. By employing techniques such as machine translation, cross-lingual embeddings, and multilingual models, and by adapting evaluation methods to account for language-specific characteristics, it is possible to create robust systems capable of handling the complexities of multilingual text. The continued advancement in this field promises to further improve our ability to process and analyze text across languages, ultimately leading to more effective and inclusive NLP solutions.

In addition to addressing the challenges of language diversity and ensuring consistent analysis, another critical aspect of handling multilingual data involves leveraging cross-lingual embeddings and multilingual models. These techniques have revolutionized the approach to processing and analyzing text across multiple languages by providing a unified representation space.

Cross-lingual embeddings aim to map text from different languages into a common vector space, allowing for direct comparison and analysis across languages. This is achieved through methods that align embeddings from different languages based on shared semantic or syntactic features. For instance, models like multilingual BERT (Bidirectional Encoder Representations from Transformers) and XLM-R (Cross-lingual Language Model - RoBERTa) provide embeddings that capture semantic similarities across languages by training on a diverse corpus of multilingual text. These embeddings facilitate tasks such as information retrieval, where a query in one language can retrieve relevant documents in another language. By representing words and phrases from different languages in a common vector space, cross-lingual embeddings enhance the ability to perform cross-lingual transfer learning and achieve better performance on multilingual tasks.

Multilingual models extend this concept by training a single model on multiple languages, thereby enabling it to handle text in various languages simultaneously. These models are typically pre-trained on large, multilingual datasets and fine-tuned for specific tasks. The advantage of multilingual models lies in their ability to transfer knowledge across languages, leveraging shared patterns and features. For example, a model trained on both English and French data can transfer learned features from one language to another, improving performance in scenarios where data in one language is scarce. This transferability is particularly valuable for low-resource languages, where direct training data might be limited.

The use of multilingual models also involves addressing issues related to model size and efficiency. Training a model on multiple languages can result in a substantial increase in the number of parameters, which can be computationally expensive and require significant memory. Techniques such as parameter sharing and model distillation are employed to manage these challenges. Parameter sharing involves using the same set of parameters for different languages, reducing the overall model size while maintaining performance. Model distillation, on the other hand, involves training a smaller model (student) to replicate the behavior of a larger, more complex model (teacher), thereby achieving a balance between performance and efficiency.

Another consideration in handling multilingual data is the incorporation of language-specific nuances and cultural contexts. Languages are not merely collections of words but are deeply intertwined with cultural and contextual meanings. This complexity is often reflected in idiomatic expressions, metaphors, and colloquialisms that vary across languages. To address these nuances, models must be trained with an understanding of the cultural contexts in which the language is used. This can involve incorporating cultural knowledge into the training data or using transfer learning to adapt models to specific cultural contexts.

Finally, evaluation of multilingual models requires a nuanced approach. Traditional evaluation metrics, such as precision and recall, may not always capture the performance of models across different languages due to variations in linguistic structures and semantics. Instead, evaluation should be tailored to reflect the specific characteristics of each language and task. This can involve using language-specific benchmarks and incorporating feedback from native speakers to ensure that the models perform effectively and appropriately in diverse linguistic contexts.

In conclusion, handling multilingual data in NLP involves a multifaceted approach that addresses language diversity, ensures consistency in analysis, and leverages advanced techniques such as cross-lingual embeddings and multilingual models. By understanding and applying these techniques, we can improve the accuracy and relevance of text analysis across different languages, enabling more effective and meaningful interactions in a globalized world.

CHAPTER 19: EVALUATING NLP MODELS

Evaluating the performance of NLP models is fundamental for understanding their effectiveness, guiding improvements, and ensuring that they meet the desired standards for accuracy and reliability. This evaluation process involves a variety of metrics and methods, each serving a specific purpose in assessing different aspects of model performance. Understanding these evaluation techniques is essential for developing robust NLP systems capable of handling real-world tasks effectively.

At the core of model evaluation are metrics such as accuracy, precision, recall, and F1 score, each providing insights into different dimensions of performance. Accuracy measures the proportion of correctly predicted instances out of the total number of instances. While accuracy is a straightforward metric, it can be misleading in cases of imbalanced datasets, where certain classes may dominate the results. In such scenarios, relying solely on accuracy can obscure the performance of the model on less frequent classes.

Precision and recall offer a more nuanced view of performance, particularly in contexts where the distribution of classes is uneven. Precision, defined as the ratio of true positives to the sum of true positives and false positives, gauges the accuracy of positive predictions. It is especially important in applications where false positives carry significant consequences, such as in medical diagnoses or spam detection. Recall, on the other hand, represents the ratio of true positives to the sum of true positives and false negatives, reflecting the model's ability to identify all relevant instances. High recall is crucial in scenarios where missing a positive instance can lead to critical errors, such as in search engines or information retrieval systems.

The F1 score, which is the harmonic mean of precision and recall, provides a balanced measure of a model's performance by combining these two metrics into a single value. The F1 score is particularly useful when dealing with imbalanced datasets, as it accounts for both false positives and false negatives, offering a comprehensive view of the model's ability to make accurate predictions across different classes.

Beyond these metrics, human evaluation plays a critical role in assessing the quality of NLP models, especially in tasks where subjective judgment and context understanding are essential. Human evaluation involves having experts or annotators assess the output of the model based on criteria such as relevance, coherence, and fluency. This approach is particularly valuable in areas like machine translation, text summarization, and dialogue systems, where automated metrics alone may not fully capture the nuances of language quality and appropriateness.

In practice, human evaluation often involves multiple annotators to ensure reliability and mitigate biases. Annotations are typically aggregated to provide a consensus rating or score, which can then be used to gauge the model's performance. Techniques such as inter-annotator agreement, measured using metrics like Cohen's kappa, help ensure the consistency and reliability of human judgments. This process is crucial for validating the results obtained from automated evaluations and for providing a more holistic assessment of model quality.

Moreover, evaluating NLP models involves a consideration of the evaluation dataset itself. The quality and representativeness of the evaluation data are critical factors that can significantly impact the results. Evaluation datasets should ideally be diverse, covering various scenarios and language variations to provide a comprehensive assessment of the model's performance. Additionally, the evaluation process should account for potential biases in the data, as biased datasets can lead to skewed results and misinterpretations of model capabilities.

Cross-validation is another technique commonly used in model evaluation to ensure robustness and generalizability. By partitioning the dataset into multiple folds and evaluating the model on different subsets, cross-validation helps mitigate issues related to overfitting and provides a more reliable estimate of the model's performance on unseen data. This technique is particularly useful for assessing model stability and performance across different data splits.

In summary, evaluating NLP models involves a multifaceted approach that includes quantitative metrics such as accuracy, precision, recall, and F1 score, as well as qualitative assessments through human evaluation. Each of these methods provides valuable insights into different aspects of model performance, contributing to a comprehensive understanding of how well the model meets its objectives. Rigorous evaluation is essential for developing reliable and accurate NLP systems that can effectively address real-world challenges and deliver meaningful results.

When evaluating NLP models, it is crucial to consider not only individual metrics but also the context and limitations of each evaluation method. Automated metrics, such as accuracy, precision, recall, and F1 score, provide quantifiable measures of performance but may not capture all the nuances of model behavior. Therefore, a comprehensive evaluation strategy often involves a combination of these metrics along with qualitative human assessments.

For instance, while automated metrics are essential for comparing model performance on standard benchmarks, human evaluation offers insights into aspects that metrics alone might miss. Human evaluators can assess the relevance, coherence, and naturalness of generated text, which are critical for applications like dialogue systems, where the quality of interaction is paramount. Evaluators typically use predefined criteria to rate outputs, such as fluency, informativeness, and grammatical correctness. This approach can help identify areas where the model may excel or struggle, providing valuable feedback for refinement.

Moreover, the evaluation process should be designed to address specific challenges associated with the application of the model. For example, in sentiment analysis, a model might achieve high accuracy but fail to capture the subtleties of sentiment expressed in complex or ambiguous sentences. Here, metrics such as sentiment-specific precision and recall, or even more sophisticated measures like sentiment-sensitivity indices, can offer a clearer picture of the model's effectiveness.

Another important consideration in evaluation is the dataset used. The quality and diversity of the evaluation dataset significantly impact the reliability of the results. A well-constructed evaluation dataset should be representative of the types of text the model will encounter in real-world applications. It should include various domains, languages, and styles to ensure that the model's performance is not biased toward a particular type of input. Additionally, datasets should be curated to reflect the complexity and variability of the tasks the model is designed to handle.

In practice, evaluation metrics should be selected based on the specific goals of the model. For example, in a named entity recognition (NER) task, precision and recall are often used to assess how well the model identifies and classifies entities. The F1 score, which balances precision and recall, provides a more holistic view of the model's performance. On the other hand, for tasks like machine translation, BLEU (Bilingual Evaluation Understudy) scores might be employed to evaluate how closely the generated translations match human references.

Moreover, cross-validation is a valuable technique in model evaluation, where the dataset is divided into multiple subsets to train and test the model across different folds. This approach helps ensure that the model's performance is robust and not overly dependent on any single subset of the data. Cross-validation also helps in understanding the generalization capabilities of the model, offering insights into how well it performs on unseen data.

It is also important to consider the computational efficiency of the evaluation process. Automated metrics offer the advantage of being scalable and reproducible, which is particularly useful when evaluating large models or datasets. However, human evaluation, while providing rich qualitative feedback, can be resource-intensive and time-consuming. Balancing these approaches often involves using automated metrics for initial screening and human evaluation for deeper analysis.

In addition to traditional evaluation methods, emerging approaches are being developed to better capture the nuances of language and context. Techniques such as adversarial evaluation, where models are tested against carefully crafted challenging examples, can reveal weaknesses that standard evaluation metrics might overlook. Furthermore, incorporating user feedback from real-world interactions can provide continuous insights into the model's performance and areas for improvement.

Ultimately, the goal of evaluation is to ensure that NLP models are reliable, effective, and aligned with the needs of their intended applications. Rigorous and comprehensive evaluation practices not only help in benchmarking model performance but also guide the iterative process of model improvement, leading to more accurate and contextually aware NLP systems. By integrating both quantitative metrics and qualitative assessments, practitioners can develop models that are not only technically proficient but also practical and user-friendly.

The effectiveness of evaluation methods can also be significantly influenced by the size and representativeness of the evaluation datasets. In smaller datasets, there is a higher risk of overfitting, where a model might perform exceptionally well on the specific data it was evaluated on but fail to generalize to new, unseen data. This issue can be mitigated by employing larger and more diverse datasets that better capture the range of possible inputs the model might encounter in real-world scenarios. Additionally, employing cross-validation techniques, where the model is trained and evaluated on different subsets of the data, can provide a more robust measure of performance and help identify potential overfitting.

Another important aspect to consider is the trade-off between model complexity and interpretability. Highly complex models, such as deep neural networks, often achieve superior performance on many metrics but can be difficult to interpret. In contrast, simpler models may offer greater transparency but at the cost of reduced accuracy. When evaluating models, it is essential to balance these factors based on the specific requirements of the application. For instance, in applications where interpretability is crucial, such as in medical diagnosis or legal text analysis, simpler, more interpretable models might be preferred despite their lower accuracy.

Moreover, the selection of appropriate evaluation metrics should also be informed by the specific characteristics of the task. In tasks such as text summarization or question answering, where the quality of the output can be subjective, automated metrics may not fully capture the nuances of performance. In these cases, combining automated metrics with human evaluation becomes even more critical. Human evaluators can provide qualitative insights into aspects like coherence, relevance, and contextual accuracy, which are difficult to quantify with automated metrics alone.

Another consideration in the evaluation process is the potential for bias in the evaluation metrics themselves. Metrics like accuracy, precision, recall, and F1 score may not always account for all types of errors or biases present in the model. For example, a model might perform well on average but exhibit systematic biases towards certain types of inputs or groups. It is essential to evaluate the model across various demographic groups and input types to ensure fairness and avoid unintended discrimination. Tools and methods for fairness evaluation, such as disparity analysis or fairness-aware metrics, can help in identifying and mitigating these biases.

Evaluating NLP models also involves understanding the impact of different training regimes and hyperparameters. The choice of training data, the size of the training set, and the specifics of model tuning can all affect performance. Therefore, evaluating how changes in these parameters impact the model's effectiveness can provide insights into optimizing training processes and improving model performance.

Finally, as NLP models are deployed in real-world applications, continuous monitoring and evaluation become necessary. Models should be periodically assessed to ensure they remain effective as they encounter new data and use cases. This ongoing evaluation can help identify any degradation in performance and facilitate adjustments to maintain the quality of the system. Establishing a robust feedback loop, where user interactions and real-world performance are continuously monitored, can provide valuable data for refining and improving models over time.

By integrating these various evaluation techniques and considerations, one can develop a more comprehensive understanding of an NLP model's performance. The goal is not only to measure how well a model performs on specific tasks but also to ensure that it meets the broader requirements of accuracy, fairness, interpretability, and relevance. This multifaceted approach to evaluation is crucial for developing NLP systems that are reliable, effective, and aligned with the needs of their users.

CHAPTER 20: ETHICAL CONSIDERATIONS IN NLP

In the realm of Natural Language Processing (NLP), ethical considerations play a pivotal role in guiding the development, deployment, and usage of technologies that increasingly permeate various aspects of daily life. As NLP systems become more sophisticated and integrated into critical applications, the ethical implications associated with their use and impact have gained prominence. This discussion explores the primary ethical concerns in NLP, including privacy, bias, and fairness, and provides frameworks for addressing these issues responsibly.

One of the foremost ethical concerns in NLP is privacy. NLP systems often require access to vast amounts of data to function effectively, including personal and sensitive information. This data can come from diverse sources such as social media, emails, or customer interactions. The collection, storage, and processing of such data raise significant privacy issues. For instance, users may not always be aware of how their data is being used or how long it is retained. Furthermore, the potential for data breaches or unauthorized access increases the risk of exposing personal information. To address these concerns, it is essential to implement robust data protection measures, including anonymization and encryption. Moreover, adhering to privacy regulations, such as the General Data Protection

Regulation (GDPR) in Europe, can help ensure that data handling practices meet established standards for privacy and security.

Bias is another critical issue in NLP. NLP systems are trained on large datasets that often reflect societal biases present in the source material. This can lead to the propagation of stereotypes or discriminatory practices. For example, language models trained on internet data might learn and replicate harmful biases related to gender, race, or ethnicity. Such biases can manifest in various ways, such as biased sentiment analysis or unfair treatment in automated decision-making systems. Addressing bias requires a multi-faceted approach, including diversifying training data to better represent various groups and contexts, implementing bias detection and mitigation techniques, and continually auditing and refining models to minimize adverse effects.

Fairness in NLP involves ensuring that systems treat all individuals and groups equitably, without perpetuating discrimination or exclusion. Achieving fairness is complex because it requires balancing competing interests and defining what constitutes fair treatment in diverse contexts. For instance, a model designed to make decisions based on historical data might inadvertently reinforce existing inequalities if the data reflects past biases. To promote fairness, it is crucial to engage in thorough impact assessments, involve stakeholders from diverse backgrounds in the design and evaluation process, and apply fairness-aware algorithms that can adjust for disparities in model performance across different groups.

The ethical implications of NLP extend beyond technical concerns to broader societal impacts. For instance, the use of NLP in surveillance technologies can raise questions about consent and autonomy. While NLP tools can enhance security and public safety, their deployment must be carefully considered to avoid infringing on individual freedoms and privacy rights. Similarly, in areas such as healthcare or legal systems, where NLP technologies can significantly influence decisions, it is vital to ensure transparency and accountability in how these technologies are used and how their recommendations are derived.

Moreover, the ethical considerations in NLP also involve addressing the potential for misuse. For example, language generation models can be exploited to create misleading or harmful content, such as deepfakes or automated misinformation campaigns. Preventing misuse requires not only technical solutions but also ethical guidelines and regulations to govern the responsible use of NLP technologies. Developers and organizations should establish clear policies and procedures for monitoring and controlling the deployment of NLP systems to mitigate risks and ensure that technologies are used ethically and responsibly.

Lastly, promoting ethical practices in NLP involves fostering a culture of responsibility and awareness within the field. This includes educating researchers, practitioners, and users about the ethical implications of their work and encouraging a commitment to ethical standards. Collaboration among stakeholders, including academic institutions, industry leaders, policymakers, and civil society, can help develop and enforce ethical guidelines and best practices. By engaging in ongoing dialogue and reflection, the NLP community can navigate the complex ethical landscape and work towards developing technologies that benefit society while respecting fundamental rights and values.

In summary, ethical considerations in NLP encompass a range of issues including privacy, bias, fairness, and the potential for misuse. Addressing these concerns requires a comprehensive approach involving robust data protection measures, bias mitigation strategies, fairness assessments, and responsible deployment practices. By integrating ethical considerations into every stage of NLP development and application, we can ensure that these technologies are used in ways that are both effective and aligned with societal values and norms.

In addressing fairness, it is essential to adopt strategies that can systematically evaluate and mitigate biases within NLP systems. Techniques such as adversarial training, where models are exposed to deliberately challenging or biased examples during training, can help in identifying and reducing undesirable biases. Additionally, fairness metrics can be employed to assess how different groups are treated by the model and to ensure that disparities are minimized. These metrics might include statistical parity, equal opportunity, and disparate impact assessments, among others. Regular audits and updates are also vital, as they allow for ongoing adjustments to address emerging issues or shifts in societal norms.

Another significant ethical concern is the potential misuse of NLP technologies. As NLP systems become more advanced, they can be employed in ways that may infringe on personal freedoms or promote harmful agendas. For instance, language models can be used to generate persuasive disinformation, deepfakes, or abusive content. The potential for such misuse highlights the necessity of implementing safeguards that limit the use of these technologies to ethical applications. This could involve creating guidelines and policies for responsible usage, as well as establishing oversight mechanisms to monitor and control how NLP systems are deployed. Engaging with stakeholders, including ethicists, legal experts, and the affected communities, can help ensure that these systems are used in ways that align with broader societal values and norms.

The transparency of NLP models is another critical aspect of ethical practice. Transparency involves making the functioning and decision-making processes of models understandable and accessible to users and stakeholders. This can include providing clear explanations of how models operate, the data they are trained on, and the rationale behind their predictions. Transparency fosters trust and accountability, allowing users to comprehend and challenge decisions made by NLP systems. Techniques such as explainable AI (XAI) can be employed to enhance model interpretability, providing insights into model behavior and helping users understand the basis for specific outputs or recommendations.

The environmental impact of training large-scale NLP models is also an important ethical consideration. Training sophisticated models often requires significant computational resources, leading to considerable energy consumption and carbon emissions. Addressing this issue involves adopting practices that minimize the environmental footprint of NLP research and development. Strategies such as optimizing model architectures to reduce resource requirements, employing energy-efficient hardware, and using renewable energy sources can help mitigate the environmental impact. Furthermore, promoting research into more efficient algorithms and encouraging practices that balance technological advancements with environmental stewardship are crucial steps toward ethical sustainability in NLP.

Furthermore, the ethical implications of NLP extend to its role in reinforcing or challenging societal power dynamics. NLP technologies can influence public opinion, shape narratives, and impact political discourse. As such, it is important to consider how these systems might affect power structures and societal inequalities. For example, NLP systems used in automated content moderation or recommendation algorithms can have significant implications for free speech and information access. Ensuring that these systems are designed to uphold democratic values and human rights is essential. This involves engaging in critical reflection on the societal impact of NLP technologies and striving to develop systems that promote inclusivity and equitable access to information.

Lastly, it is vital to involve diverse perspectives in the development and deployment of NLP technologies. Diverse teams are better equipped to identify and address potential ethical issues, as they bring a range of experiences, viewpoints, and expertise. Engaging with stakeholders from different backgrounds, including ethicists, sociologists, and representatives from affected communities, can provide valuable insights into the ethical dimensions of NLP systems. Collaborative efforts can help ensure that ethical considerations are integrated into every stage of the technology lifecycle, from design and development to deployment and evaluation.

In conclusion, addressing ethical considerations in NLP requires a multifaceted approach that encompasses privacy, bias, fairness, transparency, environmental impact, societal influence, and diversity. By implementing robust practices and engaging in continuous dialogue, stakeholders can work toward developing NLP technologies that are not only effective but also aligned with ethical principles and societal values.

Ensuring that NLP technologies do not infringe on privacy is another crucial ethical concern. Privacy issues can arise in various ways, such as through the inadvertent inclusion of sensitive information in training data or through the potential for misuse of personal data. To mitigate privacy risks, data anonymization and de-identification techniques should be employed to prevent the disclosure of personal information. Additionally, it is important to ensure that data collection practices comply with privacy regulations and standards, such as the General Data Protection Regulation (GDPR) or the California Consumer Privacy Act (CCPA). This involves obtaining informed consent from data subjects and implementing robust data security measures to protect against unauthorized access.

Ethical practices in NLP also require ongoing engagement with diverse stakeholders to ensure that the technology aligns with societal values and norms. This includes involving community representatives, policymakers, and ethicists in the development and deployment processes. Such engagement helps to identify and address potential ethical issues early in the design phase and ensures that the technology serves the broader public good. Establishing multidisciplinary teams that include not only technical experts but also individuals with expertise in ethics, social sciences, and law can provide a more comprehensive perspective on the ethical implications of NLP technologies.

Moreover, education and training in ethical practices should be integral to the development process for NLP professionals. This includes raising awareness about potential ethical challenges and providing guidance on how to address them. Training programs and resources can help practitioners understand the ethical implications of their work and make informed decisions that prioritize ethical considerations. Encouraging a culture of ethical reflection within the NLP community is crucial for fostering responsible innovation and maintaining public trust in the technology.

Finally, the development of ethical guidelines and best practices for NLP research and application is essential for ensuring that these technologies are used responsibly. Organizations and research institutions can contribute to this effort by establishing clear ethical standards and providing resources for ethical decision-making. Publicly available guidelines and frameworks can serve as valuable references for practitioners and can help promote consistency and accountability in the field.

In summary, addressing ethical considerations in NLP involves a multifaceted approach that encompasses bias mitigation, responsible usage, transparency, environmental impact, privacy protection, stakeholder engagement, and education. By integrating these principles into the development and deployment of NLP technologies, we can work towards creating systems that are not only technically advanced but also aligned with ethical standards and societal values. This comprehensive approach helps ensure that NLP technologies contribute positively to society while minimizing potential risks and harms.

CHAPTER 21: NLP IN INDUSTRY: CASE STUDIES

The integration of Natural Language Processing (NLP) into various industries has led to transformative changes, enhancing efficiency, improving decision-making, and creating new opportunities for innovation. This section delves into real-world applications of NLP across different sectors, showcasing how these technologies are used to address practical challenges and drive industry advancements. By examining specific case studies, we can gain a deeper understanding of the implementation, benefits, and impact of NLP solutions.

In the healthcare industry, NLP has become instrumental in managing and analyzing vast amounts of medical data. One notable example is the use of NLP in electronic health records (EHRs). Hospitals and healthcare providers face the challenge of extracting meaningful insights from unstructured clinical notes, which are often filled with medical jargon and varied terminology. NLP technologies, such as named entity recognition and text classification, have been employed to automate the extraction of patient information, such as diagnoses, medications, and treatment plans. For instance, a large-scale implementation at the Mayo Clinic utilized NLP to parse EHRs and identify patients at risk for certain conditions, enabling timely interventions and personalized care. This case study highlights how NLP can streamline data management, enhance patient outcomes, and support healthcare professionals in delivering high-quality care.

In the finance sector, NLP has significantly improved the analysis of financial documents and market sentiment. One prominent application is in the realm of financial news analysis. Financial institutions and investment firms leverage NLP to process and interpret vast quantities of news articles, earnings reports, and social media posts. For example, a leading hedge fund uses sentiment analysis to gauge market sentiment from financial news and social media platforms. By analyzing the tone and content of news articles, the firm can predict stock price movements and make informed investment decisions. This case study demonstrates how NLP can provide a competitive edge in financial markets by extracting actionable insights from unstructured text data, ultimately leading to more strategic investment decisions and risk management.

E-commerce is another sector where NLP has made a substantial impact, particularly in enhancing customer experiences and optimizing business operations. A prominent example is the use of NLP in chatbots and virtual assistants. Major e-commerce platforms have implemented NLP-driven chatbots to handle customer inquiries, process orders, and provide personalized recommendations. For instance, Amazon's customer service chatbot uses NLP to understand and respond to customer queries in natural language, facilitating seamless interactions and reducing the need for human intervention. Additionally, NLP techniques such as recommendation systems analyze customer reviews and browsing behavior to suggest products tailored to individual preferences. This case study illustrates how NLP can enhance user engagement, improve customer satisfaction, and drive sales growth in the e-commerce domain.

The impact of NLP is also evident in the legal industry, where it is used to streamline document review and legal research. Law firms and legal departments face the challenge of managing and analyzing large volumes of legal documents, including contracts, case law, and regulatory filings. NLP technologies, such as document classification and information retrieval, have been employed to automate these processes. For example, a leading law firm implemented an NLP-based system to assist with contract analysis and due diligence. The system uses text mining and entity recognition to identify key clauses, obligations, and potential risks in legal contracts, significantly reducing the time and effort required for manual review. This case study highlights how NLP can enhance legal research, improve accuracy, and increase efficiency in handling complex legal documents.

Another sector where NLP has made notable contributions is in the field of customer feedback and sentiment analysis. Companies across various industries use NLP to analyze customer feedback from surveys, reviews, and social media platforms. By applying sentiment analysis, businesses can gain insights into customer opinions, identify emerging trends, and address potential issues. For instance, a global consumer goods company leverages NLP to analyze customer reviews of its products. The analysis helps the company understand customer sentiments, identify common complaints, and make data-driven improvements to its products and services. This case study underscores how NLP can provide valuable feedback, inform product development, and enhance overall customer experience.

These case studies demonstrate the diverse applications of NLP across industries and highlight the transformative potential of these technologies. From healthcare to finance, e-commerce, and legal services, NLP is driving innovation, improving efficiency, and delivering tangible benefits. As NLP technologies continue to evolve, their applications are likely to expand further, offering new opportunities for solving complex problems and advancing various sectors.

Building on the initial examination of NLP applications in healthcare, finance, and e-commerce, we now delve into additional industry case studies that further illustrate the versatility and transformative potential of NLP technologies.

In the legal field, NLP is revolutionizing how legal professionals handle and process large volumes of documents. Legal research and discovery, which traditionally involved sifting through vast amounts of legal texts, case law, and contracts, has been significantly enhanced by NLP. For instance, a leading legal tech company has developed an NLP-based tool that automates contract analysis. This tool uses machine learning algorithms to extract key clauses, identify discrepancies, and highlight important legal terms across numerous documents. By reducing the time required for manual review and minimizing human error, this technology enables legal teams to focus on higher-value tasks such as strategy and negotiation. The case of this NLP application underscores its impact on efficiency and accuracy in the legal domain, making complex document review processes more manageable and less labor-intensive.

The NLP applications in customer service, beyond chatbots, also include sophisticated sentiment analysis tools. Consider a global telecommunications company that integrated sentiment analysis into its customer feedback systems. By analyzing customer reviews, support tickets, and social media mentions, the company can detect emerging issues, gauge customer satisfaction, and identify trends. This real-time analysis allows the company to address customer concerns proactively and improve service quality. For example, if sentiment analysis reveals a rising number of complaints about a specific service feature, the company can quickly investigate and make necessary adjustments, thereby enhancing customer experience and loyalty. This use of NLP illustrates how analyzing customer sentiment can drive strategic improvements and foster a more responsive and customer-centric approach.

Turning to the travel and hospitality industry, NLP technologies are also making significant strides. A prominent travel agency has implemented NLP-driven tools to enhance the booking experience and customer support. By utilizing NLP, the agency can offer more intuitive search capabilities, allowing users to input natural language queries such as "find me a beachfront hotel in Hawaii for next summer." The NLP system processes these queries, interprets user intent, and retrieves relevant results, thereby simplifying the booking process. Additionally, the same technology is used in customer support to handle booking inquiries, resolve issues, and provide travel recommendations. This application of NLP not only streamlines the user experience but also helps the agency to better understand and anticipate customer needs, leading to increased satisfaction and repeat business.

In the realm of content creation, NLP tools are being employed to automate and optimize content generation. A notable example is the use of NLP for generating product descriptions in e-commerce platforms. An e-commerce giant has adopted an NLP-driven system to automatically create compelling and SEO-friendly product descriptions based on a set of input parameters and product attributes. This system leverages language generation models to produce text that is not only informative but also engaging and persuasive, without requiring extensive manual effort. By automating this process, the company can rapidly update product listings and maintain a consistent quality of content across its platform. This case highlights how NLP can enhance content scalability and maintain high standards of written communication in commercial settings.

Further extending the application of NLP, the education sector has seen significant benefits from these technologies. In particular, NLP is being used to develop intelligent tutoring systems that offer personalized learning experiences. For instance, a leading educational technology company has created an NLP-based platform that provides students with tailored feedback on their writing assignments. The system analyzes student essays for grammar, style, and coherence, offering specific suggestions for improvement. This application of NLP not only helps students enhance their writing skills but also supports educators by reducing the time spent on grading and providing more detailed feedback. By incorporating NLP into the educational process, the platform fosters a more interactive and individualized learning environment.

These case studies illustrate the diverse ways in which NLP technologies are being leveraged across various industries. Each example underscores the transformative potential of NLP in solving practical problems, enhancing operational efficiency, and driving innovation. As NLP technologies continue to evolve, their applications are likely to expand further, offering new opportunities and solutions across a wide range of domains. Through careful implementation and ongoing refinement, businesses and organizations can harness the power of NLP to achieve significant advancements and deliver more impactful and effective outcomes in their respective fields.

In the media and entertainment sector, NLP technologies have become indispensable tools for content creation and management. For instance, a leading media organization uses NLP to automate the transcription and subtitling of video content. This application not only speeds up the content creation process but also enhances accessibility by providing subtitles in multiple languages. The NLP system employed by the organization can recognize speech with high accuracy and convert it into text, which is then translated and formatted into subtitles. This process significantly reduces the need for manual transcription and translation work, allowing media professionals to focus on content quality and creative aspects. Moreover, the ability to generate subtitles quickly and in multiple languages expands the reach of content to a global audience, increasing its impact and viewership.

In the realm of scientific research, NLP has shown remarkable potential in managing and analyzing research literature. Consider a case where a research institution implemented an NLP-powered tool to sift through thousands of research papers and extract relevant information. The tool utilizes named entity recognition and topic modeling to identify key concepts, research trends, and potential collaborators. By automatically summarizing research findings and categorizing them based on relevance and subject matter, the NLP system aids researchers in staying up-to-date with the latest developments in their field. This application not only accelerates the literature review process but also enhances the efficiency of knowledge discovery, enabling researchers to make informed decisions and drive scientific progress.

In the realm of personalized marketing, NLP technologies have been leveraged to enhance customer engagement through tailored content recommendations. A prominent e-commerce platform employs NLP algorithms to analyze user behavior, preferences, and past interactions to deliver personalized product recommendations. The system processes natural language queries and user reviews to understand individual preferences and suggest relevant products. For example, if a user frequently searches for eco-friendly products, the NLP system can prioritize and highlight similar items in their recommendations. This targeted approach not only improves the relevance of the content presented to users but also boosts sales and customer satisfaction by providing a more customized shopping experience.

Another notable application of NLP is in financial services, particularly in fraud detection and compliance monitoring. Financial institutions utilize NLP to analyze transactional data and identify suspicious patterns that may indicate fraudulent activities. By applying NLP techniques to parse and interpret vast amounts of unstructured data, such as transaction descriptions and customer communications, these systems can flag anomalies and generate alerts for further investigation. For example, if a transaction description contains unusual patterns or keywords indicative of fraudulent behavior, the NLP system can raise a red flag for review. This proactive approach enhances the ability to detect and prevent fraudulent activities, safeguarding both the institution and its customers.

In the educational sector, NLP is transforming the way learning materials are created and accessed. A notable example is the development of intelligent tutoring systems that utilize NLP to provide personalized feedback and support to students. These systems analyze students' written responses and assess their understanding of the material based on predefined criteria. For instance, an intelligent tutoring system might evaluate a student's essay for coherence, grammar, and adherence to the topic, offering constructive feedback and suggestions for improvement. By providing personalized guidance and immediate feedback, these NLP-driven systems support student learning and development more effectively than traditional methods.

In summary, the diverse applications of NLP across various industries highlight its transformative potential and versatility. From automating legal document review to enhancing customer service, personalizing marketing strategies, and advancing scientific research, NLP technologies are driving innovation and improving efficiency in numerous domains. Each case study presented illustrates the practical benefits of NLP, showcasing how these technologies are leveraged to address specific challenges and deliver tangible results. As NLP continues to evolve, its impact on industry practices and problem-solving will undoubtedly grow, offering new opportunities for advancement and transformation.

CHAPTER 22: ADVANCED NEURAL NETWORK ARCHITECTURES

In recent years, the field of natural language processing (NLP) has witnessed transformative advancements driven by the development of advanced neural network architectures. This section will explore some of the most influential models, including Transformers, BERT, and GPT. Each of these architectures represents a significant leap forward in the way machines understand and generate human language. By examining these models, I aim to elucidate the innovations they introduced and their profound impact on language modeling.

The Transformer architecture, introduced in the seminal paper "Attention is All You Need" by Vaswani et al., marks a pivotal shift in NLP. Prior to Transformers, neural network-based models largely relied on recurrent neural networks (RNNs) and their variants, such as long short-term memory networks (LSTMs). While these models were effective in capturing sequential dependencies, they struggled with long-range dependencies due to their inherently sequential processing nature. Transformers addressed this limitation through the introduction of self-attention mechanisms.

Self-attention allows the model to weigh the importance of

different words in a sentence relative to each other. Instead of processing words sequentially, Transformers process all words in parallel, enabling the model to capture complex relationships between words irrespective of their position in the sequence. This capability is crucial for understanding context and nuances in language. For example, in the sentence "The cat sat on the mat because it was tired," self-attention enables the model to link "it" with "cat" rather than "mat," thus improving the understanding of the sentence's meaning.

The Transformer's architecture consists of an encoder and a decoder. The encoder processes the input sequence and generates a set of attention-based representations. The decoder then generates the output sequence based on these representations. This design allows for efficient parallel processing and has led to significant improvements in translation tasks, among others. The introduction of the Transformer model laid the groundwork for subsequent innovations in NLP by demonstrating that attention mechanisms could effectively capture and utilize contextual information.

Building upon the Transformer framework, BERT (Bidirectional Encoder Representations from Transformers) introduced a new paradigm for pre-training language models. Developed by Devlin et al., BERT is unique in its bidirectional approach to language modeling. Unlike previous models that processed text in a unidirectional manner (either left-to-right or right-to-left), BERT considers the entire context of a word by looking at both directions. This bidirectional approach enhances the model's ability to understand the nuances and context of language more effectively.

BERT's training involves two primary tasks: masked language modeling (MLM) and next sentence prediction (NSP). In MLM, random words in a sentence are masked, and the model is trained to predict these masked words based on their context.

This task helps the model learn to capture the meaning of words in their given context. NSP, on the other hand, involves predicting whether a given sentence follows another, which helps in understanding sentence relationships and coherence. By combining these training tasks, BERT achieves a deep understanding of language, leading to improved performance on a variety of NLP tasks, such as question answering and sentiment analysis.

Following BERT, the GPT (Generative Pre-trained Transformer) series, developed by OpenAI, represents another significant advancement in language modeling. GPT models are autoregressive transformers designed for generating coherent and contextually relevant text. Unlike BERT, which is bidirectional and primarily focused on understanding text, GPT is unidirectional and optimized for generating text. GPT models are pre-trained on a large corpus of text using unsupervised learning techniques and then fine-tuned for specific tasks.

The key innovation of GPT is its use of a large-scale transformer model with extensive pre-training on diverse text data. This pre-training allows the model to learn a wide range of language patterns and structures. For instance, GPT-3, one of the largest models in the GPT series, contains 175 billion parameters and demonstrates impressive capabilities in generating human-like text. Its ability to perform tasks such as translation, summarization, and creative writing with minimal task-specific training underscores the effectiveness of large-scale pre-training in capturing intricate language features.

The development of these advanced neural network architectures—Transformers, BERT, and GPT—has fundamentally reshaped the landscape of NLP. Each model has introduced novel techniques and improvements, leading to significant advancements in language understanding and generation. Transformers' self-attention mechanism enhanced the ability to process long-range dependencies, BERT's bidirectional approach improved contextual understanding, and GPT's autoregressive generation enabled more coherent and versatile text production.

The impact of these models extends beyond academic research and into real-world applications. They have set new benchmarks in various NLP tasks, including machine translation, text summarization, and conversational AI. By leveraging these architectures, practitioners can build more sophisticated and effective NLP systems that better understand and generate human language. The continued evolution of these models promises further innovations and improvements in the field, driving the development of even more advanced language technologies.

BERT's bidirectional approach represents a profound shift in how language models understand context. By training on masked language modeling (MLM) and next sentence prediction (NSP), BERT learns to predict missing words within a sentence and to discern the relationship between sentence pairs. In MLM, random words in the input sequence are masked, and the model is tasked with predicting these masked words based on the surrounding context. This approach forces BERT to consider both preceding and following words, thereby capturing the nuances of context from both directions. For NSP, BERT is trained to predict whether one sentence follows another, which enhances its ability to understand relationships between sentences.

The impact of BERT on various NLP tasks has been remarkable. By providing pre-trained representations that can be fine-tuned on specific tasks, BERT has achieved state-of-the-art performance on benchmarks like the Stanford Question Answering Dataset (SQuAD) and the General Language Understanding Evaluation (GLUE) benchmark. This versatility has made BERT a foundational model in NLP, enabling applications such as question answering, sentiment analysis, and entity recognition to benefit from its deep contextual understanding.

Following BERT, the GPT (Generative Pre-trained Transformer) series by OpenAI introduced another significant advancement in language modeling. GPT builds on the Transformer architecture but focuses on autoregressive modeling, where the model generates text one word at a time, conditioned on the previous words. Unlike BERT, which is designed to understand and represent text, GPT is optimized for generating coherent and contextually relevant text. The GPT models are trained using a large corpus of text in an unsupervised manner, learning to predict the next word in a sequence given the previous words. This training strategy enables GPT to generate human-like text with remarkable fluency and coherence.

The evolution from GPT to GPT-3 demonstrates the power of scaling up neural network models. GPT-3, with its 175 billion parameters, exemplifies the principle that increasing model size can significantly enhance performance across a wide range of NLP tasks. GPT-3's size and extensive training data allow it to perform few-shot and zero-shot learning, where it can generate text or answer questions with minimal or no task-specific training. This capability highlights the model's ability to generalize from its vast training data and perform tasks that it was not explicitly trained for.

Despite their impressive capabilities, both BERT and GPT models come with challenges. One notable concern is their computational and resource demands. Training such large models requires substantial hardware resources, including powerful GPUs or TPUs and extensive memory. This has implications for accessibility and the environmental impact of training large-scale models. Additionally, while these models perform exceptionally well on many tasks, they are not without limitations. For instance, they can produce biased or problematic outputs based on the biases present in their training data. Addressing these issues requires ongoing research and development to create more ethical and equitable models.

Furthermore, the use of large language models raises questions about their interpretability. Understanding how these models arrive at their predictions or generated text remains a challenge, which complicates efforts to diagnose and correct errors or biases in the models. Techniques such as attention visualization and probing tasks are being explored to improve interpretability, but this remains an active area of research.

In summary, the development of advanced neural network architectures like Transformers, BERT, and GPT has revolutionized the field of NLP, enabling more sophisticated and context-aware language understanding and generation. These models have set new standards for performance on a range of NLP tasks, demonstrating the power of deep learning techniques in capturing the intricacies of human language. However, the challenges associated with their computational demands, biases, and interpretability underscore the need for continued research and responsible development practices. As the field advances, these models will likely continue to evolve, driving further innovations and applications in natural language processing.

Transformers, BERT, and GPT represent major strides in neural network architectures for natural language processing. As we explore these advanced models, it becomes evident how they have collectively shaped the landscape of language understanding and generation.

The Transformer architecture itself, introduced in the seminal paper "Attention is All You Need," revolutionized NLP by dispensing with the recurrent structures that had previously dominated the field. Instead, it relies on self-attention mechanisms to process sequences of data. Self-attention allows the model to weigh the importance of each word in a sequence relative to others, providing a nuanced understanding of context and relationships within the text. This mechanism enables Transformers to handle long-range dependencies and maintain context over extensive text, addressing limitations inherent in earlier architectures like LSTMs and GRUs.

Transformers consist of an encoder-decoder structure, where the encoder processes input text and the decoder generates output. However, in many NLP tasks, the encoder-only or decoder-only configurations of the Transformer are utilized. For instance, BERT employs a Transformer encoder to generate bidirectional contextual representations, which significantly enhances its understanding of context. GPT, conversely, uses a Transformer decoder for autoregressive text generation, making it adept at producing coherent and contextually relevant text sequences.

The evolution from the Transformer to BERT and GPT illustrates how specific adaptations of the architecture can address different NLP challenges. BERT's bidirectional approach, using masked language modeling and next sentence prediction, allows it to understand the intricacies of language with greater depth. This model's ability to consider context from both directions—left-to-right and right-to-left—enables it to capture subtle nuances and relationships in the text. Its success in various NLP benchmarks underscores the effectiveness of this approach.

GPT's autoregressive modeling, on the other hand, emphasizes the model's capacity for text generation. By predicting the next word in a sequence based on prior words, GPT can generate text that is contextually coherent and stylistically consistent. The advancements seen from GPT to GPT-3, including the scale of parameters and data, have pushed the boundaries of what is possible in text generation. GPT-3's ability to perform few-shot and zero-shot learning further exemplifies the power of large-scale models, where minimal additional training allows it to tackle a diverse array of tasks.

As these models have advanced, they have not been without challenges and limitations. One significant issue is the computational cost associated with training and deploying large-scale models. Models like GPT-3 require substantial computational resources, both in terms of hardware and energy consumption. This raises concerns about the environmental impact of training large models and the accessibility of such technology. Moreover, the sheer size of these models can make them difficult to interpret, leading to challenges in understanding and explaining their decision-making processes.

Another challenge is the potential for these models to perpetuate or even exacerbate existing biases present in training data. Since these models are trained on vast datasets gathered from the internet, they may inadvertently learn and reproduce biases related to race, gender, and other socio-cultural factors. Addressing these biases is an ongoing area of research, with efforts focused on developing techniques for bias detection and mitigation. Ensuring that NLP models are fair and unbiased is crucial for their responsible deployment and acceptance in real-world applications.

The advancements in neural network architectures have paved the way for innovative applications across various domains. In healthcare, for example, models based on these architectures are being used for tasks such as medical text classification, named entity recognition, and patient data analysis. In finance, they are applied to sentiment analysis, fraud detection, and automated customer service. E-commerce benefits from these models through enhanced product recommendations, customer feedback analysis, and personalized shopping experiences.

Looking ahead, the continued development of neural network architectures will likely focus on improving model efficiency, interpretability, and ethical considerations. Researchers are exploring methods for reducing the computational requirements of large models, such as through model pruning, quantization, and efficient training techniques. Efforts to make models more interpretable aim to provide insights into their inner workings and decision-making processes, enhancing trust and understanding.

The ethical implications of these advancements will also remain a central concern. As NLP models become increasingly integrated into various aspects of society, it is essential to address issues related to privacy, bias, and fairness proactively. Ensuring that these technologies are developed and deployed responsibly will be critical in maximizing their benefits while mitigating potential risks.

In conclusion, the advancements in neural network architectures like Transformers, BERT, and GPT have fundamentally transformed the field of NLP. These models have demonstrated unprecedented capabilities in language understanding and generation, driving significant progress across various applications. As the field continues to evolve, addressing the associated challenges and ethical considerations will be crucial in shaping the future of NLP and its impact on society.

CHAPTER 23: FUTURE TRENDS IN NLP

As we advance into the future, the field of natural language processing (NLP) is poised for transformative changes that will significantly influence its trajectory. This exploration into emerging trends and future directions offers a glimpse into how the integration of NLP with other AI technologies, advancements in model efficiency, and the evolution of research developments are expected to shape the landscape of NLP.

One of the most promising areas of development is the integration of NLP with other artificial intelligence technologies. This synergy is increasingly evident as NLP models are combined with computer vision, robotics, and knowledge graphs to create more comprehensive AI systems. For instance, combining NLP with computer vision can enhance the understanding of multimedia content by allowing systems to interpret and generate text based on visual inputs. This integration is crucial for applications such as automated video description, where the system needs to understand both the visual content and the accompanying text to generate accurate and relevant descriptions.

In robotics, NLP is playing a vital role in enabling more sophisticated human-robot interactions. Robots equipped with advanced NLP capabilities can understand and respond to natural language commands with greater accuracy, making them more useful in various environments, from home assistants to industrial automation. The fusion of NLP with robotics opens new possibilities for developing intelligent systems that can engage in meaningful conversations, provide contextually appropriate responses, and perform complex tasks based on verbal instructions.

Knowledge graphs, which represent relationships between concepts and entities, are another area where NLP integration is proving beneficial. By linking NLP with knowledge graphs, systems can leverage structured information to enhance their language understanding and generation capabilities. This integration enables more accurate information retrieval, better contextual understanding, and improved responses in applications such as virtual assistants and question-answering systems.

Advancements in model efficiency are also a significant focus for the future of NLP. As models become more complex and data-intensive, there is an increasing need to optimize their performance and reduce computational costs. Techniques such as model distillation, pruning, and quantization are being explored to create smaller, more efficient versions of large models without sacrificing their accuracy. Model distillation involves training a smaller model to mimic the behavior of a larger, more complex one, effectively transferring knowledge while reducing the computational burden. Pruning techniques selectively remove less important parameters from a model, while quantization reduces the precision of model parameters to lower memory usage and computation requirements.

Another promising area is the development of more efficient training methods. Researchers are investigating techniques such as few-shot learning and transfer learning to reduce the amount of data and computational resources needed to train NLP models. Few-shot learning allows models to perform well on tasks with minimal training examples, making it possible to adapt to new domains with limited data. Transfer learning, on the other hand, involves leveraging pre-trained models on large datasets to improve performance on specific tasks, thus reducing the need for extensive training from scratch.

The evolution of research in NLP is also driving significant advancements. Emerging techniques in deep learning, such as self-supervised learning and unsupervised learning, are expanding the capabilities of NLP models. Self-supervised learning enables models to learn from unlabeled data by predicting parts of the input based on other parts, thereby reducing the reliance on labeled datasets. Unsupervised learning approaches are also gaining traction as they allow models to discover patterns and structures in data without explicit supervision, offering new avenues for improving language understanding.

Moreover, ethical considerations and fairness in NLP are becoming increasingly important as the field progresses. As models become more integrated into societal systems, addressing biases and ensuring equitable treatment in NLP applications is crucial. Researchers are focusing on developing techniques to identify and mitigate biases in training data and model predictions. Ensuring transparency and accountability in NLP systems is essential for maintaining public trust and fostering responsible AI development.

Looking ahead, the future of NLP is set to be shaped by a confluence of technological advancements and evolving research paradigms. The integration of NLP with other AI technologies promises to create more capable and versatile systems, while advancements in model efficiency and training methods will drive innovation and accessibility. As researchers continue to explore new techniques and address ethical challenges, the field of NLP is poised for exciting developments that will enhance its applications and impact across various domains.

The trajectory of natural language processing (NLP) is increasingly influenced by emerging research developments and technological advancements. One area that warrants attention is the shift toward more personalized and context-aware NLP systems. The future of NLP will see an emphasis on tailoring interactions to individual users, which involves incorporating user-specific data and preferences to enhance the relevance and accuracy of responses. This personalization can significantly improve user experiences in applications ranging from customer support to personal assistants.

Personalized NLP systems rely on advanced user modeling techniques, which involve understanding user behavior, preferences, and context. By leveraging historical interaction data and contextual cues, these systems can generate responses that are more aligned with individual needs. For example, in customer service applications, a personalized NLP system could remember past interactions with a customer to provide more accurate and contextually appropriate support. This approach not only improves user satisfaction but also fosters a more engaging and effective interaction between humans and machines.

Another critical trend is the development of multilingual and cross-lingual NLP models. As global communication becomes increasingly interconnected, there is a growing need for models that can seamlessly handle multiple languages and cross-lingual tasks. Advances in transfer learning and pre-trained multilingual models, such as mBERT and XLM-R, have laid the groundwork for this trend. These models are designed to process text in various languages and facilitate cross-lingual understanding, making them highly valuable for applications such as international customer support and global content management.

The future of NLP will also be shaped by advancements in low-resource language processing. Many languages around the world lack sufficient data and resources for effective NLP development. Addressing this gap requires innovative approaches to model training and data augmentation. Techniques such as zero-shot and few-shot learning enable models to perform tasks in low-resource languages by leveraging knowledge from high-resource languages. Additionally, synthetic data generation and transfer learning can help create resources for languages with limited training data.

In parallel with these developments, there is an increasing focus on the ethical considerations of NLP technologies. As NLP systems become more prevalent, it is essential to address issues related to bias, fairness, and transparency. The design and implementation of NLP models must account for potential biases in training data, which can lead to discriminatory outcomes and reinforce societal inequalities. Researchers and practitioners are working on methods to detect, mitigate, and prevent bias in NLP systems, ensuring that these technologies are fair and inclusive.

Transparency in NLP models is another critical concern. As models become more complex, understanding their decision-making processes can be challenging. Efforts to improve interpretability and explainability are crucial for building trust in NLP systems and ensuring their responsible use. Techniques such as model introspection and visualization can help users and developers understand how models arrive at their predictions, facilitating better decision-making and accountability.

Looking ahead, the integration of NLP with emerging technologies, such as augmented reality (AR) and virtual reality (VR), presents exciting possibilities. NLP can enhance AR and VR experiences by enabling more natural and intuitive interactions within these immersive environments. For example, users could engage in conversational interactions with virtual characters or access real-time language translation in AR applications. The convergence of NLP with AR and VR technologies promises to create new opportunities for user engagement and interaction.

Furthermore, advancements in hardware and computational infrastructure will continue to impact the development and deployment of NLP models. The rise of specialized hardware, such as GPUs and TPUs, has already accelerated the training and inference of large-scale models. Future innovations in hardware and distributed computing will further enhance the efficiency and scalability of NLP systems, enabling researchers and practitioners to tackle increasingly complex tasks and datasets.

In conclusion, the future of NLP is characterized by a convergence of trends that emphasize personalization, multilingual capabilities, ethical considerations, and integration with emerging technologies. As the field continues to evolve, researchers and practitioners must remain vigilant in addressing challenges and seizing opportunities to advance NLP applications. By staying at the forefront of these developments, we can shape a future where NLP technologies are more effective, equitable, and seamlessly integrated into our daily lives.

The integration of NLP with other AI technologies represents a transformative trend in the field. One of the most significant integrations is between NLP and computer vision, which has given rise to multimodal AI systems. These systems combine textual and visual data to perform complex tasks that were previously beyond the capabilities of single-modality models. For instance, in the realm of automated content generation, models that can analyze both images and accompanying text are now able to produce more coherent and contextually appropriate descriptions. This capability is crucial for applications like automated image captioning and visual question answering, where understanding and generating content based on both modalities is essential.

Similarly, the fusion of NLP with reinforcement learning is advancing the development of intelligent agents capable of interactive and adaptive behaviors. In this scenario, NLP models are employed to understand and generate human-like responses in dialogue systems, while reinforcement learning algorithms are used to optimize the agents' behavior based on feedback from their interactions with users. This combination enhances the ability of AI systems to engage in complex, real-time conversations and adapt to user preferences and goals over time.

The trend towards improving model efficiency is also paramount. With the growing complexity of state-of-the-art NLP models, there is a pressing need to make these models more computationally efficient and less resource-intensive. Techniques such as model pruning, quantization, and knowledge distillation are being employed to reduce the size and complexity of models while maintaining their performance. For instance, knowledge distillation involves training a smaller, more efficient model (the student) to replicate the behavior of a larger, pre-trained model (the teacher). This approach helps in deploying high-performance NLP models on devices with limited computational resources, such as mobile phones and embedded systems.

Moreover, the development of sparse transformers is another promising avenue for enhancing model efficiency. Sparse transformers aim to reduce the computational burden associated with dense attention mechanisms by focusing only on a subset of input tokens at each layer. This approach can lead to substantial improvements in both speed and memory usage, making it feasible to apply large-scale models in real-time applications and resource-constrained environments.

Another key aspect of future trends in NLP involves the expansion of research into novel architectures and learning paradigms. One notable area is the exploration of self-supervised learning techniques, which leverage vast amounts of unlabelled data to pre-train models in a way that captures complex linguistic patterns and structures. Self-supervised learning has proven to be highly effective in creating representations that are transferable across various NLP tasks. By continuously evolving these techniques, researchers aim to enhance the versatility and robustness of NLP models.

The impact of new research developments on NLP is multifaceted. Breakthroughs in areas such as neural architecture search (NAS) and automated machine learning (AutoML) are poised to revolutionize how NLP models are designed and optimized. NAS involves using algorithms to automatically search for the most effective neural network architectures, which can lead to the discovery of novel and more efficient designs. Similarly, AutoML aims to simplify the process of model selection and hyperparameter tuning, making advanced NLP technologies more accessible to practitioners with varying levels of expertise.

As NLP continues to advance, it will also benefit from the integration of cross-disciplinary research. Collaborations between NLP researchers and experts in fields such as cognitive science, linguistics, and human-computer interaction can provide deeper insights into the nuances of human language and improve the design and functionality of NLP systems. For example, incorporating findings from cognitive science can lead to more natural and human-like interactions in conversational agents, while linguistic research can enhance the understanding of semantic and syntactic nuances in language processing.

In conclusion, the future of NLP is being shaped by a confluence of technological advancements, integration with other AI domains, and ongoing research into more efficient and effective models. These trends promise to push the boundaries of what NLP systems can achieve, leading to more sophisticated, context-aware, and user-friendly applications. As we move forward, it is crucial for researchers, practitioners, and policymakers to remain vigilant about the ethical implications of these advancements, ensuring that the benefits of NLP technologies are realized in a manner that is fair, transparent, and inclusive.

CHAPTER 24: INFORMATION RETRIEVAL AND SEARCH ENGINES

Information retrieval (IR) encompasses the methodologies and systems used to extract relevant information from extensive repositories, such as databases or the internet. Central to this process is the ability to index, query, and rank data effectively, ensuring that users receive pertinent and accurate results in response to their information needs. As we delve into the fundamentals of IR, we will explore the core components and techniques that underpin modern search engines, highlighting the role of natural language processing (NLP) in enhancing search capabilities.

The first crucial step in information retrieval is indexing. Indexing involves organizing data in a way that allows for efficient retrieval. Traditional indexing methods, such as inverted indexing, create a mapping from terms to their occurrences within documents. This structure supports rapid lookups by mapping each word or term in the corpus to the documents in which it appears, thus facilitating quick access to relevant content. An inverted index is particularly effective for handling large volumes of text, as it compresses the data and reduces the complexity of searches.

Building on this foundation, querying is the next critical component. When a user submits a search query, the system must translate this input into a form that can be efficiently processed against the index. This process often involves tokenization, stemming, and normalization. Tokenization breaks the query into discrete units, or tokens, such as words or phrases. Stemming reduces words to their root forms, which helps in matching variations of a term. Normalization, on the other hand, involves converting text to a uniform format, such as lowercase, to ensure consistent processing. Together, these techniques ensure that queries are processed in a way that maximizes the chances of retrieving relevant documents.

The third key aspect is ranking algorithms, which determine the order in which search results are presented to users. Ranking algorithms assess the relevance of documents based on various factors, including term frequency, document frequency, and term proximity. The term frequency (TF) reflects how often a search term appears in a document, while the document frequency (DF) indicates how common the term is across the entire corpus. Term proximity measures the closeness of search terms within a document. More sophisticated ranking models, such as the BM25 algorithm, refine these basic measures by incorporating probabilistic models of relevance.

Advancements in NLP have significantly enhanced search engine performance by improving the way queries and documents are understood and matched. One of the primary contributions of NLP to IR is semantic search, which moves beyond keyword matching to understand the context and meaning behind user queries. Semantic search involves techniques such as word embeddings, which represent words in a high-dimensional space based on their contextual relationships. These embeddings allow search engines to capture synonyms, related terms, and contextual meanings, thereby improving the accuracy of search results.

Another pivotal NLP advancement is the integration of named entity recognition (NER) into search engines. NER identifies and categorizes entities such as people, organizations, and locations within text. By recognizing these entities, search engines can better understand the specific topics or entities that a user is interested in, thereby refining search results to match the intended context. For example, a search query for "Apple" can be disambiguated to distinguish between the technology company and the fruit, depending on the surrounding context.

Furthermore, the application of deep learning models has revolutionized the field of information retrieval. Models such as BERT (Bidirectional Encoder Representations from Transformers) and GPT (Generative Pre-trained Transformer) leverage large-scale language understanding to improve search relevance. BERT, with its bidirectional attention mechanism, can grasp the context of words within a query more effectively than traditional models, leading to better comprehension of user intent and more accurate search results. Similarly, GPT's generative capabilities allow it to produce coherent and contextually appropriate responses, enhancing the ability of search engines to handle complex queries and conversational searches.

In addition to these advancements, search engines are increasingly incorporating user interaction data to refine search results. User feedback, such as click-through rates and dwell times, provides valuable insights into the effectiveness of search results. Machine learning models can analyze this data to adjust ranking algorithms and improve the relevance of future searches. By continuously learning from user interactions, search engines can adapt to evolving user preferences and trends, resulting in a more personalized and efficient search experience.

Overall, the integration of NLP techniques into information

retrieval systems has significantly improved the performance and relevance of search engines. From semantic search and named entity recognition to deep learning models and user interaction data, these advancements have enabled search engines to deliver more accurate, contextually relevant, and personalized search results. As the field of NLP continues to evolve, further innovations in information retrieval will undoubtedly enhance our ability to access and utilize information in increasingly sophisticated ways.

The integration of natural language processing (NLP) techniques has transformed information retrieval, enhancing search engine capabilities and user experiences. NLP advancements have enabled more sophisticated methods for understanding and processing queries, leading to improvements in the relevance and accuracy of search results. As we delve deeper, it is essential to explore how these techniques have been applied to refine indexing, querying, and ranking processes.

One of the primary NLP innovations in search engines is semantic search, which moves beyond traditional keyword matching to understand the meaning and context of queries. Semantic search utilizes techniques such as word embeddings, which map words into continuous vector spaces where semantically similar words are positioned close to each other. This representation allows search engines to better comprehend synonyms and context, providing more accurate results even when exact keywords are not used. For instance, if a user searches for "how to fix a leaky faucet," a semantic search system can recognize that "leaky faucet" and "plumbing repair" are related, delivering relevant results for both terms.

Another significant advancement is the incorporation of named entity recognition (NER) into search engines. NER identifies and classifies entities such as people, organizations, and locations within text. By recognizing and indexing these entities, search engines can enhance query understanding and retrieval accuracy. For example, if a user searches for "Elon Musk's companies," a search engine equipped with NER will accurately identify "Elon Musk" as a person and retrieve documents related to his associated companies, such as SpaceX and Tesla, even if the query does not explicitly mention these companies.

Contextual understanding has also been improved through the use of deep learning models, particularly those based on transformer architectures. Models like BERT (Bidirectional Encoder Representations from Transformers) and GPT (Generative Pre-trained Transformer) have revolutionized how search engines interpret queries and documents. BERT, for instance, enhances search engines' ability to understand the context of words in a sentence by analyzing both preceding and following words, thereby improving comprehension of complex queries and ambiguous terms. GPT, on the other hand, excels in generating human-like text and understanding nuanced language, enabling more natural interactions and more relevant search results.

Beyond individual queries, search engines have adopted advanced ranking strategies driven by NLP. One such method is the use of relevance feedback, where search engines refine their results based on user interactions. For example, if users frequently select specific documents from search results, the system learns to rank similar documents higher in future queries. This adaptive approach leverages user behavior data to continually improve ranking accuracy.

Additionally, query expansion techniques have become prevalent, where search engines automatically broaden queries to include related terms or concepts. NLP-based query expansion uses semantic understanding to suggest relevant terms or synonyms, thus enhancing search results. For example, if a user searches for "travel tips," the system might expand the query to include related terms like "vacation advice" or "holiday planning," ensuring a more comprehensive set of results.

Machine learning techniques also play a critical role in optimizing search engine performance. Algorithms such as support vector machines (SVMs) and neural networks are employed to classify and rank documents based on features extracted from both the queries and the indexed content. These models are trained on large datasets to learn patterns and relationships that contribute to better search result rankings. For instance, a machine learning model might be trained to recognize high-quality sources and prioritize them in search results based on past performance and user feedback.

The fusion of NLP and information retrieval technologies extends to personalized search experiences as well. By analyzing user profiles, search history, and interaction patterns, search engines can tailor results to individual preferences and needs. NLP techniques enable more effective personalization by understanding user intent and context, which helps in delivering search results that are not only relevant but also tailored to the user's specific interests and historical behavior.

In conclusion, the advancements in NLP have significantly enhanced information retrieval processes, leading to more accurate, relevant, and context-aware search results. From semantic search and named entity recognition to deep learning models and personalized search experiences, these innovations have transformed how search engines operate and interact with users. As technology continues to evolve, the integration of NLP with information retrieval systems will undoubtedly drive further improvements and new capabilities, shaping the future of search engines and their applications in diverse domains.

The evolution of search engine technologies is profoundly influenced by advances in natural language processing (NLP), which have led to significant enhancements in information retrieval systems. These improvements are not only about refining the core algorithms but also about incorporating novel approaches that leverage the complexity and subtlety of human language. To fully appreciate the transformation, it is crucial to explore how NLP techniques are applied in various stages of the search process, from query expansion and relevance feedback to personalized search and multimodal search integration.

One of the pivotal applications of NLP in search engines is query expansion, which involves broadening the scope of a user's search query to include related terms and concepts. Traditional keyword-based search engines may miss relevant results due to limited query specificity or variations in terminology. NLP techniques address this by using word embeddings and thesauri to identify and incorporate synonyms, related phrases, and contextual meanings into the search process. For instance, a query for "best laptop for gaming" might be expanded to include terms like "gaming laptop reviews" or "top gaming notebooks," thus improving the likelihood of retrieving comprehensive and relevant results.

Another advanced application of NLP in search engines is relevance feedback. This technique involves adjusting the search results based on user interactions with the initial set of results. For example, if users consistently select certain results as useful, the search engine can infer that similar documents are likely to be relevant. NLP models facilitate this process by analyzing user behavior, including click patterns and dwell times, to refine the ranking algorithms. This dynamic adjustment improves the accuracy of search results over time, adapting to user preferences and evolving search trends.

Personalized search represents a significant leap forward in tailoring search results to individual users. By leveraging user-specific data, such as search history, location, and preferences, NLP techniques can customize results to better meet the unique needs of each user. For example, a user frequently searching for vegan recipes may receive tailored search results that prioritize vegan-friendly options and exclude non-relevant content. This personalization is achieved through sophisticated NLP models that analyze user behavior and contextual information to predict and deliver content that aligns with individual interests and past interactions.

Multimodal search integration is an emerging trend where search engines combine textual and non-textual data, such as images and audio, to enhance the search experience. NLP plays a crucial role in this integration by enabling the processing and understanding of diverse data types. For example, an image search engine might use image recognition algorithms to identify objects within photos, while NLP models interpret textual descriptions to match these images with relevant content. Similarly, voice search systems utilize speech recognition and natural language understanding to process spoken queries and deliver accurate results. This fusion of modalities allows for more intuitive and versatile search experiences, accommodating various user inputs and enhancing the overall efficacy of retrieval systems.

Additionally, advancements in NLP have introduced context-aware search functionalities, which consider the broader context of a query rather than treating it in isolation. Contextual search leverages the user's previous queries, current session activity, and even real-time events to refine search results. For instance, a user searching for "weather" might receive different results depending on their location and recent activities, such as recent searches related to travel plans or current weather conditions in nearby cities. Context-aware search systems provide a more nuanced understanding of user intent, leading to more accurate and relevant search outcomes.

The development of advanced neural network architectures, such as transformers, has further propelled the capabilities of search engines. These architectures excel in capturing complex linguistic patterns and relationships within text, facilitating deeper comprehension and more sophisticated search functionalities. Transformers, with their self-attention mechanisms, allow for more effective handling of long-range dependencies and contextual nuances, resulting in improved query understanding and retrieval performance.

In conclusion, the integration of NLP techniques into information retrieval and search engines has revolutionized the field, enhancing the precision, relevance, and personalization of search results. Through innovations in query expansion, relevance feedback, personalized search, multimodal integration, and context-aware functionalities, NLP continues to drive significant advancements in how information is retrieved and presented. As search technologies evolve, the continued application and refinement of NLP methods will be essential in meeting the growing demands for more accurate and user-centric search experiences.

CHAPTER 25: QUESTION ANSWERING SYSTEMS

The landscape of question answering (QA) systems has evolved considerably, transitioning from rule-based approaches to sophisticated neural network architectures that provide more nuanced and accurate answers. At the core of these systems lies a complex interplay of knowledge bases, retrieval-based methods, and generative approaches. Understanding each component and their interactions is crucial for grasping how modern QA systems deliver precise and contextually relevant responses to user queries.

The architecture of question answering systems typically begins with a robust knowledge base or corpus of information. This knowledge base serves as the foundational repository from which the system retrieves and synthesizes answers. Knowledge bases can vary widely, from structured databases like SQL and RDF, which organize information into predefined schemas, to unstructured text corpora such as encyclopedias or web pages. The choice of knowledge base influences the QA system's ability to handle different types of questions, whether they require precise factual information or more open-ended, exploratory responses.

Retrieval-based methods form the first stage of a QA system's processing pipeline. These methods focus on identifying and extracting relevant information from the knowledge base in response to a user's query. Traditional retrieval-based approaches use techniques such as keyword matching and vector space models to locate pertinent documents or passages. These methods rely heavily on the quality of the indexing and the relevance of the retrieved content. For example, a question like "What are the symptoms of the flu?" would trigger the system to search through medical texts or databases for passages that contain information about flu symptoms.

Advancements in NLP have significantly enhanced retrieval-based methods through the incorporation of more sophisticated semantic understanding. Modern techniques involve embedding-based retrieval, where words and phrases are transformed into dense vectors that capture their contextual meanings. Models like BERT (Bidirectional Encoder Representations from Transformers) and its variants have revolutionized this process by allowing for bidirectional context understanding, improving the system's ability to retrieve relevant passages even when queries are phrased in complex or varied ways.

The second stage involves the generation of answers, which is where generative approaches come into play. Unlike retrieval-based methods, generative approaches do not simply extract information but instead create answers from scratch based on the retrieved content. This requires a deeper level of comprehension and synthesis. Neural network models, particularly those based on transformer architectures, have made significant strides in this area. Models like GPT (Generative Pre-trained Transformer) are trained on vast amounts of text data to generate coherent and contextually appropriate answers.

Generative approaches pose their own set of challenges. One major issue is ensuring that the generated responses are not only accurate but also relevant and contextually appropriate. Unlike retrieval-based methods, which have a direct link to the source material, generative methods must navigate the subtleties of human language to produce answers that align with user expectations. This challenge is compounded by the need for the system to maintain consistency and avoid generating incorrect or misleading information.

To address these challenges, QA systems incorporate various strategies to refine their generative capabilities. Contextual understanding is crucial, as it allows the system to generate answers that are aligned with the user's query and the context in which it is asked. Techniques such as fine-tuning pre-trained models on specific datasets or using domain-specific knowledge can improve the relevance and accuracy of generated answers. For instance, a QA system trained specifically on legal texts will perform better in answering legal questions compared to a general-purpose model.

Another important aspect of QA systems is their ability to handle ambiguous or multi-faceted questions. Systems must be equipped to interpret and disambiguate user queries, which often involves understanding the nuances of language and context. Techniques such as question decomposition, where complex queries are broken down into simpler sub-questions, can help in generating more precise answers. Additionally, incorporating user feedback and iterative learning processes can enhance the system's ability to handle a wider range of questions effectively.

The integration of external knowledge sources, such as knowledge graphs and ontologies, further enriches QA systems by providing additional context and structure to the information retrieval and generation processes. Knowledge graphs, for instance, offer a structured representation of entities and their relationships, enabling the system to infer connections and generate more insightful responses.

In summary, question answering systems have progressed

from simple keyword-based retrieval methods to sophisticated models that leverage deep learning and semantic understanding. The architecture of these systems involves a combination of knowledge bases, retrieval-based techniques, and generative models, each contributing to the overall effectiveness of the system. As advancements in NLP continue to drive innovation, the focus remains on improving the accuracy, relevance, and contextual understanding of answers, ultimately enhancing the user experience and the utility of QA systems across various domains.

In the context of question answering systems, generative models play a crucial role in producing coherent and contextually appropriate answers. These models are fundamentally different from retrieval-based approaches in that they are capable of generating responses from scratch rather than merely selecting and presenting pre-existing information. The shift towards generative methods has been largely driven by advancements in deep learning, particularly with the development of transformer architectures.

Transformers, as a class of neural network models, represent a significant leap forward in natural language processing. They leverage self-attention mechanisms to weigh the relevance of different parts of the input data, allowing the model to understand and generate text with greater context and coherence. This mechanism enables models to handle complex queries that may involve multiple layers of context and nuance. For example, when faced with a question like "How does climate change impact marine life?" a generative model can synthesize information from various sources and generate a comprehensive answer that addresses multiple aspects of the query.

The advent of large pre-trained language models such as GPT (Generative Pre-trained Transformer) has further pushed the boundaries of what is possible in question answering. These models are trained on vast amounts of text data and are capable of understanding and generating human-like text based on the patterns learned during training. GPT, for instance, can generate detailed and contextually relevant answers by leveraging its deep understanding of language patterns and contextual relationships. The pre-training process involves exposing the model to a diverse array of texts, which helps it build a rich representation of language that can be fine-tuned for specific QA tasks.

Despite these advancements, generative QA systems face several challenges. One of the primary issues is ensuring the accuracy and reliability of the generated answers. Generative models, while powerful, can sometimes produce plausible-sounding but incorrect or nonsensical responses. This is particularly problematic in applications where the correctness of the information is critical, such as in medical or legal contexts. To mitigate this risk, ongoing research focuses on improving the training data quality, incorporating external knowledge sources, and developing techniques for better answer validation and verification.

Another challenge is maintaining context-awareness in generated responses. For a QA system to provide accurate answers, it must not only understand the query but also consider the broader context in which the question is asked. This includes the user's prior interactions, the specific domain of the query, and any relevant contextual information that might influence the answer. Transformers and other advanced models have made strides in handling context, but there is still ongoing research to improve their ability to maintain and utilize context over extended interactions.

In addition to the technical challenges, there are practical considerations related to the deployment and scaling of QA systems. For instance, integrating these systems into real-world applications requires efficient handling of computational resources and ensuring that the systems can operate in a user-friendly manner. High-performance QA systems must be optimized to balance the trade-offs between computational complexity and response time, ensuring that users receive timely and accurate answers without undue delay.

To address these challenges, researchers and practitioners are exploring various strategies. One approach involves the use of hybrid models that combine retrieval-based and generative methods. Such models can first retrieve relevant information using traditional search techniques and then refine or generate answers using advanced generative methods. This hybrid approach leverages the strengths of both retrieval and generation, aiming to improve the overall accuracy and relevance of the responses.

Another strategy is the development of domain-specific QA systems that are tailored to particular fields or applications. By focusing on a specific domain, these systems can be fine-tuned with specialized data and algorithms that enhance their performance within that context. Domain-specific models can provide more accurate and relevant answers by leveraging expertise and knowledge particular to the field, whether it be healthcare, finance, or any other specialized area.

In conclusion, the evolution of question answering systems reflects the rapid advancements in natural language processing and machine learning. The shift from retrieval-based methods to generative approaches, driven by transformer architectures and large-scale pre-trained models, has significantly enhanced the capabilities of QA systems. However, challenges related to accuracy, context-awareness, and practical deployment remain. Ongoing research and development efforts continue to address these challenges, striving to create more accurate, reliable, and contextually aware question answering systems that can effectively meet the needs of users across diverse applications.

The advancement in question answering systems has been

significantly influenced by the integration of knowledge bases with NLP techniques. Knowledge bases provide a structured repository of information that can be queried to retrieve factual answers, enhancing the accuracy and reliability of responses. These databases, often curated and maintained by experts, offer a wealth of domain-specific information that retrieval-based systems can leverage to answer queries more effectively.

Incorporating knowledge bases into question answering systems involves several key steps. Initially, the data from these repositories must be preprocessed and indexed in a manner that facilitates efficient querying. This preprocessing involves cleaning the data, structuring it into a format suitable for the retrieval algorithms, and creating indices that allow for fast lookups. Once the data is indexed, retrieval-based methods can leverage these indices to quickly locate relevant information in response to user queries.

A common approach in retrieval-based question answering systems is the use of traditional search algorithms, such as Boolean queries or vector space models. Boolean queries rely on simple keyword matching and logical operators to filter results, while vector space models represent documents and queries as vectors in a high-dimensional space. The relevance of documents is determined based on their proximity to the query vector, which allows for a more nuanced retrieval process. More advanced techniques, such as Latent Semantic Analysis (LSA) and Latent Dirichlet Allocation (LDA), further enhance retrieval by capturing semantic relationships between terms and documents.

Recent advancements have introduced neural retrieval methods that leverage deep learning techniques to improve the performance of question answering systems. These methods often involve training neural networks to understand and retrieve relevant information based on the semantic meaning of the query. For instance, models like Dense Passage Retrieval

(DPR) use bi-encoder architectures to encode queries and documents into dense vectors, which are then compared to retrieve the most relevant passages. This approach enhances the system's ability to handle complex queries and retrieve contextually appropriate answers.

Generative models, such as those based on the Transformer architecture, have also contributed to significant improvements in question answering systems. Unlike retrieval-based approaches, generative models generate answers by predicting the most likely text given the query and the context. These models are trained on large datasets to learn the patterns and structures of natural language, enabling them to produce coherent and contextually relevant responses. Transformer-based models, such as BERT and GPT, have set new benchmarks in QA performance by leveraging self-attention mechanisms to capture complex relationships between words and phrases.

Despite their effectiveness, generative models face challenges related to the generation of accurate and reliable answers. One notable issue is the risk of generating hallucinated or incorrect information, where the model produces plausible-sounding but factually incorrect answers. Addressing this challenge involves incorporating mechanisms for answer validation and fact-checking. Techniques such as leveraging external knowledge sources, implementing post-generation filtering, and fine-tuning models on domain-specific datasets can help mitigate the risks associated with answer accuracy.

Another challenge in the realm of question answering systems is ensuring that the generated responses are contextually appropriate and relevant. Context-awareness is crucial for providing answers that align with the user's query and the broader conversational context. Techniques for improving context-awareness include incorporating conversational history into the model's input, using domain-specific knowledge to tailor responses, and employing user feedback to refine and enhance the system's performance.

Recent advancements have also focused on creating more interactive and user-friendly question answering systems. These systems are designed to engage users in a more natural and intuitive manner, allowing for iterative interactions and follow-up questions. Techniques such as active learning and reinforcement learning are employed to improve the system's ability to handle dynamic and evolving queries, ultimately leading to a more engaging user experience.

In summary, the field of question answering systems has seen remarkable progress through the integration of knowledge bases, retrieval-based methods, and generative approaches. While each of these methods offers distinct advantages, ongoing research and development continue to address the challenges of accuracy, context-awareness, and user engagement. By combining these approaches and incorporating advancements in machine learning and NLP, question answering systems are poised to provide increasingly accurate and contextually relevant responses, enhancing their utility and effectiveness in a wide range of applications.

CHAPTER 26: SENTIMENT ANALYSIS IN DEPTH

Sentiment analysis, a critical aspect of natural language processing, aims to determine the emotional tone conveyed in a piece of text. This chapter delves into advanced techniques for sentiment analysis, providing a comprehensive exploration of how sentiment can be dissected and understood at a granular level. We will examine both aspect-based sentiment analysis and the challenges associated with sentiment analysis in multilingual contexts. Additionally, the application of these techniques across various domains, such as customer feedback and social media monitoring, will be discussed in detail.

To begin with, aspect-based sentiment analysis (ABSA) extends traditional sentiment analysis by focusing on the different aspects or components of a product, service, or entity mentioned in a text. Unlike general sentiment analysis, which provides a broad overview of sentiment, ABSA seeks to identify specific aspects and determine the sentiment associated with each aspect. For example, in a product review, while a general sentiment analysis might categorize the review as positive or negative overall, ABSA would break it down further to evaluate sentiments regarding particular aspects like the product's quality, price, or customer service.

The process of aspect-based sentiment analysis involves

several steps. Initially, it requires aspect extraction, where key attributes or components of the entity are identified from the text. This can be accomplished using techniques such as named entity recognition (NER) or topic modeling. Once the aspects are identified, sentiment classification is performed to determine the sentiment expressed towards each aspect. This often involves using supervised machine learning models or advanced deep learning approaches that are trained on annotated datasets to classify sentiment into categories such as positive, negative, or neutral.

A notable challenge in ABSA is handling the contextual nuances of language. Sentiment towards different aspects can be influenced by the context in which they are mentioned. For instance, a mention of "poor battery life" in a smartphone review could be negative, while the same mention in a review of a portable charger might be viewed positively. To address such nuances, sophisticated models that incorporate context-aware embeddings, such as BERT or GPT, are employed. These models understand the context of words and phrases, enhancing the accuracy of sentiment classification for specific aspects.

Sentiment analysis in multilingual contexts presents a different set of challenges. Language diversity adds complexity to the sentiment analysis process, as models trained on data from one language may not perform well on texts in another language. Issues such as linguistic variations, idiomatic expressions, and cultural differences can affect the accuracy of sentiment analysis across languages. To mitigate these challenges, approaches such as cross-lingual embeddings and multilingual transformers are utilized. Cross-lingual embeddings project words from different languages into a shared vector space, allowing sentiment analysis models to generalize across languages. Multilingual transformers, like mBERT or XLM-R, are pretrained on multiple languages and can be fine-tuned for specific sentiment analysis tasks in various languages.

In practice, sentiment analysis is applied extensively in domains such as customer feedback and social media monitoring. In customer feedback, businesses leverage sentiment analysis to gauge customer satisfaction and identify areas for improvement. For instance, analyzing feedback from surveys, reviews, and support tickets helps companies understand customer perceptions of their products or services. Aspect-based sentiment analysis further refines this understanding by pinpointing specific aspects that drive positive or negative sentiments.

Similarly, in social media monitoring, sentiment analysis enables organizations to track public opinion and brand reputation in real-time. Social media platforms generate vast amounts of data, and analyzing this data helps in identifying trends, detecting emerging issues, and measuring the impact of marketing campaigns. Techniques such as topic modeling and sentiment clustering are used to categorize and summarize sentiments expressed in social media posts, providing actionable insights for businesses and policymakers.

Advanced sentiment analysis techniques also find applications in areas like political analysis and market research. By analyzing public sentiment towards political candidates or policies, researchers can gauge voter opinions and predict electoral outcomes. In market research, sentiment analysis helps in understanding consumer preferences and trends, aiding in product development and strategic planning.

The continuous evolution of sentiment analysis techniques, driven by advancements in NLP and machine learning, holds promise for even more nuanced and accurate sentiment detection. As we progress, the integration of sentiment analysis with other AI technologies, such as emotion recognition and contextual understanding, will further enhance our ability to interpret and respond to the emotional tone of text. This ongoing development will not only improve the effectiveness of sentiment analysis in various domains but also contribute to the broader field of human-computer interaction, enabling more empathetic and intelligent systems.

The complexity of sentiment analysis in multilingual contexts arises from the inherent differences between languages, including syntactic structures, idiomatic expressions, and cultural nuances. Models trained on data from one language often encounter difficulties when applied to others due to these variations. To tackle this, several strategies are employed, ranging from cross-lingual models to language-specific adaptations.

Cross-lingual models aim to bridge the gap between different languages by leveraging shared semantic spaces. Techniques such as multilingual embeddings, which map words from different languages into a common vector space, enable models to understand sentiment across various languages. For instance, models like mBERT (Multilingual BERT) are designed to handle multiple languages simultaneously by training on a diverse corpus. These models use contextualized embeddings that capture the meaning of words in different linguistic contexts, improving sentiment analysis performance across languages.

Another approach involves fine-tuning pre-trained multilingual models on specific language datasets. This technique allows models to adapt to the peculiarities of individual languages while retaining the benefits of cross-lingual understanding. By training on large corpora of annotated sentiment data in multiple languages, these models can better capture sentiment nuances unique to each language. Additionally, incorporating domain-specific knowledge and language resources, such as lexicons and translation tools, further enhances the accuracy of sentiment analysis in diverse linguistic settings.

In practical applications, sentiment analysis is widely used in various domains, including customer feedback, social media monitoring, and market research. Each application area presents unique challenges and opportunities for leveraging sentiment analysis techniques.

In the domain of customer feedback, sentiment analysis plays a crucial role in understanding customer satisfaction and identifying areas for improvement. By analyzing reviews and feedback from customers, businesses can gain valuable insights into product performance, service quality, and overall customer experience. Aspect-based sentiment analysis is particularly useful here, as it allows businesses to pinpoint specific aspects of their products or services that are praised or criticized. For example, a review mentioning "fast delivery" and "friendly staff" may indicate positive sentiments about those specific aspects, even if the overall review is mixed.

Social media monitoring presents a different set of challenges due to the informal and often fragmented nature of social media language. Users frequently employ slang, abbreviations, and emojis, which can complicate sentiment analysis. To address these challenges, advanced techniques such as sentiment lexicons tailored for social media and deep learning models trained on social media data are used. These models can effectively interpret the sentiment behind social media posts, tweets, and comments, providing insights into public opinion and emerging trends.

In market research, sentiment analysis helps businesses and organizations understand consumer perceptions and preferences. By analyzing sentiments expressed in online discussions, surveys, and focus groups, companies can identify market trends, evaluate brand reputation, and make data-driven decisions. Sentiment analysis models can be integrated into market research tools to provide real-time insights and predictions, aiding strategic planning and competitive analysis.

The continuous evolution of sentiment analysis techniques

is driven by advancements in machine learning and natural language processing. Researchers and practitioners are exploring new methodologies to improve the accuracy and applicability of sentiment analysis across different languages and domains. Innovations in model architecture, training techniques, and data sources contribute to the ongoing enhancement of sentiment analysis capabilities, making it an increasingly valuable tool for understanding human emotions and opinions in a wide range of contexts.

In summary, sentiment analysis has evolved significantly, with advanced techniques addressing both aspect-based analysis and multilingual challenges. The integration of sophisticated models and approaches has expanded the scope of sentiment analysis applications, providing deeper insights into customer feedback, social media interactions, and market dynamics. As technology continues to advance, sentiment analysis will remain a pivotal tool in extracting meaningful information from textual data, enabling more informed decision-making and strategic planning across various industries.

One of the significant challenges in sentiment analysis, particularly in social media contexts, is dealing with the informal nature of language used by individuals. Social media platforms are replete with abbreviations, slang, emoticons, and hashtags, which can significantly alter the sentiment conveyed in a text. Traditional sentiment analysis models, which rely on formal language structures and lexicons, often struggle with these idiosyncrasies. To overcome this, recent advancements have focused on incorporating more sophisticated language models that are trained specifically on social media data.

These specialized models utilize large datasets from social media platforms to better understand the nuances of informal language. For example, embeddings trained on Twitter data can capture the meaning of slang terms and abbreviations more effectively than general-purpose models. Additionally, sentiment lexicons tailored for social media, such as those that include emoticons and hashtags, can improve the accuracy of sentiment classification. These lexicons are often built through crowdsourcing or domain-specific annotation, ensuring they reflect the latest trends and expressions used by users.

Another crucial advancement in sentiment analysis involves the integration of sentiment analysis with other NLP tasks, such as entity recognition and topic modeling. By combining sentiment analysis with these tasks, it is possible to gain deeper insights into how sentiment varies with different topics or entities. For instance, in customer feedback analysis, combining sentiment analysis with entity recognition allows businesses to understand not only the sentiment towards a product but also how specific features of the product contribute to that sentiment. This multi-faceted approach can provide a more comprehensive understanding of customer opinions and preferences.

Topic modeling techniques, such as Latent Dirichlet Allocation (LDA), can be used alongside sentiment analysis to identify and analyze the themes present in large volumes of text. This combination helps in uncovering patterns and trends related to sentiment in different contexts or time periods. For example, during a product launch, topic modeling can reveal which aspects of the product are being discussed most frequently and how the sentiment around these aspects evolves over time. This temporal analysis can be particularly valuable for tracking the impact of marketing campaigns or product updates.

The integration of sentiment analysis with predictive analytics is another promising area of research. Predictive analytics leverages historical sentiment data to forecast future trends and outcomes. By applying machine learning techniques to sentiment data, it is possible to predict customer behavior, market trends, and other business-related metrics. For instance, businesses can use sentiment analysis to predict customer churn by identifying negative sentiment patterns that may indicate dissatisfaction or likelihood of leaving. Similarly, sentiment trends can be used to forecast stock market movements or assess the impact of public relations efforts.

Despite these advancements, several challenges remain in the field of sentiment analysis. One major issue is the difficulty in accurately capturing the sentiment of ambiguous or complex sentences. Sentiments are not always expressed in a straightforward manner, and sarcasm, irony, and mixed sentiments can complicate analysis. To address these challenges, ongoing research focuses on improving the sophistication of sentiment models through enhanced contextual understanding and multi-modal data integration. For example, combining text-based sentiment analysis with visual sentiment analysis, which interprets sentiment from images or videos, could provide a more holistic view of user sentiment.

Another challenge is ensuring the robustness and generalizability of sentiment analysis models across different domains and languages. Models that perform well in one context may not necessarily translate to others due to variations in language use and cultural differences. Continuous evaluation and adaptation of models are essential to maintain their effectiveness across diverse settings. This includes updating models with new data, refining lexicons, and incorporating feedback from real-world applications.

In conclusion, the field of sentiment analysis has made significant strides with the advent of advanced techniques and models. From handling the complexities of multilingual texts to addressing the informal language of social media, ongoing research and innovation are driving improvements in sentiment analysis capabilities. By integrating sentiment analysis with other NLP tasks and predictive analytics, we can gain richer insights into emotional tones and their implications across various domains. However, addressing the remaining challenges and ensuring the adaptability of models will be crucial for the continued evolution and application of sentiment analysis in real-world scenarios.

CHAPTER 27: TEXT SUMMARIZATION METHODS

Text summarization is a fundamental task in natural language processing that involves condensing a longer text into a shorter form, preserving its core ideas and essential information. This process is invaluable in numerous applications, including news aggregation, document summarization, and information retrieval. The goal of summarization is to make large volumes of text more accessible and comprehensible by highlighting the most important content.

To achieve effective text summarization, methods are typically categorized into two broad approaches: extractive and abstractive summarization. Each approach has its own set of algorithms and techniques, offering different advantages and challenges.

Extractive summarization involves selecting key sentences, phrases, or sections from the original text and combining them to form a coherent summary. This method relies on identifying and extracting portions of the text that are deemed important based on various criteria. Algorithms used in extractive summarization include frequency-based methods, where the importance of sentences is determined by the frequency of key terms or phrases. Another common technique is the use of graph-based algorithms, such as TextRank, which build a graph of sentences and rank them based on their significance within the document.

One popular extractive approach is the use of sentence ranking algorithms, which evaluate sentences based on their relevance to the overall content. Techniques such as Latent Semantic Analysis (LSA) and Term Frequency-Inverse Document Frequency (TF-IDF) are employed to measure the importance of sentences. LSA captures the underlying semantic structure of the text, while TF-IDF focuses on the term frequencies and their inverse document frequencies to determine sentence relevance. These methods help in identifying sentences that best represent the main ideas of the document.

Abstractive summarization, on the other hand, involves generating new sentences that capture the essence of the original text. This approach is more complex as it requires the model to understand and rephrase the content rather than simply selecting parts of the text. Abstractive summarization methods often employ advanced neural network architectures, such as sequence-to-sequence models, which consist of an encoder and a decoder. The encoder processes the input text and converts it into a latent representation, while the decoder generates the summary from this representation.

Recent advancements in abstractive summarization have been driven by transformer-based models, such as BERT and GPT. These models leverage attention mechanisms to better capture the context and relationships between words in the text. For instance, models like GPT-3 can generate coherent and contextually appropriate summaries by learning from large-scale datasets. Transformer-based models excel in creating summaries that are more fluent and human-like compared to traditional methods.

The evaluation of summarization quality is a critical aspect of developing effective summarization systems. Metrics such as

ROUGE (Recall-Oriented Understudy for Gisting Evaluation) are commonly used to assess the quality of generated summaries. ROUGE evaluates summaries based on their overlap with reference summaries, measuring aspects such as precision, recall, and F1 score. This metric provides insights into how well the summary captures the essential information from the original text.

In real-world applications, text summarization is employed in various domains to enhance information accessibility and user experience. In news aggregation, summarization techniques are used to condense news articles into brief summaries, enabling readers to quickly grasp the key points without reading the full text. This is particularly useful in keeping up with the rapidly changing news cycle and managing information overload.

Document summarization is another application where summarization methods play a crucial role. For instance, in legal and medical fields, summarizing lengthy documents or research papers helps professionals quickly identify relevant information. Automated summarization tools assist in extracting key findings, recommendations, and conclusions, streamlining the review process.

In addition to these applications, text summarization techniques are increasingly being integrated into search engines and digital assistants to provide users with concise answers and summaries. By leveraging summarization methods, these systems can deliver more relevant information, improving the efficiency of information retrieval and user satisfaction.

Overall, text summarization methods, whether extractive or abstractive, play a pivotal role in managing and understanding large volumes of text. By continuously advancing these methods and integrating them into practical applications, we can enhance our ability to process and interpret information in an increasingly data-rich world.

In the realm of abstractive summarization, the advent of transformer-based models has revolutionized the field. These models, particularly those employing self-attention mechanisms, offer a significant leap in generating summaries that are both coherent and contextually relevant. Transformer models like BERT and GPT have shown remarkable performance improvements due to their ability to capture complex dependencies within the text and generate summaries that are more human-like in their phrasing.

BERT, or Bidirectional Encoder Representations from Transformers, functions by creating deep contextual embeddings for each word in a sentence, taking into account both preceding and following words. This bidirectional approach allows BERT to understand the context of words more effectively than traditional unidirectional models. When applied to summarization tasks, BERT-based methods can better capture the semantic nuances of the text, leading to more accurate and contextually appropriate summaries. For instance, BERTSUM, an adaptation of BERT for extractive summarization, has been shown to outperform previous methods by leveraging these deep contextual embeddings to identify the most relevant sentences in a document.

GPT, or Generative Pre-trained Transformer, takes a different approach. Unlike BERT, GPT generates text in a unidirectional manner, predicting the next word in a sequence based on previous words. This autoregressive model excels in generating coherent and fluent text, making it particularly suited for abstractive summarization. The ability of GPT to generate summaries that are not merely extracts but are phrased in natural language allows for the creation of summaries that better capture the essence of the original text in a more readable form.

An important aspect of evaluating text summarization systems is the use of metrics that assess the quality and effectiveness of the summaries produced. Traditional evaluation metrics for extractive summarization include ROUGE (Recall-Oriented Understudy for Gisting Evaluation), which measures the overlap between the generated summaries and reference summaries. ROUGE scores, such as ROUGE-N, ROUGE-L, and ROUGE-W, evaluate different aspects of the summary's quality, including n-gram overlap, longest common subsequence, and weighted overlap, respectively. While ROUGE is widely used due to its simplicity and effectiveness, it has limitations, particularly in capturing the semantic accuracy and coherence of abstractive summaries.

To address these limitations, recent advancements have introduced more sophisticated evaluation metrics. For example, BLEU (Bilingual Evaluation Understudy) is commonly used in machine translation but has also been adapted for summarization tasks. BLEU evaluates the precision of n-grams in the generated summary relative to the reference summaries. Additionally, newer metrics such as BERTScore leverage the contextual embeddings provided by models like BERT to assess the semantic similarity between the generated summary and reference summaries, providing a more nuanced evaluation of the summary's quality.

Beyond these metrics, human evaluation remains crucial for assessing the effectiveness of summarization systems. Human judges can evaluate summaries based on criteria such as informativeness, coherence, and fluency, which may not be fully captured by automated metrics. Human evaluations often involve comparative assessments, where judges compare summaries from different systems and provide feedback on their relative quality.

In practical applications, text summarization is employed in a variety of domains. In news aggregation, summarization algorithms are used to condense news articles into brief summaries that provide readers with the essential information without requiring them to read lengthy articles. This application is particularly valuable in keeping readers informed in a time-efficient manner, especially when dealing with high volumes of news content.

Document summarization, another significant application, involves generating concise summaries of longer documents, such as research papers, legal documents, or reports. This application aids professionals by providing them with quick insights into the content of documents, helping them to efficiently locate and extract relevant information.

Additionally, text summarization plays a critical role in enhancing information retrieval systems. By generating summaries of documents or search results, summarization techniques can improve the user experience by providing concise previews of content, allowing users to quickly assess the relevance of search results.

As summarization technologies continue to evolve, the integration of advanced machine learning models and evaluation techniques promises to further enhance the quality and applicability of text summarization systems. The continued research and development in this area are expected to lead to more accurate, contextually aware, and human-like summaries, driving innovation and efficiency across various applications and industries.

In addition to the conventional metrics like ROUGE and BLEU, which focus on overlap and n-gram precision, newer evaluation methods are emerging to provide a more nuanced understanding of summarization quality. For instance, METEOR (Metric for Evaluation of Translation with Explicit ORdering) extends the capabilities of BLEU by incorporating synonymy and stemming, which enables a more flexible comparison of generated summaries with reference summaries. This flexibility is crucial for abstractive summarization where generated text may not match reference phrases exactly but conveys similar meanings.

Furthermore, human evaluation remains a gold standard in assessing the quality of summaries. Despite the progress in automatic metrics, human judgment is essential to evaluate aspects such as coherence, readability, and informativeness—dimensions that automated metrics often overlook. In practice, human evaluators rate summaries based on predefined criteria such as overall quality, relevance to the input text, and clarity. This approach provides insights that metrics alone may not capture, though it is more resource-intensive and less scalable.

The practical applications of text summarization are extensive and diverse. In news aggregation, summarization systems are employed to distill information from a plethora of sources, providing readers with concise and relevant news updates. This task is particularly challenging given the dynamic nature of news and the need for summaries to be not only accurate but also timely. Techniques such as extractive summarization are frequently used in this domain to ensure that key facts are retained while removing redundant or less relevant content.

Document summarization, on the other hand, involves condensing longer documents, such as academic papers or legal contracts, into more manageable summaries. Here, the focus is on preserving essential details and ensuring that the summary accurately reflects the document's content. Abstractive methods are particularly useful in this context as they allow for more flexibility in how information is presented, potentially making complex or technical content more accessible.

In the realm of customer service, summarization technologies are used to aggregate customer interactions and feedback. By summarizing customer queries and complaints, organizations can identify common issues and trends, enabling more efficient and targeted responses. This application benefits from both extractive and abstractive techniques, as it requires capturing specific details as well as generating insights from broader patterns in the data.

Another significant area where summarization techniques are making an impact is in academic research. Researchers often deal with vast amounts of literature and data, and summarization tools help in sifting through this information to highlight relevant findings and trends. Automated summarization systems can assist researchers by providing concise summaries of research papers, facilitating quicker review of literature and more informed decision-making.

In recent years, there has been a growing interest in integrating summarization methods with other NLP technologies, such as named entity recognition and topic modeling. For instance, by combining summarization with named entity recognition, systems can produce summaries that not only convey the main ideas but also highlight key entities and their relationships. This integration enhances the utility of summaries by providing additional context and facilitating deeper insights.

As summarization technologies continue to evolve, there are several key challenges that need to be addressed. One of the primary challenges is handling the diversity of text types and domains. Summarization methods that perform well on news articles may not necessarily be effective for legal documents or scientific papers due to differences in structure and content. Therefore, developing domain-specific summarization models and techniques remains an ongoing area of research.

Another challenge is the generation of summaries that are both informative and concise without introducing bias or distortion. Ensuring that summaries faithfully represent the original content while maintaining brevity and clarity is a delicate balance that requires continuous refinement of algorithms and evaluation methods.

Overall, the advancements in text summarization methods

reflect the dynamic nature of the field and its growing importance across various applications. By leveraging both extractive and abstractive techniques, and by continuously improving evaluation metrics, researchers and practitioners are making strides toward creating more effective and reliable summarization systems. The ongoing development and application of these methods promise to enhance information accessibility and comprehension in an increasingly information-rich world.

CHAPTER 28: NAMED ENTITY RECOGNITION (NER) APPLICATIONS

Named Entity Recognition (NER) is a crucial task in natural language processing (NLP) that focuses on identifying and classifying named entities within text. Named entities are typically proper nouns representing specific people, organizations, locations, dates, and other categories of interest. The accuracy and efficiency of NER are pivotal in various applications, from information extraction to knowledge graph construction. To understand the role and functionality of NER, it is essential to explore the different methodologies used and their practical implementations.

Traditionally, NER systems were developed using rule-based approaches. These methods rely on handcrafted rules and patterns to identify named entities. For instance, regular expressions and dictionaries of names and locations are used to match patterns in the text. Although rule-based systems can achieve high precision when the rules are well-crafted and the domain is well-defined, they often struggle with flexibility and adaptability. The primary drawback is their inability to handle the variability in language and the emergence of new names and entities without extensive manual updates.

To address the limitations of rule-based methods, statistical approaches were introduced. These methods leverage machine learning algorithms to automatically learn patterns from annotated data. One of the earliest statistical approaches involved Conditional Random Fields (CRFs), which model the sequence of tokens in a text and assign labels to each token based on its context. CRFs are particularly effective for handling the sequential nature of text and capturing dependencies between tokens. However, statistical methods still face challenges in understanding complex linguistic features and relationships between entities.

In recent years, neural network-based methods have significantly advanced NER capabilities. These approaches utilize deep learning techniques to model complex relationships and representations of text. Neural networks, particularly recurrent neural networks (RNNs) and their variants such as Long Short-Term Memory (LSTM) networks, have shown impressive performance in named entity recognition tasks. These models are trained on large corpora of annotated text, learning to identify entities by capturing contextual information and dependencies across the entire sequence.

The introduction of Transformer models has further revolutionized NER. Transformers, such as BERT (Bidirectional Encoder Representations from Transformers) and its variants, have demonstrated exceptional performance in various NLP tasks, including NER. Unlike traditional models, Transformers can capture bidirectional context, which allows for a more nuanced understanding of entities in different contexts. For example, BERT can differentiate between "Washington" as a location and "Washington" as a person's name based on the surrounding text. This capability is particularly valuable in disambiguating entities and improving recognition accuracy.

NER applications are diverse and span multiple domains. In information extraction, NER plays a vital role in identifying and categorizing key entities from unstructured text. This process involves extracting relevant information from documents, such as identifying all mentions of companies, people, or locations in news articles or scientific papers. Accurate NER enhances the efficiency of information retrieval systems by enabling more precise querying and indexing based on entity types.

In knowledge graph construction, NER contributes to building comprehensive and structured representations of knowledge. Knowledge graphs are networks of entities and their relationships, and NER provides the foundational data required to populate these graphs. For instance, in a knowledge graph about historical events, NER can identify and categorize entities such as historical figures, events, and locations. This structured representation allows for advanced querying and reasoning over the relationships between entities, facilitating more intelligent information retrieval and decision-making.

NER is also instrumental in enhancing search engines and recommendation systems. By accurately identifying entities within user queries and documents, search engines can deliver more relevant results. For example, when a user searches for "Apple," an NER system can distinguish between the technology company and the fruit based on the query context. Similarly, in recommendation systems, NER helps in personalizing content by recognizing user interests and preferences related to specific entities, such as brands, products, or celebrities.

Furthermore, NER is valuable in social media analysis, where it helps in monitoring and analyzing mentions of entities across various platforms. By identifying and categorizing mentions of brands, public figures, or events, businesses and organizations can gain insights into public sentiment, track brand reputation, and identify emerging trends. This application of NER supports targeted marketing strategies and informed decision-making by providing actionable intelligence from social media data.

In summary, Named Entity Recognition is a foundational task in NLP with a wide range of applications. From rule-based and statistical methods to advanced neural network-based approaches, NER has evolved to handle the complexities of modern text and deliver high-quality results. Its applications in information extraction, knowledge graph construction, search engines, and social media analysis underscore its significance in transforming unstructured text into actionable insights. The continued advancements in NER technologies promise further improvements in accuracy, adaptability, and applicability across diverse domains.

Named Entity Recognition (NER) finds extensive application across various domains, where its ability to accurately identify and classify named entities enhances information retrieval and processing tasks. One of the primary applications of NER is in information extraction. In this context, NER is used to extract structured information from unstructured text, which is particularly valuable in fields like news aggregation and document summarization. For example, in news articles, NER can be employed to identify entities such as people, organizations, and locations, which can then be used to organize and categorize news content. This extraction process facilitates the generation of summaries and the creation of databases that support more efficient information retrieval and analysis.

In the domain of search engines, NER contributes significantly by improving the relevance and precision of search results. By identifying key entities within search queries and documents, NER systems can enhance search algorithms' understanding of user intent and context. For instance, if a user searches for "Apple," a well-trained NER system can distinguish whether the query pertains to the technology company or the fruit, based on the surrounding context. This capability not only refines search results but also aids in personalizing search experiences by aligning results with users' specific interests and needs.

Another significant application of NER is in the creation and enrichment of knowledge graphs. Knowledge graphs are structured representations of information where entities and their relationships are captured and organized in a graph format. NER plays a crucial role in populating these graphs by identifying and linking entities from diverse data sources. For example, in a medical knowledge graph, NER can be used to identify diseases, drugs, and patient names from clinical records and research papers. This automated process helps build comprehensive and up-to-date knowledge bases that can be leveraged for various applications, including research, clinical decision support, and data analysis.

In the realm of social media monitoring, NER is employed to track and analyze public sentiment and trends. By extracting entities from social media posts, companies and researchers can gain insights into public opinions, emerging trends, and potential issues. For instance, a brand might use NER to monitor mentions of its products or services across social media platforms, identifying not just the brand names but also related entities such as competitors and key influencers. This information can be invaluable for managing brand reputation, understanding market dynamics, and formulating marketing strategies.

NER also finds applications in financial analysis and fraud detection. In the financial sector, accurate identification of entities such as companies, stock symbols, and financial terms is crucial for analyzing market trends, monitoring financial news, and detecting anomalies. For example, NER can be used to identify company names and their associated financial metrics in earnings reports, aiding analysts in extracting relevant information and making informed decisions. Additionally, in fraud detection, NER can help identify unusual patterns or entities involved in fraudulent activities, enhancing the ability to detect and prevent financial crimes.

The healthcare industry benefits from NER through the extraction of critical information from medical texts, such as electronic health records (EHRs) and research publications. By identifying entities such as patient names, medical conditions, and treatment protocols, NER facilitates the organization and analysis of medical data. This capability supports various tasks, including patient record management, clinical research, and the development of decision support systems.

Despite its advancements, NER continues to face challenges that impact its performance and applicability. Variability in entity names, context-dependent meanings, and the emergence of new entities pose ongoing difficulties. To address these challenges, continuous improvements in NER techniques are necessary, including the integration of more sophisticated models, such as those based on deep learning and transfer learning. The development of domain-specific models and the incorporation of user feedback are also crucial for enhancing NER systems' adaptability and accuracy.

The future of NER holds promise with the ongoing evolution of NLP technologies. Advances in pre-trained language models, such as BERT and GPT, offer new opportunities for improving entity recognition across diverse contexts and languages. As these models become more sophisticated, they are expected to drive further innovations in NER applications, making them more robust, context-aware, and capable of handling complex linguistic and semantic challenges.

In summary, Named Entity Recognition is a fundamental component of modern NLP systems, with wide-ranging applications that impact information extraction, search engine performance, knowledge graph construction, social media monitoring, financial analysis, and healthcare. As NER continues to evolve, its ability to accurately and efficiently identify and classify named entities will play a critical role in shaping the future of information processing and analysis across various domains.

In addition to information extraction, knowledge graph

creation, and social media monitoring, Named Entity Recognition (NER) has important applications in several other domains, including customer service, financial analysis, and legal document processing. Each of these areas benefits from the precise identification and categorization of named entities to enhance data usability and operational efficiency.

In customer service, NER is employed to improve the effectiveness of automated systems such as chatbots and virtual assistants. By recognizing and categorizing entities like customer names, product types, and service issues, these systems can provide more accurate and contextually relevant responses. For instance, if a customer inquires about "returning an iPhone," a well-tuned NER system can identify "iPhone" as a product and understand the context of a return process, enabling the chatbot to offer specific guidance on the return policy and procedures related to the iPhone.

In financial analysis, NER plays a critical role in processing and analyzing vast amounts of financial documents and reports. By extracting entities such as company names, stock tickers, financial terms, and monetary values, NER systems facilitate more efficient data analysis and reporting. For example, in the context of earnings reports, NER can identify key financial figures and company names, which can then be used to generate summaries or feed into financial models for predicting market trends and assessing investment opportunities.

The legal field also benefits significantly from NER, particularly in the processing of legal documents and case law. Legal professionals often deal with large volumes of text, including contracts, legal briefs, and court rulings. NER can automate the extraction of relevant entities such as party names, legal terms, and case citations, which simplifies document review and enhances legal research. For instance, in contract analysis, NER can help identify and categorize entities such as the parties involved, contract terms, and obligations, streamlining the process of contract review and compliance checking.

Despite its many advantages, NER is not without challenges. One significant challenge is handling ambiguities and context-dependent entities. Named entities can have multiple interpretations depending on their context. For example, the term "Washington" could refer to the U.S. state, the U.S. capital, or a historical figure, depending on the text's context. To address such ambiguities, NER systems must leverage advanced contextual understanding and disambiguation techniques. Modern neural network-based approaches, such as those using transformers, offer promising solutions by incorporating contextual information from surrounding text to better resolve ambiguities.

Another challenge is dealing with the diversity and variability of entity names, especially in multilingual or cross-cultural contexts. Names and entities can vary significantly across languages and cultures, requiring NER systems to be adaptable and capable of handling diverse naming conventions and entity types. Multilingual NER systems are designed to address this challenge by incorporating language-specific models and cross-lingual transfer learning techniques to improve entity recognition across different languages.

Furthermore, the evolving nature of entities and terminology presents an ongoing challenge. Entities such as brand names, geographic locations, and even people's names can change over time, and new entities can emerge. To stay relevant and effective, NER systems must be continuously updated and trained on current data to reflect these changes. Incorporating mechanisms for dynamic updating and retraining can help maintain the accuracy and relevancy of NER systems over time.

In summary, Named Entity Recognition is a powerful tool with a wide range of applications across various domains, from enhancing customer service and financial analysis to streamlining legal document processing. While challenges such as context ambiguity, multilingual variability, and evolving entities must be addressed, ongoing advancements in NER technologies, particularly those leveraging neural network-based approaches, continue to enhance the effectiveness and versatility of entity recognition systems. As these technologies evolve, their ability to accurately and efficiently handle complex and diverse text data will only improve, further expanding their applicability and impact across different fields.

CHAPTER 29: HANDLING AMBIGUITY AND POLYSEMY

Ambiguity and polysemy represent fundamental challenges in natural language processing, arising from the inherent complexity of human language. Ambiguity occurs when a word or phrase has multiple meanings, while polysemy involves a single word having multiple related meanings. Addressing these challenges requires sophisticated techniques to disambiguate words and phrases and accurately interpret their intended meanings within different contexts.

The first line of defense against ambiguity and polysemy is context-based disambiguation. Context-based methods leverage surrounding text to discern the intended meaning of an ambiguous term. This approach hinges on understanding the broader linguistic environment in which a word is used. For instance, the word "bank" could refer to a financial institution or the side of a river, depending on the context in which it appears. By examining the words and sentences surrounding "bank," a language model can infer whether the text is discussing financial transactions or geographical features.

Contextual disambiguation often employs machine learning algorithms, particularly those based on neural network architectures. Recurrent Neural Networks (RNNs) and their more advanced variant, Long Short-Term Memory (LSTM) networks, have been widely used to capture contextual dependencies and improve disambiguation accuracy. These models process sequences of text and use learned representations to predict the most likely meaning of a word based on its surrounding context. For example, an LSTM network trained on a large corpus of text can learn to associate the word "bank" with financial terms like "account" or "loan" when discussing financial topics, while associating it with words like "river" or "fishing" in environmental contexts.

Recent advancements in NLP have introduced transformer-based models, such as BERT and GPT, which have further enhanced the ability to handle ambiguity and polysemy. These models use self-attention mechanisms to weigh the importance of different words in a sentence, allowing them to capture more nuanced relationships and context-dependent meanings. BERT, for example, employs bidirectional context, meaning it considers both the preceding and following words in a sentence to determine the meaning of an ambiguous term. This approach enables a more comprehensive understanding of context and improves the model's ability to disambiguate polysemous words effectively.

Semantic analysis complements context-based methods by focusing on the deeper meanings of words and their relationships. Techniques such as word embeddings, which represent words as dense vectors in a high-dimensional space, facilitate semantic analysis by capturing word meanings based on their usage across large text corpora. Word embeddings like Word2Vec and GloVe encode semantic similarities between words, enabling models to recognize related meanings and contextually appropriate interpretations. For instance, if a word embedding model learns that "bank" is closely related to terms like "finance" and "river," it can use this knowledge to resolve ambiguity by selecting the meaning most consistent with the surrounding semantic context.

Another important aspect of semantic analysis involves leveraging knowledge bases and ontologies, which provide structured information about concepts and their interrelationships. Knowledge bases like WordNet and ConceptNet offer valuable resources for disambiguating words by providing detailed semantic information and hierarchical relationships between concepts. By integrating these resources into NLP systems, models can gain access to rich semantic knowledge that aids in resolving ambiguities and understanding polysemous terms.

In addition to context-based methods and semantic analysis, addressing ambiguity and polysemy often involves incorporating domain-specific knowledge. Different domains may have specialized meanings for the same words or phrases, necessitating tailored approaches for disambiguation. For instance, medical texts may use terms like "stroke" with specific medical connotations, while legal documents may use the same term in a legal context. Domain-specific language models trained on specialized corpora can improve the accuracy of disambiguation by incorporating relevant knowledge and context.

Despite these advances, handling ambiguity and polysemy remains a complex challenge. Ambiguity can arise from various sources, including syntactic structure, word sense variations, and cultural differences. Moreover, polysemous words often exhibit fine-grained distinctions in meaning that may not always be captured by existing models. To address these challenges, ongoing research focuses on developing more sophisticated techniques and models that can better understand and interpret the subtleties of human language. For example, approaches such as few-shot learning and transfer learning are being explored to enhance the ability of models to generalize across different contexts and domains, thereby improving their performance in handling ambiguous and polysemous terms.

Ultimately, the goal is to develop NLP systems that can accurately and reliably interpret language, even in the presence of ambiguity and polysemy. By combining context-based methods, semantic analysis, domain-specific knowledge, and advanced modeling techniques, researchers and practitioners can continue to advance the field and address these fundamental challenges in natural language understanding.

When tackling ambiguity and polysemy, semantic analysis offers another crucial layer of understanding. Semantic analysis focuses on the meaning and relationships between words, phrases, and sentences to address the deeper linguistic nuances that context alone may not fully resolve. This method involves creating models that understand not just the surface-level text but the underlying concepts and relationships between them. By employing semantic representations, we can enhance our ability to discern the intended meaning of ambiguous terms based on their conceptual associations.

One effective approach within semantic analysis is the use of word embeddings. Word embeddings represent words as vectors in a continuous vector space, capturing their meanings based on their usage in large corpora. These embeddings are generated using models such as Word2Vec, GloVe, and FastText, which map words with similar meanings close to each other in the vector space. For instance, synonyms like "bank" (as a financial institution) and "financial institution" will have similar embeddings, making it easier to discern their shared meanings. This semantic proximity allows models to infer meanings based on the closeness of word vectors.

Beyond word embeddings, semantic role labeling (SRL) provides another method to handle polysemy by identifying the roles that different words play in a sentence. SRL parses sentences to determine who is doing what to whom, which helps in understanding the context in which ambiguous words are used. For example, in the sentence "She went to the bank to withdraw money," SRL can identify "bank" as the location where the action of withdrawing occurs, thereby distinguishing it from the financial institution sense.

Deep semantic understanding can also be augmented by using knowledge graphs, which represent knowledge in a structured form where entities and their relationships are explicitly defined. Knowledge graphs like WordNet, ConceptNet, or custom-built domain-specific graphs provide a rich resource for disambiguation. They link words to their meanings, synonyms, antonyms, and related concepts. For instance, if a system encounters the word "apple" in different contexts, it can refer to a knowledge graph to distinguish between the fruit and the tech company based on the surrounding text and known relationships.

Furthermore, another significant challenge in disambiguation arises when dealing with multilingual contexts. Words that are polysemous in one language may have different polysemous structures in another, creating additional complexity for NLP systems operating across multiple languages. To address this, cross-lingual embeddings and multilingual models like mBERT (Multilingual BERT) have been developed. These models are trained on data from various languages and are capable of capturing semantic similarities and differences across languages. By aligning word representations in a shared space, these models facilitate the resolution of ambiguity in a multilingual setting by leveraging parallel corpora and linguistic resources.

In addition to these methods, machine learning techniques for disambiguation often incorporate ensemble approaches that combine multiple models or methods. For instance, a hybrid model might use both context-based and semantic-based methods to improve accuracy. By integrating outputs from different models, these approaches can provide a more robust solution to the challenge of polysemy, capturing a wider range of contextual and semantic nuances.

Evaluation of disambiguation systems typically involves using benchmark datasets and evaluation metrics tailored to measure accuracy in handling ambiguity and polysemy. Common metrics include precision, recall, and F1 score, which assess how well the system can correctly identify and classify the intended meanings of ambiguous words. Evaluating systems on diverse datasets, including those with various levels of ambiguity and polysemy, helps ensure their robustness and generalizability.

Despite these advances, challenges remain in fully resolving ambiguity and polysemy. Variations in context, the complexity of natural language, and the evolving nature of word meanings all contribute to the difficulty of achieving perfect disambiguation. Ongoing research aims to improve disambiguation accuracy by developing more sophisticated models, incorporating richer contextual information, and refining semantic understanding.

The pursuit of more effective disambiguation techniques is integral to advancing NLP capabilities. By continuously enhancing context-based and semantic methods, and addressing the nuances of multilingual contexts, we can develop systems that more accurately interpret and generate human language, ultimately contributing to more intelligent and responsive language technologies.

Addressing ambiguity and polysemy in multilingual contexts requires specialized techniques tailored to the nuances of different languages. Translating polysemous words between languages often introduces additional layers of complexity. Words that are polysemous in one language may have multiple distinct equivalents in another, each representing a different sense of the word. To manage this, we must integrate cross-lingual models that leverage knowledge across languages. These models use parallel corpora, where sentences are aligned across languages, to learn correspondences between polysemous terms and their meanings in various languages. Techniques such as multilingual embeddings and cross-lingual transfer learning help align the semantic spaces of different languages, enabling better handling of ambiguity across linguistic boundaries.

Additionally, machine translation systems, which are essential for handling polysemy in a multilingual context, incorporate context-aware mechanisms to disambiguate terms during translation. Contextual embeddings, such as those produced by BERT (Bidirectional Encoder Representations from Transformers) or its successors, are pivotal in this regard. These embeddings provide a dynamic representation of words based on their surrounding context, allowing translation models to generate more accurate translations by considering the broader context in which a polysemous word appears. For example, the term "bark" in English might be translated into different words in other languages depending on whether it refers to the sound a dog makes or the outer layer of a tree. Contextual embeddings help the model disambiguate these meanings based on the sentence's context.

An important aspect of managing ambiguity is the continuous evolution of language. Language is dynamic, with new words, phrases, and meanings emerging regularly. This poses a challenge for static models that may not be updated frequently enough to account for new usages and meanings. To address this, models need to be retrained or fine-tuned with up-to-date data, incorporating recent changes and trends in language usage. Techniques such as online learning or incremental learning can help models adapt to new linguistic patterns and maintain relevance over time.

Another key approach involves leveraging human feedback and crowdsourcing to refine models and address ambiguities. Human annotators can provide valuable insights into the meanings of ambiguous terms, especially in nuanced or context-specific cases that automated systems may struggle with. Crowdsourcing platforms, where multiple annotators provide input on the meaning of ambiguous terms, can enhance the accuracy of disambiguation efforts and provide a more comprehensive understanding of polysemy.

In practical applications, handling ambiguity and polysemy is crucial for various NLP tasks. In information retrieval systems, for example, accurately interpreting user queries that contain polysemous words is essential for retrieving relevant documents. Improved disambiguation techniques lead to better search results and user satisfaction. Similarly, in sentiment analysis, correctly understanding the sentiment associated with polysemous terms ensures accurate sentiment classification, which is important for analyzing customer feedback or social media content.

In summary, effectively addressing ambiguity and polysemy in NLP requires a multifaceted approach that combines context-based methods, semantic analysis, and multilingual considerations. By integrating advanced techniques such as contextual embeddings, cross-lingual models, and human feedback, we can enhance the accuracy of language models and improve their ability to handle the complexities of polysemous terms. As language continues to evolve and diversify, ongoing research and adaptation will be essential in maintaining the effectiveness of NLP systems in disambiguating and understanding the nuanced meanings of words and phrases.

CHAPTER 30: NLP FOR SPEECH PROCESSING

The integration of natural language processing (NLP) with speech processing has revolutionized how we interact with technology through spoken language. This synthesis of fields encompasses several key areas: speech recognition, speech synthesis, and speaker identification. Each of these domains presents unique challenges and has seen significant advancements through the application of NLP techniques.

In speech recognition, the goal is to convert spoken language into written text. This process involves several stages, beginning with acoustic modeling, which transforms audio signals into phonetic units. Modern speech recognition systems utilize deep learning models, particularly recurrent neural networks (RNNs) and their variants, such as long short-term memory (LSTM) networks and transformers. These models are adept at capturing temporal dependencies in speech, which is crucial for understanding spoken language. Acoustic models are trained on vast amounts of audio data, learning to recognize patterns associated with different phonemes, words, and phrases.

Following acoustic modeling, the process incorporates language modeling, which leverages NLP techniques to predict and correct the transcriptions based on linguistic patterns. Language models, such as those based on n-grams or neural network architectures like BERT and GPT, enhance the accuracy of speech recognition systems by providing context-based predictions. For instance, context-aware language models help resolve ambiguities by considering the broader context in which words are spoken, improving transcription accuracy even in noisy environments or with accents and dialects.

Speech synthesis, or text-to-speech (TTS), involves generating spoken language from text. The goal is to produce natural and intelligible speech that closely resembles human speech patterns. Advanced TTS systems use concatenative synthesis or parametric synthesis techniques. Concatenative synthesis involves stringing together pre-recorded units of speech, while parametric synthesis generates speech waveforms based on acoustic models and statistical parameters. Recent advancements have been driven by neural network-based methods, such as WaveNet and Tacotron, which produce more natural-sounding and expressive speech by modeling the complex relationships between text and speech waveforms. These systems utilize end-to-end learning approaches that map text directly to speech, enhancing the quality and fluidity of synthetic voices.

Speaker identification and verification are critical components of speech processing, focusing on recognizing and confirming the identity of individuals based on their voice characteristics. Speaker identification involves determining who is speaking from a given set of known speakers, while speaker verification confirms whether a speaker matches a claimed identity. These tasks rely on extracting speaker-specific features from audio signals, such as pitch, tone, and speaking style. Techniques such as speaker embeddings, which represent unique vocal traits in a high-dimensional space, have proven effective in distinguishing between speakers. Machine learning models, particularly deep neural networks, are employed to train these embeddings, enabling robust and accurate speaker recognition even in varied acoustic conditions.

Despite significant progress in these areas, several challenges remain in speech processing. One major challenge is handling diverse accents, dialects, and speech impairments, which can significantly impact the performance of speech recognition and synthesis systems. To address this, speech processing models must be trained on diverse datasets that include a wide range of accents and speech patterns. Moreover, ongoing research focuses on developing more adaptive systems that can fine-tune themselves based on individual speaker characteristics and acoustic environments.

Another challenge is managing the ambiguity inherent in spoken language. Speech recognition systems often struggle with homophones and context-dependent meanings, where words sound the same but have different meanings. NLP techniques, such as context-aware language models and disambiguation algorithms, are crucial in resolving these ambiguities and improving the accuracy of transcriptions.

In addition to technical challenges, ethical and privacy concerns also play a significant role in the development and deployment of speech processing technologies. The collection and processing of voice data raise questions about consent, data security, and potential misuse. Ensuring transparency, obtaining informed consent, and implementing robust data protection measures are essential for addressing these concerns and building trust with users.

As speech processing technologies continue to evolve, their applications expand into various domains, including voice assistants, automated transcription services, and customer service automation. Voice assistants, such as Siri and Alexa, integrate speech recognition and synthesis to provide conversational interfaces that facilitate user interactions with technology. Automated transcription services leverage speech recognition to convert spoken content into written form, supporting a wide range of use cases from legal documentation to media content creation. Customer service automation employs speech processing to handle routine queries and provide personalized responses, improving efficiency and user satisfaction.

In conclusion, the integration of NLP with speech processing encompasses a range of technologies and techniques that transform how we interact with spoken language. Advances in speech recognition, synthesis, and speaker identification continue to drive innovation, making interactions with technology more natural and intuitive. Addressing challenges related to diversity, ambiguity, and ethical considerations is crucial for advancing these technologies and ensuring their responsible and effective application.

As we delve deeper into the realm of speech processing, it is essential to explore the intricacies of integrating NLP techniques with the tasks of speech recognition, synthesis, and speaker identification. Each of these areas presents unique challenges and opportunities for innovation.

In speech recognition, after the initial acoustic and language modeling stages, the process involves incorporating advanced techniques to handle diverse linguistic and acoustic variations. One significant challenge is the variability in speech patterns, including accents, dialects, and speaking rates. To address these issues, modern speech recognition systems employ large-scale, diverse training datasets and sophisticated algorithms designed to generalize across different speech patterns. This approach includes the use of transfer learning, where models pre-trained on vast amounts of data are fine-tuned on specific languages or dialects, enhancing the system's ability to accurately recognize and transcribe speech from various speakers.

Moreover, speech recognition systems must be robust to noisy environments and background sounds. Noise robustness is achieved through techniques such as spectral subtraction, noise masking, and the integration of advanced signal processing algorithms. Recent advancements in deep learning have also introduced end-to-end models that directly map audio features to text, bypassing traditional intermediate stages and improving the system's ability to handle real-world conditions.

Speech synthesis, or text-to-speech (TTS), has evolved significantly with the advent of neural network-based methods. Neural TTS systems, such as those using WaveNet and Tacotron architectures, generate speech with unprecedented naturalness and expressiveness. WaveNet, for instance, models raw audio waveforms using deep generative networks, resulting in high-quality, lifelike speech. Tacotron, on the other hand, utilizes sequence-to-sequence models to convert text into spectrograms, which are then used to generate audio waveforms. These advancements have enabled TTS systems to produce speech that is not only intelligible but also carries the nuances of natural human expression, such as intonation, stress, and emotion.

Furthermore, TTS systems now incorporate prosody modeling to enhance the naturalness of generated speech. Prosody refers to the rhythm, stress, and intonation patterns in spoken language. Accurate prosody modeling involves predicting these patterns from text and applying them to the synthesized speech, resulting in more natural-sounding outputs. Techniques such as attention mechanisms and contextual embeddings play a crucial role in improving the alignment between text and speech, ensuring that the generated speech closely mirrors human-like prosody.

In the domain of speaker identification and verification, the focus shifts to distinguishing and authenticating speakers based on their vocal characteristics. Speaker identification involves determining the identity of a speaker from a known set of individuals, while speaker verification confirms whether a speaker is indeed who they claim to be. Both tasks rely on extracting distinctive features from speech signals, such as pitch, timbre, and formant frequencies.

Advancements in speaker recognition have been driven

by the application of deep learning techniques, including convolutional neural networks (CNNs) and recurrent neural networks (RNNs). These models excel in learning and representing the complex patterns present in speaker-specific features. For instance, embedding-based approaches, where speaker embeddings are learned and compared, have shown remarkable performance in identifying and verifying speakers. These embeddings capture the unique vocal traits of each individual, enabling accurate and reliable speaker recognition even in challenging conditions.

The integration of NLP with speech processing extends to real-world applications, such as voice assistants and transcription services. Voice assistants, like Siri, Alexa, and Google Assistant, leverage speech recognition to understand user queries and NLP to interpret and respond to them. These systems combine speech-to-text conversion with sophisticated language understanding algorithms to perform tasks such as answering questions, setting reminders, and controlling smart devices. Continuous improvements in both speech recognition accuracy and language understanding have significantly enhanced the user experience, making voice assistants more intuitive and responsive.

Transcription services benefit from advancements in speech recognition and synthesis to provide accurate and efficient conversion of spoken content into text. This technology is used in various contexts, including meeting transcription, legal documentation, and content generation. High-quality transcription services rely on accurate speech recognition algorithms and robust language models to handle diverse vocabulary and terminologies, ensuring that the transcriptions are precise and contextually relevant.

As we conclude this exploration of NLP in speech processing, it is clear that the integration of these technologies has transformed how we interact with spoken language. From improving the accuracy of speech recognition systems to advancing the naturalness of speech synthesis and enhancing speaker identification, the advancements in NLP and speech processing continue to drive innovation and improve the accessibility and functionality of voice-based technologies.

In the domain of speaker identification, the integration of NLP techniques with speech processing also presents intriguing challenges and advancements. Speaker identification involves determining the identity of a speaker based on their vocal characteristics. This task is distinct from speaker verification, which involves confirming a speaker's claimed identity. Speaker identification can be crucial in applications ranging from security systems to personalized user experiences.

A core component of speaker identification is feature extraction, where distinctive characteristics of a speaker's voice, such as pitch, accent, and speech rate, are analyzed. Techniques such as Mel-frequency cepstral coefficients (MFCCs) and deep neural network-based embeddings are commonly used to extract these features. MFCCs capture the short-term power spectrum of speech and are effective in representing phonetic content, while embeddings from deep learning models can encapsulate more complex, high-level features of a speaker's voice.

Recent advancements in this area leverage deep learning approaches to improve the accuracy and robustness of speaker identification systems. Convolutional Neural Networks (CNNs) and Recurrent Neural Networks (RNNs) have been adapted to process audio signals, enhancing the model's ability to handle variabilities such as background noise, speaker age, and emotional state. For example, CNNs are used to extract hierarchical patterns from spectrograms, while RNNs capture temporal dependencies in speech, which are crucial for modeling the dynamic aspects of a speaker's voice.

In addition to feature extraction, speaker identification systems often employ speaker models or profiles, which are created by analyzing a speaker's voice during a training phase. These profiles are used to compare against incoming speech to make identification decisions. Advanced techniques include the use of probabilistic models, such as Gaussian Mixture Models (GMMs) and Hidden Markov Models (HMMs), as well as more recent approaches using neural networks that can handle large-scale, diverse datasets to build more accurate speaker profiles.

The integration of NLP in speech processing also addresses the challenge of multilingual and cross-lingual applications. For instance, speech recognition systems that support multiple languages must handle diverse phonetic systems, grammar rules, and vocabulary. To tackle this, models are trained on multilingual corpora, and techniques such as transfer learning are used to adapt models to new languages with limited data. This involves leveraging knowledge from one language to improve performance in another, enhancing the system's ability to handle varied linguistic inputs.

Moreover, advancements in neural machine translation (NMT) have contributed to improving speech processing systems in multilingual contexts. NMT models, which translate text from one language to another, can be integrated with speech synthesis to provide coherent and contextually appropriate translations in spoken form. This is particularly relevant in applications such as real-time translation devices and multilingual virtual assistants, where seamless and natural language interaction is essential.

Applications of speech processing technologies, particularly in voice assistants and transcription services, demonstrate the practical impact of these advancements. Voice assistants, such as Amazon's Alexa or Google Assistant, utilize speech recognition to understand user commands and provide relevant responses. These systems rely on continuous improvements in NLP and speech processing to enhance their accuracy, contextual understanding, and naturalness of interaction. The ability to handle diverse accents, noisy environments, and complex queries is critical for delivering a satisfactory user experience.

Similarly, transcription services benefit from advances in speech recognition and synthesis. Automatic transcription systems convert spoken language into written text, which is invaluable in settings like meetings, conferences, and legal proceedings. The accuracy of these systems hinges on the effectiveness of speech recognition models and their ability to handle various speakers, accents, and domain-specific terminology. Additionally, real-time transcription services that support live captioning rely on low-latency processing and high accuracy to ensure that users receive timely and accurate text representations of spoken content.

In conclusion, the integration of NLP techniques with speech processing tasks is a dynamic and evolving field, addressing complex challenges and enabling a wide range of applications. From enhancing speech recognition accuracy and generating natural-sounding speech to identifying speakers and supporting multilingual interactions, advancements in this area continue to shape the future of human-computer interaction and communication technologies. The continuous development of algorithms, models, and applications underscores the importance of combining linguistic insights with sophisticated computational techniques to push the boundaries of what is possible in speech processing.

CHAPTER 31: ETHICAL CONSIDERATIONS IN NLP

The advent of natural language processing (NLP) technologies brings with it a myriad of ethical considerations that need careful examination. As NLP systems become increasingly integrated into daily life, addressing issues related to bias, privacy, and responsible use of language models is crucial. These concerns are not just theoretical but have real-world implications for individuals and society at large.

One of the primary ethical challenges in NLP is bias. Bias in NLP models can manifest in various forms, including gender, racial, and socioeconomic biases. These biases often reflect and perpetuate societal inequalities present in the training data. For instance, if a model is trained on text data that contains biased language or stereotypes, it is likely to replicate those biases in its predictions or outputs. This can result in harmful consequences, such as reinforcing stereotypes or making discriminatory decisions in automated systems.

Addressing bias involves several strategies. One approach is to carefully curate and preprocess training data to mitigate the impact of biased language. This includes identifying and removing biased terms or phrases, and ensuring that the data represents diverse and inclusive perspectives. Another strategy is to implement fairness-aware algorithms that adjust the model's behavior to reduce biased outcomes. Techniques such as adversarial debiasing, which involves training a secondary model to detect and correct for biases, can also be effective. Additionally, continuous evaluation and monitoring of NLP systems for biased behavior are essential to ensure that models perform fairly across different demographic groups.

Privacy is another critical ethical concern in NLP. NLP systems often require access to large amounts of personal data, including sensitive information such as health records, communication content, and personal preferences. The collection, storage, and processing of this data must be conducted with stringent privacy safeguards to protect users from unauthorized access and misuse. Techniques such as data anonymization and encryption are commonly used to enhance privacy. Anonymization involves removing or obfuscating personally identifiable information from data, while encryption protects data by encoding it into a format that can only be deciphered by authorized parties.

Furthermore, ensuring user consent and transparency in data collection practices is vital. Users should be informed about what data is being collected, how it will be used, and who will have access to it. This transparency builds trust and allows users to make informed decisions about their participation. Privacy policies and consent forms should be clear and accessible, and users should have the option to opt out of data collection if they choose.

The responsible use of language models also raises important ethical considerations. Language models have the potential to generate harmful or misleading content, such as fake news, hate speech, or manipulative propaganda. Ensuring that NLP technologies are used ethically involves implementing safeguards to prevent misuse and promoting transparency in how these technologies are applied. For instance, platforms that deploy language models should have clear guidelines and monitoring mechanisms to detect and address abusive or deceptive content.

Additionally, the ethical deployment of NLP technologies requires considering the broader societal impact. This includes evaluating how these technologies affect employment, social dynamics, and access to information. For example, automated content generation and moderation tools can influence public discourse and potentially displace jobs in content creation or moderation roles. Understanding and addressing these societal impacts involves engaging with stakeholders, including affected communities, to ensure that the benefits of NLP technologies are distributed fairly and that potential harms are mitigated.

In conclusion, ethical considerations in NLP are multifaceted and require a comprehensive approach to address issues related to bias, privacy, and responsible use. By implementing strategies to mitigate bias, protecting user privacy, and ensuring that NLP technologies are used ethically, we can foster a more equitable and responsible application of these powerful tools. This involves ongoing research, dialogue, and collaboration among researchers, developers, and policymakers to navigate the complex ethical landscape of NLP and its impact on society.

As we delve further into the ethical considerations surrounding natural language processing (NLP), the responsible use of language models emerges as a crucial area of concern. NLP technologies, such as language generation models and conversational agents, possess the power to influence and shape public discourse. The ethical implications of deploying such models need careful scrutiny to prevent misuse and ensure that they contribute positively to society.

One significant ethical issue in the responsible use of language models is the potential for generating misleading or harmful content. Language models, especially those based on advanced neural networks, are capable of producing highly convincing text that can be indistinguishable from human-written content.

This ability raises concerns about the dissemination of false information, misinformation, and propaganda. For instance, automated content generation tools could be exploited to create and spread fake news or deceptive marketing messages. To address these risks, it is essential to implement safeguards that limit the potential for misuse. This may include incorporating mechanisms to detect and filter out harmful content, as well as developing guidelines for ethical use and deployment of these models.

Another aspect of responsible use involves ensuring that language models do not perpetuate or amplify harmful stereotypes and biases. Despite efforts to mitigate bias during training, models can still inadvertently produce biased or prejudiced outputs if not properly monitored. For example, a language model might generate gendered or culturally insensitive responses based on the biases present in the training data. To combat this, it is important to establish robust evaluation processes that regularly assess the model's performance for fairness and inclusivity. Engaging diverse teams in the development and testing phases can also help identify and address potential issues more effectively.

Transparency and accountability are also crucial in the ethical use of NLP technologies. Users and stakeholders should be aware of how these models operate and the potential risks associated with their use. Transparency can be achieved by providing clear explanations of how models are trained, what data is used, and the limitations of their capabilities. Additionally, accountability mechanisms should be in place to address any negative consequences arising from the deployment of NLP systems. This includes establishing protocols for reporting and addressing instances where the technology causes harm or fails to meet ethical standards.

Furthermore, the ethical use of NLP technologies must consider the impact on job markets and economic structures. As NLP systems become more sophisticated, there is a growing concern about their effect on employment, particularly in fields such as content creation, customer service, and translation. While these technologies can enhance efficiency and productivity, they also have the potential to displace workers and disrupt traditional job roles. It is important to balance the benefits of automation with strategies that support workforce transition and retraining. Policies that promote education and skill development in areas complementary to NLP technologies can help mitigate adverse economic effects and support a more equitable transition.

In addition to these considerations, the ethical framework for NLP should address issues of consent and user autonomy. For instance, users interacting with conversational agents or receiving personalized content should have control over their data and the extent of their engagement with the system. Ensuring that users can opt-out or modify their interactions based on their preferences respects individual autonomy and aligns with ethical principles of user agency.

Lastly, the ethical landscape of NLP research and development requires ongoing dialogue and collaboration among researchers, practitioners, policymakers, and the public. Establishing interdisciplinary forums and partnerships can facilitate the exchange of ideas and best practices, and promote the development of standards and guidelines that reflect diverse perspectives and values. Engaging in continuous reflection and adaptation of ethical practices will help address emerging challenges and ensure that NLP technologies contribute positively to society.

In summary, the ethical considerations in NLP encompass a range of issues including bias, privacy, responsible use, transparency, accountability, economic impact, and user autonomy. Addressing these challenges requires a multi-faceted approach involving thoughtful design, rigorous evaluation, and proactive engagement with all stakeholders. By adhering to ethical principles and implementing robust strategies, we can harness the potential of NLP technologies while mitigating risks and ensuring that their benefits are distributed fairly and responsibly.

The potential impact of NLP technologies on job markets and economic structures also necessitates ethical scrutiny. As these systems become increasingly adept at performing tasks traditionally handled by humans, there is a pressing need to address the implications for employment. The automation of roles in content generation, customer service, and other sectors could lead to significant job displacement. To mitigate these effects, it is crucial to promote policies that support workforce retraining and reskilling. Investing in education and training programs can help individuals transition to new roles that leverage human skills that complement NLP technologies. Additionally, fostering discussions about the future of work and ensuring that the benefits of automation are distributed equitably can help in addressing the broader economic impacts.

Privacy considerations also play a significant role in the ethical deployment of NLP technologies. Many NLP applications rely on large volumes of data, including sensitive and personal information, to function effectively. The collection, storage, and use of this data raise important questions about user consent and data protection. Ensuring that user data is handled with the utmost care involves implementing stringent data protection measures, such as anonymization and encryption. It is also essential to establish clear policies regarding data collection and use, providing users with transparent information about how their data will be used and ensuring that they have control over their own information. By adhering to privacy principles and regulations, organizations can build trust with users and mitigate the risks associated with data handling.

Another ethical concern is the potential for NLP technologies to be used in ways that infringe on individual rights or freedoms. For example, language models used in surveillance systems could lead to invasions of privacy or be employed for unethical purposes, such as political repression. To prevent such abuses, it is vital to establish ethical guidelines and legal frameworks that govern the use of NLP technologies in sensitive areas. This includes ensuring that the deployment of these systems aligns with fundamental human rights and freedoms. Regular audits and oversight mechanisms can help ensure compliance with ethical standards and prevent misuse.

In addressing these ethical considerations, a collaborative approach involving researchers, practitioners, policymakers, and the broader public is essential. Engaging in interdisciplinary dialogue can help identify potential ethical issues early and develop solutions that balance technological advancements with societal values. Encouraging ethical practices within the research and development process involves not only adhering to established guidelines but also actively seeking to anticipate and address emerging challenges. By fostering a culture of responsibility and accountability in the development and deployment of NLP technologies, we can work towards ensuring that these tools are used in ways that benefit society while minimizing potential harms.

Ultimately, the ethical landscape of NLP is complex and continually evolving. As the field advances, ongoing reflection and adaptation of ethical practices will be necessary to address new challenges and opportunities. By prioritizing ethical considerations and implementing proactive measures, we can contribute to the responsible and equitable advancement of NLP technologies.

CHAPTER 32: NLP IN REAL-WORLD APPLICATIONS

The integration of Natural Language Processing (NLP) into real-world applications has revolutionized various industries, demonstrating its versatility and impact across diverse fields. In healthcare, NLP technologies facilitate the extraction of meaningful information from unstructured medical texts, such as electronic health records (EHRs), clinical notes, and research papers. One prominent application is the development of systems that can automatically identify and categorize medical conditions, treatments, and outcomes from text data. These systems aid in improving patient care by enabling more efficient retrieval of relevant information, enhancing diagnostic accuracy, and supporting clinical decision-making. For example, NLP algorithms can be employed to mine patient records for insights related to disease progression, treatment efficacy, and adverse drug reactions, thus contributing to personalized medicine.

A noteworthy case study in healthcare is the implementation of NLP-driven systems in oncology, where such technologies have been utilized to analyze large volumes of cancer-related literature and patient records. By extracting and synthesizing data from these sources, researchers and clinicians can gain insights into emerging trends, treatment responses, and patient outcomes. This application not only accelerates the pace of research but also enables more informed clinical decisions, ultimately leading to improved patient outcomes. Another application in healthcare involves the use of NLP for patient interaction, such as virtual health assistants that can interpret patient queries, provide information, and even schedule appointments, thereby enhancing patient engagement and accessibility.

In the financial sector, NLP plays a crucial role in sentiment analysis, which involves assessing the emotional tone of text data from sources such as financial news, social media, and earnings reports. By analyzing sentiments expressed in these texts, financial analysts can gain insights into market trends, investor sentiment, and potential risks. For instance, NLP algorithms can process news articles and social media posts to gauge public opinion on a particular stock or economic event, providing valuable information for investment decisions. Additionally, NLP techniques are employed in automated trading systems to analyze market reports and execute trades based on predefined criteria, enhancing trading efficiency and responsiveness.

A case study highlighting the impact of NLP in finance is the use of sentiment analysis for predicting stock market movements. Financial institutions have developed NLP models that analyze news headlines, financial statements, and analyst reports to forecast market trends and make investment recommendations. These models can process vast amounts of data in real-time, offering a competitive edge in decision-making and risk management. Moreover, NLP is used in fraud detection and compliance monitoring, where it helps identify suspicious activities and ensure adherence to regulatory requirements by analyzing transaction records and communications.

In the legal domain, NLP technologies are increasingly being applied to streamline the processing of legal documents and support legal research. One significant application is the use of

NLP for contract analysis, where algorithms can identify key clauses, obligations, and terms within contracts. This capability helps legal professionals review and manage contracts more efficiently, reducing the time and effort required for manual analysis. NLP is also utilized in legal research to assist in finding relevant case law and legal precedents by analyzing vast collections of legal texts and summarizing pertinent information.

A prominent case study in legal document processing involves the use of NLP for e-discovery, a process in which large volumes of electronic documents are reviewed to identify relevant evidence for legal cases. NLP tools can automate the identification and categorization of documents, significantly speeding up the e-discovery process and improving accuracy. Additionally, NLP-driven systems are employed in legal chatbots and virtual assistants that provide legal information and answer queries related to legal procedures, enhancing accessibility to legal services.

Overall, the application of NLP in these diverse fields demonstrates its transformative potential in enhancing efficiency, accuracy, and decision-making. By leveraging advanced NLP techniques, industries can unlock valuable insights from text data, automate routine tasks, and improve overall performance. As NLP technology continues to evolve, its applications are expected to expand further, driving innovation and contributing to advancements across various sectors.

In the legal domain, NLP is transforming how legal professionals handle and analyze vast amounts of textual information. Legal document processing is one area where NLP has shown significant promise. Tasks such as contract review, case law analysis, and legal research benefit greatly from NLP technologies. For instance, automated contract review systems utilize NLP to identify key clauses, flag potential issues, and ensure compliance with legal standards. These systems can parse through extensive legal documents, extract pertinent information, and highlight areas that require attention, thus saving time and reducing the risk of human error.

One notable application of NLP in the legal field is the development of legal research tools that leverage natural language understanding to assist attorneys in finding relevant case law and statutes. Traditional legal research methods are often labor-intensive and time-consuming, involving manual searches through extensive legal databases. NLP-driven tools, on the other hand, can analyze legal texts to identify relevant precedents and legal arguments quickly. For example, platforms such as ROSS Intelligence and LexisNexis use NLP to enable lawyers to pose queries in natural language and receive contextually relevant case law and legal interpretations.

Additionally, NLP technologies have been applied to predictive legal analytics, where they analyze historical case data to predict case outcomes and assist in legal strategy development. By examining patterns and trends in past legal decisions, NLP models can provide insights into likely case outcomes, aiding legal professionals in making more informed decisions. This predictive capability can significantly impact litigation strategy, settlement negotiations, and overall case management.

In the realm of customer service, NLP-driven chatbots and virtual assistants have become increasingly prevalent. These technologies are designed to handle customer queries, provide support, and process requests efficiently. For example, companies like IBM and Google have developed conversational agents that can understand and respond to customer inquiries in natural language, improving customer experience and operational efficiency. These systems use NLP to parse customer inputs, identify intent, and generate appropriate responses, often employing machine learning techniques to continuously improve their performance based on interactions.

Moreover, NLP has found applications in market research and consumer feedback analysis. Businesses use sentiment analysis tools to gauge customer opinions and emotions from reviews, social media posts, and surveys. By analyzing the sentiment expressed in customer feedback, companies can gain insights into customer satisfaction, identify areas for improvement, and tailor their products and services to better meet customer needs. For instance, companies like Amazon and Netflix utilize sentiment analysis to evaluate user feedback on their platforms, informing product development and enhancing user experience.

Another significant application of NLP is in automated content generation and summarization. Content creation tasks, such as generating news articles, reports, or marketing materials, can be streamlined using NLP techniques. For example, tools like OpenAI's GPT-3 can generate coherent and contextually relevant text based on given prompts, assisting in content creation for various purposes. Automated summarization techniques, both extractive and abstractive, help distill lengthy documents or articles into concise summaries, making it easier for users to access key information quickly.

In the field of education, NLP applications are enhancing learning experiences and supporting educational outcomes. Intelligent tutoring systems use NLP to provide personalized feedback to students on their writing, helping them improve grammar, style, and content organization. These systems analyze student submissions, identify areas for improvement, and offer tailored suggestions. Additionally, NLP-based tools for language learning assist users in acquiring new languages by providing practice exercises, grammar corrections, and conversational practice with virtual tutors.

The integration of NLP in various industries demonstrates its transformative potential and underscores its growing importance in addressing real-world challenges. By leveraging NLP technologies, organizations can improve efficiency, enhance decision-making, and offer more personalized services. As NLP continues to evolve, its applications are likely to expand further, driving innovation and creating new opportunities across diverse domains.

In the realm of healthcare, NLP plays a pivotal role in medical text analysis, transforming how medical data is processed and utilized. Electronic Health Records (EHRs), clinical notes, and medical literature contain vast amounts of unstructured text that, if analyzed properly, can yield critical insights for patient care and research. NLP techniques are employed to extract meaningful information from these sources, such as patient symptoms, diagnoses, treatments, and outcomes.

One prominent application is the extraction of key medical concepts from clinical narratives. For instance, NLP algorithms can identify and categorize mentions of diseases, medications, and medical procedures within clinical notes. This information is crucial for tasks such as identifying adverse drug reactions, tracking disease prevalence, and supporting clinical decision-making. Systems like MetaMap and cTAKES (Clinical Text Analysis and Knowledge Extraction System) utilize NLP to facilitate the indexing and retrieval of medical information from free-text clinical documents, enhancing the efficiency of medical research and patient care.

Another significant application of NLP in healthcare is in the realm of predictive analytics. By analyzing historical patient data, NLP models can help predict patient outcomes, identify high-risk individuals, and suggest personalized treatment plans. For example, NLP can be used to analyze patient records to predict the likelihood of hospital readmissions or to identify patients who may benefit from specific interventions. This predictive capability supports proactive healthcare management and improves patient outcomes.

Financial sentiment analysis is another area where NLP has made considerable strides. The financial industry relies heavily on the analysis of news articles, financial reports, and social media to gauge market sentiment and inform investment decisions. NLP techniques are used to analyze the tone and sentiment of financial news, earnings reports, and analyst comments, providing investors with actionable insights.

Sentiment analysis in finance involves classifying textual data into categories such as positive, negative, or neutral, and assessing the impact of these sentiments on market behavior. Advanced models can capture nuances in language and context, allowing for more accurate predictions of market trends. For example, algorithms developed by companies like Bloomberg and Thomson Reuters analyze financial news and social media to provide real-time sentiment scores, which can influence trading strategies and investment decisions.

In addition to sentiment analysis, NLP is employed for information extraction and summarization in financial contexts. Investors and analysts use NLP tools to extract key information from financial reports, such as revenue figures, profit margins, and management commentary. These tools can also generate summaries of lengthy financial documents, making it easier for stakeholders to access relevant information quickly and make informed decisions.

The impact of NLP on improving efficiency and decision-making is evident across various domains. In healthcare, NLP facilitates the processing of vast amounts of unstructured data, enabling more effective patient management and research. In finance, NLP provides tools for analyzing market sentiment and extracting critical information, enhancing decision-making and strategic planning.

As NLP continues to advance, its applications in these and other industries will likely expand, offering new opportunities for improving efficiency, accuracy, and decision-making. The ongoing development of NLP technologies promises to drive further innovations and improvements across diverse fields, contributing to the advancement of knowledge and the enhancement of various professional practices.

CHAPTER 33: FUTURE TRENDS IN NLP

The field of Natural Language Processing (NLP) is undergoing a profound transformation driven by rapid advancements in technology and methodology. As we look to the future, several key trends are emerging that promise to shape the next wave of innovations in NLP. These trends include advancements in deep learning, the continued rise of transformer models, and the integration of NLP with other artificial intelligence (AI) technologies.

Deep learning, a subset of machine learning, has revolutionized NLP by enabling models to learn from vast amounts of data and make highly accurate predictions. This approach leverages neural networks with multiple layers, allowing for the extraction of complex patterns and features from textual data. The evolution of deep learning techniques has led to the development of sophisticated models that can perform a variety of NLP tasks with impressive accuracy. Future advancements in deep learning are likely to focus on improving model efficiency, reducing computational requirements, and enhancing the interpretability of neural networks. Techniques such as neural architecture search and meta-learning are expected to play a significant role in this regard, as they offer ways to optimize model performance and adapt to new tasks with minimal human intervention.

The rise of transformer models represents another pivotal trend in NLP. Introduced with the "Attention Is All You

Need" paper by Vaswani et al. in 2017, transformers have since become the backbone of many state-of-the-art NLP systems. Unlike traditional recurrent neural networks (RNNs) and long short-term memory (LSTM) networks, transformers rely on self-attention mechanisms to process entire sequences of text simultaneously. This approach allows for more efficient handling of long-range dependencies and enables the model to capture intricate relationships between words and phrases.

As transformer models continue to advance, we can expect to see innovations that enhance their scalability and adaptability. For instance, research is actively exploring ways to reduce the size and computational cost of transformer models while maintaining their performance. Techniques such as knowledge distillation, pruning, and quantization are being investigated to create smaller, more efficient models that can be deployed in resource-constrained environments. Additionally, the development of more specialized transformer architectures, such as those tailored for specific languages or domains, will likely contribute to further advancements in NLP.

Another emerging trend is the integration of NLP with other AI technologies, such as computer vision and robotics. This interdisciplinary approach aims to create more holistic AI systems capable of understanding and interacting with the world in a more nuanced manner. For example, combining NLP with computer vision enables systems to interpret and generate textual descriptions of visual content, facilitating applications such as automated image captioning and visual question answering. Similarly, the integration of NLP with robotics allows for more sophisticated human-robot interactions, where robots can understand and respond to natural language commands in a contextually relevant manner.

The future of NLP also holds promise for advancements in multimodal learning, where models are trained to process and understand data from multiple modalities, such as text, audio, and images. Multimodal NLP systems aim to enhance the richness of machine understanding by leveraging diverse sources of information. For instance, models that combine text and audio data can improve speech recognition and synthesis, while those that integrate text and visual data can enhance content generation and scene understanding.

In addition to these technological advancements, the future of NLP will be influenced by ongoing research into ethical and societal implications. As NLP systems become more pervasive, addressing issues related to bias, fairness, and transparency will be crucial. Researchers are working on developing techniques to mitigate biases present in training data and ensure that NLP systems operate in a manner that respects ethical standards and promotes inclusivity. Furthermore, the responsible deployment of NLP technologies will require careful consideration of privacy concerns and the potential impact on individuals and communities.

Finally, the evolution of NLP will be shaped by its applications across various domains. The continued expansion of NLP into new areas, such as healthcare, finance, and education, will drive the development of specialized models and tools tailored to specific industry needs. For instance, in healthcare, NLP advancements will focus on improving clinical decision support and patient care through more accurate and efficient medical text analysis. In finance, the integration of NLP with financial forecasting and risk management will enhance decision-making capabilities and market insights. In education, NLP technologies will support personalized learning experiences and intelligent tutoring systems, contributing to more effective and adaptive educational practices.

As we move forward, the field of NLP will continue to evolve in response to technological advancements, interdisciplinary collaborations, and societal needs. The convergence of deep learning, transformer models, and AI integration will pave the way for new applications and capabilities, shaping the future of how we interact with and understand language.

Building on the foundation of deep learning and transformer models, the integration of NLP with other AI technologies is setting the stage for transformative advancements across various domains. One significant area of integration is the fusion of NLP with computer vision. This multidisciplinary approach is aimed at creating systems that can understand and generate language in conjunction with visual data. For example, image captioning and visual question answering are applications that leverage both visual and textual information to generate descriptions or answer questions about images. These systems utilize joint embeddings and multimodal transformers to align text and image features, enabling more nuanced interactions with visual content.

Another noteworthy area of convergence is the integration of NLP with robotics. In this domain, natural language understanding is combined with robotic control systems to enable more intuitive human-robot interactions. For instance, robots equipped with advanced NLP capabilities can interpret and execute complex verbal commands, enhancing their utility in tasks such as home automation and industrial operations. The development of dialogue systems for robots involves training models to understand context, manage conversation flows, and adapt to dynamic environments, thereby making robots more versatile and user-friendly.

Moreover, advancements in few-shot and zero-shot learning are pushing the boundaries of NLP capabilities. Few-shot learning refers to the ability of a model to learn new tasks with only a few examples, while zero-shot learning allows a model to perform tasks without any direct training examples by leveraging its knowledge from related tasks. These techniques are particularly useful in scenarios where annotated data is scarce or expensive to obtain. The progress in this area is driven by models like GPT-3 and GPT-4, which demonstrate impressive few-shot learning abilities by leveraging extensive pre-training on diverse datasets.

Additionally, the trend towards personalized NLP models is gaining momentum. Personalization involves tailoring language models to individual user preferences, contexts, and histories to provide more relevant and engaging interactions. This approach can be applied to various applications, from virtual personal assistants to content recommendation systems. The challenge in developing personalized NLP systems lies in balancing user privacy with the need for personalized experiences. Techniques such as federated learning, which enables model training across decentralized data sources while preserving privacy, are emerging as solutions to this challenge.

As NLP technologies become more advanced, ethical considerations and responsible AI practices will play an increasingly critical role. The development and deployment of NLP systems must be guided by principles that ensure fairness, transparency, and accountability. For instance, addressing issues related to algorithmic bias requires rigorous evaluation and mitigation strategies to prevent the reinforcement of harmful stereotypes or discriminatory practices. Furthermore, as NLP systems become more integrated into everyday life, it is essential to establish frameworks for safeguarding user data and ensuring that models are used responsibly and ethically.

Looking forward, the future of NLP is likely to be characterized by continued innovation and expansion into new domains. The convergence of NLP with other AI fields, along with advancements in model efficiency and personalization, will drive new applications and capabilities. However, it is crucial to approach these developments with a commitment to ethical practices and a focus on addressing the broader societal impacts of NLP technologies. As researchers, practitioners, and policymakers navigate the evolving landscape of NLP, collaborative efforts will be essential to harness the potential of these technologies while ensuring they contribute positively to society.

Looking forward, the intersection of NLP and ethical AI presents both challenges and opportunities. As NLP systems become increasingly sophisticated and embedded in daily life, ensuring that these systems operate in an unbiased, transparent, and equitable manner is paramount. Addressing biases in training data, which can perpetuate existing societal inequalities, is a crucial aspect of developing responsible NLP technologies. Researchers and practitioners are focusing on developing methodologies for bias detection and mitigation, such as fairness-aware algorithms and diverse training datasets. Moreover, the establishment of ethical guidelines and frameworks for NLP development is essential to safeguard against misuse and unintended consequences.

The advancements in NLP are also expected to influence and enhance various sectors beyond those previously mentioned. For instance, in the realm of education, personalized learning experiences powered by NLP can revolutionize how educational content is delivered and tailored to individual learning needs. Intelligent tutoring systems can use NLP to assess student progress, provide real-time feedback, and adapt learning materials based on student responses and comprehension levels. This personalized approach has the potential to improve educational outcomes and make learning more engaging and effective.

Similarly, the integration of NLP into healthcare systems promises significant improvements in patient care and clinical decision-making. NLP technologies can analyze electronic health records (EHRs), extract relevant information from medical literature, and assist in diagnosing and predicting patient outcomes. By enabling more efficient data extraction and knowledge synthesis, NLP can support clinicians in making informed decisions and developing personalized treatment plans. Additionally, NLP can facilitate patient interaction through conversational agents that offer health advice, schedule appointments, and answer medical queries, thus enhancing patient engagement and access to healthcare services.

In the financial sector, NLP is poised to transform how market trends are analyzed and financial decisions are made. Sentiment analysis and opinion mining, powered by advanced NLP models, can provide insights into market sentiment and investor behavior by analyzing news articles, social media posts, and financial reports. This capability enables financial analysts to detect emerging trends, assess market risks, and make more informed investment decisions. Moreover, NLP can streamline compliance and regulatory processes by automating the review of legal documents and detecting anomalies or potential violations.

The continued development of NLP models also holds promise for improving accessibility and inclusivity. For individuals with disabilities, NLP technologies can enhance communication and interaction with digital platforms. Speech-to-text and text-to-speech systems, as well as automatic translation services, can bridge communication gaps and provide greater access to information and services. By focusing on user-centric design and incorporating feedback from diverse user groups, NLP can help create more inclusive digital environments that accommodate a wide range of needs.

As NLP technologies advance, the importance of interdisciplinary collaboration cannot be overstated. The complexity of natural language understanding and generation requires expertise from various fields, including linguistics, computer science, cognitive science, and ethics. Collaboration among researchers, practitioners, and policymakers is essential to address the multifaceted challenges and ensure that NLP technologies are developed and deployed in a manner that benefits society as a whole. The ongoing dialogue between these stakeholders will play a crucial role in shaping the future of NLP and its impact on various domains.

In summary, the future of NLP is marked by rapid technological advancements, interdisciplinary integration, and a growing emphasis on ethical considerations. As we look ahead, the potential for NLP to drive innovation and improve various aspects of human life is immense. By addressing current challenges and leveraging emerging trends, researchers and practitioners can continue to advance the field and harness the power of NLP for positive societal impact.

CHAPTER 34: CONCLUSION AND NEXT STEPS

In this concluding section, we will encapsulate the critical insights and advancements discussed throughout the book, providing a comprehensive summary of the key concepts in Natural Language Processing (NLP). Reflecting on the breadth of topics covered—from foundational principles to cutting-edge applications—will offer a cohesive understanding of the field and its trajectory.

The exploration began with the core techniques of NLP, including tokenization, part-of-speech tagging, and parsing. These foundational elements are essential for breaking down and analyzing language at a granular level. We delved into the intricacies of syntactic and semantic analysis, which are pivotal for understanding sentence structure and meaning. The journey continued with an examination of more advanced methods, such as machine learning approaches for text classification and sequence labeling, which have significantly enhanced the capabilities of NLP systems.

One of the pivotal advancements in NLP is the development and application of deep learning techniques, particularly neural networks and transformer models. The rise of architectures like BERT, GPT, and their successors has revolutionized the field by enabling more nuanced and context-aware text generation and understanding. These models, with their ability to capture intricate linguistic patterns and semantic relationships, have set new benchmarks for performance in various NLP tasks.

The book also highlighted the integration of NLP with speech processing technologies. The synergy between NLP and speech recognition has led to significant improvements in voice assistants and transcription services, showcasing how NLP can extend beyond text-based applications to interact with spoken language. Similarly, advancements in speech synthesis have enhanced the naturalness and intelligibility of synthetic speech, making interactions with technology more seamless and human-like.

As we examined various applications of NLP, it became clear that its impact spans multiple domains. In healthcare, NLP facilitates medical text analysis and aids in clinical decision-making. Financial sentiment analysis leverages NLP to interpret market trends and investor sentiments. Legal document processing benefits from NLP's ability to streamline the review and extraction of pertinent information. Each application underscores NLP's transformative potential in enhancing efficiency, accuracy, and decision-making across different sectors.

However, alongside these advancements, ethical considerations have emerged as a critical area of focus. Addressing biases in NLP models, safeguarding user privacy, and ensuring responsible use of language technologies are essential for maintaining trust and integrity in NLP applications. The ongoing efforts to mitigate biases, implement transparency measures, and develop ethical guidelines are crucial for advancing NLP in a manner that benefits all users while minimizing adverse impacts.

Looking ahead, the future of NLP is poised to be shaped by several promising trends and research directions. Continued advancements in deep learning and neural architectures will likely drive further improvements in language models, enhancing their ability to understand and generate human-like text. The integration of NLP with other AI technologies, such as computer vision and robotics, opens new possibilities for creating more sophisticated and versatile systems.

To further explore and contribute to the field of NLP, several avenues are worth pursuing. For those interested in deepening their understanding, engaging with the latest research through academic journals, conferences, and workshops is essential. Participating in open-source projects and contributing to collaborative efforts can provide practical experience and foster innovation. Additionally, pursuing advanced studies and specialized courses in NLP and related disciplines can offer deeper insights and open new research opportunities.

In conclusion, the field of NLP continues to evolve rapidly, with ongoing advancements and emerging technologies driving its growth. The importance of continuous innovation and research cannot be overstated, as these efforts will shape the future of language and communication. By staying informed, engaging with the latest developments, and addressing ethical considerations, we can contribute to the responsible and transformative evolution of NLP. The journey of exploration and discovery in NLP is far from complete, and the path forward promises exciting opportunities and challenges for those invested in understanding and advancing this dynamic field.

The examination of ethical challenges and the commitment to responsible NLP practices highlight the crucial need for ongoing vigilance and improvement. As NLP technologies become more pervasive, it is imperative to develop frameworks and guidelines that promote fairness and accountability. Ensuring that NLP models operate without reinforcing harmful stereotypes or privacy violations is not merely an ethical obligation but also a necessity for maintaining public trust and advancing the field in a positive direction.

Reflecting on the advancements in NLP, it is evident that the field is in a state of rapid evolution. The integration of NLP with other AI technologies, such as computer vision and robotics, is opening new avenues for research and application. The synergy between these domains promises to create more sophisticated and capable systems, such as autonomous agents that can understand and interact with the world in increasingly complex ways. For example, the combination of NLP and computer vision has enabled systems to interpret visual data in conjunction with text, leading to advancements in tasks like image captioning and visual question answering.

The trajectory of NLP also points toward more personalized and adaptive technologies. Future NLP systems are likely to leverage advancements in user modeling and context-awareness to provide more tailored interactions. This could range from personalized content recommendations to adaptive language models that adjust their responses based on individual user preferences and historical interactions. Such developments hold the potential to significantly enhance user experiences across various applications, from virtual assistants to educational tools.

Looking forward, several potential research directions stand out as promising avenues for exploration. One area of interest is the development of more interpretable and explainable NLP models. While current models like transformers have demonstrated impressive performance, their complexity often obscures their decision-making processes. Advancing techniques for model interpretability could help demystify how these systems arrive at their conclusions, making them more transparent and trustworthy. This would not only improve user confidence but also facilitate better debugging and refinement of NLP technologies.

Another critical area for future research is addressing the

challenges associated with multilingual and cross-lingual NLP. As NLP models are predominantly trained on English and other major languages, there is a growing need to extend their capabilities to a broader range of languages and dialects. This involves developing models that can effectively handle the diversity of linguistic structures and cultural contexts, which is essential for creating more inclusive and globally accessible NLP applications.

The potential for NLP to impact various fields underscores its transformative power. In education, for instance, NLP technologies can be employed to create intelligent tutoring systems that adapt to students' needs, providing personalized feedback and support. In journalism, NLP can assist in automating content generation and fact-checking, thereby improving the efficiency and reliability of news production. The application of NLP in these domains, and others, highlights its role in shaping the future of communication and information dissemination.

In conclusion, the field of NLP is poised for continued innovation and growth. The advancements discussed throughout this book provide a foundation for understanding the current state of NLP, while also pointing toward exciting future developments. As researchers, practitioners, and stakeholders in the field move forward, the emphasis should remain on fostering ethical practices, embracing new technological possibilities, and exploring the vast potential of NLP to enhance and transform how we interact with language and information. The journey of NLP is ongoing, and its future holds the promise of further breakthroughs that will redefine our relationship with language and communication.

In considering the future trajectory of NLP, we must also reflect on the implications of emerging technologies and methodologies. One significant trend is the growing emphasis on ethical AI and the integration of fairness and accountability measures into NLP systems. As NLP applications become increasingly embedded in critical areas such as healthcare, finance, and law, the need for robust ethical frameworks becomes even more pressing. This includes addressing issues related to algorithmic fairness, where models might inadvertently perpetuate biases present in training data, and ensuring transparency in how decisions are made.

To further enhance the field, it is crucial to invest in interdisciplinary research. NLP intersects with many domains, including cognitive science, neuroscience, and human-computer interaction. Collaboration with experts from these fields can provide valuable insights into creating more nuanced and effective language models. For example, incorporating findings from cognitive science can help design NLP systems that better simulate human-like understanding and reasoning, leading to more natural and intuitive interactions.

The development of more sophisticated evaluation metrics is another area where future work is needed. Traditional metrics, such as BLEU for machine translation or F1 score for named entity recognition, have their limitations and often fail to capture the full spectrum of language understanding. New evaluation frameworks that consider the context, pragmatics, and overall quality of generated text will be essential for advancing NLP capabilities. This might involve developing metrics that assess not only the accuracy but also the appropriateness and coherence of language models in various scenarios.

Moreover, as NLP continues to evolve, the integration of NLP with other AI technologies will likely lead to new and innovative applications. For instance, combining NLP with advancements in robotics could enable more advanced human-robot interactions, where robots not only understand and generate language but also respond in ways that are contextually relevant and emotionally intelligent. Similarly, integrating NLP with augmented reality (AR) and virtual reality (VR) could lead to immersive experiences where users interact with virtual environments through natural language.

The impact of NLP on various sectors is profound and far-reaching. In healthcare, NLP has the potential to revolutionize patient care through advanced medical record analysis and decision support systems. By extracting and synthesizing information from vast amounts of medical texts, NLP can assist in diagnosing conditions, personalizing treatment plans, and identifying trends that inform public health strategies. Similarly, in finance, NLP-driven sentiment analysis can provide real-time insights into market trends and investor sentiment, helping firms make informed investment decisions.

In legal contexts, NLP can streamline document processing and case management. Legal professionals can benefit from tools that automatically extract relevant information from legal texts, perform legal research, and assist in drafting documents. Such tools can significantly reduce the time and effort required for these tasks, allowing legal experts to focus on more strategic and complex aspects of their work.

As we look towards the future, ongoing innovation in NLP will play a crucial role in transforming how we interact with technology and each other. The advancements in deep learning, the rise of transformer models, and the integration with other AI technologies are paving the way for increasingly sophisticated and capable systems. These developments hold promise for creating more intuitive, efficient, and effective language technologies that can enhance various aspects of our lives.

To continue exploring NLP and stay at the forefront of the field, it is essential to engage with the latest research and developments. Attending conferences, participating in workshops, and contributing to scholarly publications are valuable ways to stay informed and involved. Additionally, exploring online resources, such as specialized courses and tutorials, can provide further insights into emerging techniques and applications.

In summary, the field of NLP is poised for exciting advancements, driven by innovations in technology and a growing understanding of language and communication. The commitment to ethical practices, interdisciplinary collaboration, and continued research will be key to harnessing the full potential of NLP and ensuring its positive impact on society. As we move forward, it is essential to remain adaptable and forward-thinking, embracing new opportunities and challenges in the ever-evolving landscape of NLP.

www.ingramcontent.com/pod-product-compliance
Lightning Source LLC
Chambersburg PA
CBHW052142220526
45471CB00004B/1487